Bullets In The Fire

Biography Of New York Red

Edward Roy

Bullets In The Fire

Biography Of New York Red

Edward Roy

Copyright © 2023 by Edward Roy

Published by Edward Roy in Collaboration with Mosaic Inc.

4222 Fortuna Plaza Center Suite 645 Dumfries,
Virginia 22025

Bullets In The Fire

Biography Of New York Red
ISBN: 978-1-7357658-4-6

Printed in the United States of America

Dedication

This book is dedicated to Erma Louise Hill, also known on the streets of Harlem as New York Red. She developed into one of Harlem's most celebrated Number Writers and Bankers. She also became a tireless advocate for the well-being of her children and for the residents of Harlem. She unapologetically established her own rules, lived by them, and died by them.

I wish to thank her for her love, unselfish dedication, and sacrifices in laying an exceptional foundation for me, my brother, my sisters, her grandchildren, and her great-grandchildren to build our dreams upon.

She often told us:
"Do as I say, do, not as I do. I am throwing bricks at the jailhouse, so you won't have to. Bullets in the Fire."

Acknowledgments

This biography is a true story based on my family's history passed down through stories and documents told or given to me by my family elders, family friends, my mother's associates, my personal experiences, and memory. For this reason, many names, dates, and places may not be confirmable.

I wish to thank my two sisters, Vernetta and Pandora, for their love and support. Their only instruction to me in writing Mommy's biography was to tell the unapologetic truth. A thank you also to my wife, Dale, who for 52 years has hung in there with me during the difficult times with sacrifice, dedication, and love.

Respectfully, I wish to thank all my mother's customers, who knew her as New York Red, the residents of Harlem, and the City of New York for your prayers and support over the years. Your financial support and resources invested in us were well spent. I acknowledged as many of you as I could at the conclusion of this publication.

Also, I wish to thank the New York City Police Department, especially the "honest old school" police officers, who knew who the real criminals were and who protected my mother as best as they could.

Likewise, I will always appreciate *New York Times* reporter, Charles Grutzner, who in 1964 told it like it really was.

Additionally, I wish to thank my editor, Denise Powell, graphic and cover designers, Alex Gottardy and Maureen Leahy, along with the Schomburg Museum, New York City Public Library, The Amsterdam News, Ancestry.com, a host of online resources, historical associations, and other sources without which this publication would not have been possible.

Finally, I wish to thank the Tikar women and men in my family, whose lineage stretches back to Cameroon, Africa. They suffered unimaginable abuses to arrive and survive in America. But they never allowed their suffering to diminish the courage that was required for them to push forward, thereby enabling me to prosper and tell my mother's dynamic story, as if it were being told in her own voice.

Table of Content

Chapter I

Prophet Or Pariah?

Planted cotton last year and the boll weevils ate it. Planted corn this year and the drought took it. Plan to plant peanuts next year and the fungus will destroy it—no matter what George Washington Carver said.

- In 1933, the news man said on the radio, "Due to a cold, snowy winter in Russia, hungry wolves attacked a train." Heat waves, floods, droughts, and famines, killed hundreds of thousands of people in China. The heat caused a road to explode in New Jersey.

- In 1934, 80% of the United States suffered from drought. All 48 states had temperatures higher than 100 degrees in June, with 14 days straight higher than 100 degrees and killing more than 600 Americans. Global warming caused 81 of the Swiss glaciers to retreat.

- In 1935, the worst dust storm in history moved across Kansas City. There were 50 dust storms in 104 days and 124-degree heat that blasted India.

- In 1936, the Italian Alps Glaciers shrunk and the bodies of WWI Army servicemen were uncovered after the glaciers melted. Violent tornadoes ravaged the south, causing 300 deaths. Alaska's 10-day heat wave peaked higher than 108 degrees.

- In 1937, Russian explorers said that the world's climate was growing warmer.

- I hoped 1938 would be a better year. But this summer was another hot one. It has been like this for a long time; no different and no matter what you do.

Bullshit! Mother Nature is just a mean bitch. All life and death are in her hands. The Lord giveth and she taketh away. Trying to earn a living from farming was like pissing into the wind. Whose side was Mother Nature on, anyway? Is she *Prophet or Pariah?*

Trying to please Mother Nature with meager efforts will only bear you meager fruit. Minimal effort will only produce just enough to sustain her until you can mount a greater effort next time, and possibly, please her. When one makes a supreme effort for her, a no holds barred effort, only then will a roadway to her heart open. She reminds me of a beautiful, sultry, and enticing woman that her lover will never, ever please. She simply punishes him for his meager efforts and never, ever tells him what he did wrong. Therefore, he must go for the whole hog because he is doomed if he settles for the pig's feet. Prophet or Pariah?

The road to Mother Nature's heart is unfortunately paved with the discarded bones of those who did not please her. Their discarded bones are the foundation of lessons learned that others that follow build their dreams upon. Mother Nature says there are two kinds of people in this world: those who are clever or shrewd, and those who are insensible, or stupid. Both have a place in her world. The clever are here to build their dreams on the missteps of the insensible. They achieve their dreams only when they please her. *Prophet or Pariah?*

Mother Nature will allow you to make your own rules, clever or insensible. But as sole judge and juror she makes you live and die by them. She reminds me of myself. If you make the supreme effort to please me by working hard at it, I may respond in kind. If not, my severe wrath awaits you.

Of course, how well you satisfy me depends on my disposition. Naturally, I believe everyone and everything placed on this planet is here for my benefit, my pleasure, and my comfort. All I have to do is reach for it and retrieve it. *Prophet or Pariah?*

This year, I will be 14 years old. Good jobs that are not in farming are hard to come by in Plains, Georgia. Getting a good job here has nothing to do with how rich your parents are or what your skin color is. Plains is mostly absent from the severe racial policies of other southern towns, but it's still the pits. White people suffer right along with

Negroes. It is all Mother Nature's fault. Is she *Prophet or Pariah?*

Most young men here have already headed north for greener pastures. Their departures have left slim pickings for us young girls left behind. Most of my brothers were thinking of doing the same. They were simply waiting long enough to grow a few inches to their limbs and put a little more fat on their bones to feel fit enough to make the trip. They were all about gone, except for my youngest brother, Fred, who was already tired of shaking peanuts and picking cotton. Truth be told, he was ready to leave now.

My family was hard working and saved what we could. We were lucky not to miss many meals and asked no one for anything. Money? What was that? No one here earned much money, even in good years. We were so poor that it seemed we couldn't even afford sunshine. Whose side was Mother Nature on anyway?

Mama, Freddie Mae Hill, who everyone called Daught, loved us all. But she was gone most of the time looking for work out of town. I do not remember much about my father, John Butler. But I do remember him and Mama having an ugly argument over whether I was really his daughter. He disowned me that day. And when I got old enough, I disowned him. I refused to use his name. I remained a Hill, Erma Louise Hill, although my birth papers said my last name was Butler. And I am better known as Kitty.

Daught broke up with John Butler after that argument and she did not waste much time worrying about it either. She hooked up right after with George Mac Wilson and had six children by him. I don't think they ever really got married—at least I never saw a marriage license. I am pretty sure that they simply told people they were married to try to keep the churchwomen from gossiping about them. The marriage lasted a long time, and ended after she hospitalized his behind for slapping her. That single slap left our grandmother, Victoria Hill, who everyone called Ma Babe, alone with six more mouths to feed and me to take care of.

Daught traveled far and wide looking for work and income, with or without George Mac Wilson. Sometimes she traveled all the way to Brunswick, Georgia or to Pensacola, Florida. When she heard of an out-of-town job, she just got up and went, leaving her children behind. No one knew where she had gone until a letter arrived written by a friend letting on where she was. I had to care for my siblings for weeks at a time. How food got into the house sometimes I really did not know. But it did. Sometimes food would arrive at the house from C. L. Walker's Grocery Store, on Main Street in Plains, with a note attached to it that read, "Hope you all are doing well."

Ma Babe said it was from Dr. Chappell, her oldest son Arthur's father, and known to us as Uncle Fass.

Come Friday, if you didn't catch Daught before she heard the "Jungle Music" wailing in the air from the Roadhouses, she would be "broke" before Sunday morning. You had to put horse blinders on her to get her to the Western Union office so she could wire money back to Ma Babe. If you missed her, the money would be in the collection plate at the Roadhouse's sunrise service. When that happened, it was a tough week for us kids.

Daught wasn't lazy. She did not mind hard work. She just loved to party and go. She partied as hard as she worked. Outside of work, her life was only partying, baseball, and courting. She was a tall, good-looking woman who was built like a Georgia pine— all legs. But, like so many other young, attractive, brown-skinned girls here in Plains, she was forced to live by a man's rules.

Daught was an underhand pitcher on the Plains, Georgia Mud Clots softball team. They were the top colored girls' softball team in Sumter County. They traveled from town to town, riding in the back of Uncle Fass's truck, taking on all female comers. If they didn't win the game, they won the fight. The snacks concession at the ball games were run by Uncle Fass. Uncle Luther was the team's manager and he demanded a share of the concession money from Uncle Fass. But Uncle Fass refused to give anyone a share. He even charged the team for their transport.

Ma Babe was a nurse's assistant at the Plains Sanitarium, a well-known, local hospital here. Ma Babe was working at the hospital in Plains before they built the Wise Sanitarium that Drs. Samuel, Thaddeus, and Bowman Wise built in 1921. They were sons of Dr. Burr T. and

Laura Wise who were early settlers of Plains, Georgia. It was a state-of-the-art hospital known as "The Mayo Clinic of the South." The Plains Sanitarium was one of the first small hospitals in the state of Georgia accredited by the American College of Surgeons and the American Medical and Hospital Association. It also served as an accreditation school for nurses, treating Negro patients in a separate building at the rear of the main building. Negroes received the same quality care as white folks.

It was here that Lillian Cordy Carter received her training in nursing. Jimmy Carter, son of Earl and Lillian Carter, and who would become the 39th President of the United States, was born here on October 1, 1924. It was the same year I was born. He was also the first President of the United States to be born in a hospital.

On January 21, 1936, a fire damaged this building. Right after the fire, Dr. S. Wise and Dr. T. Wise moved their practice to Americus, Georgia, and Dr. Bowman Wise opened an office here in Plains. Often, Mama worked as his assistant when he made house calls in Plains. Dr. Bowman J. Wise was Granny's (Ma Babe's mother's) doctor. He treated her while she was alive and pronounced her dead by signing her death certificate in 1921.

Ma Babe married Robert (Bob) Hill in 1896. She had five children by him: Nora, Roy, Effie, Freddie Mae, Daught (Mama), and Leila (Aunt Touchy), and two others that died at birth. Bob, my grandfather, a hard-working dedicated man, was killed on a Friday evening while he was gambling on the side of the house with his brothers and nephews. All of them were drinking and his drunk nephew shot him during an argument over a dice call. It was the same year Aunt Touchy was born so, she was never held by her father because Ma Babe was pregnant at the time. Ma Babe never got over it or got married again after my grandfather's death. The "old church hens" here in Plains said Ma Babe thought she was too good for a Negro man. I think she thought she was too good for any man.

Even without much formal education, she was smart and feisty. And she learned things very quickly. That is why they hired her at the hospital. She taught herself how to read, but she did not let anyone know it. If you left personal letters from your boyfriends lying around at night, the next day Ma Babe knew all your business.

She worked all times of day and night, mostly at night. And she put in lots of extra hours. I doubted whether she received pay for much of her overtime. If she wanted to keep her job, she had to jump through white men's hoops. One of those hoops resulted in the birth of my Uncle Arthur (Fass) Hill. He was Doctor Chappell's son.

She tried to fend off his advances, but Dr. Chappell was always 'at her.' She told him, "No!" so many times that she just stopped responding when he asked. It only made matters worse when she let him know that she was telling him no because she was a virgin and was saving herself for her future husband. When he learned that his mind went off like a firecracker. He decided he was not accepting no from a young, attractive, Negro, virgin woman. Southern white men have had a historical fetish for robbing the virginity of young Negro women.

I often heard people refer to Uncle Fass behind his back as "Chappell's boy." He cursed the gossipers and denied the rumor, but even he knew it was true. For whatever reason, his nickname was Fass, he looked just like Dr. Chappell, and he was as white as could be for a Black man. He even passed for white whenever he left Plains. As I said, Ma Babe would not talk about it, but she never denied it. He was her first child and she conceived him at the age of 16, which was considered old for a woman's first birth here in Plains. Some girls got married at 11 years old if they started menstruating.

Despite everything, she loved Fass to death and didn't complain about the tongue wagging by the churchwomen concerning who his father was. She was a very strong woman. She simply sucked it up and continued loving and caring for her children and grandchildren and let people talk.

Ma Babe refused to discuss who Uncle Fass's father was with anyone, but my Aunt Nora knew what happened and she told it all. Dr. Chappell took good care of her and the baby though until the Plains' churchwomen started to interfere with their gossip. Once problems started for her, she told him, "It's not wise for you to come around to the house anymore."

By that time, she had already taken up with Robert Hill. They got married in 1896. That is how we got the family name Hill. Some say Hill was our slave master's name.

I say that is not true. It is definitely British, but both Ma Babe and I chose the name ourselves—not any slave master. That is why there are so many Negroes with the names Lincoln, Jefferson, and Washington. These were the only names they knew after they were freed from slavery.

Dr. Chappell was one of the few doctors that made house calls for Negro folk. And he made them in his black buggy with his old mule named Stanford pulling it. He loved that mule. And if you could not pay him, a drink of good shine would do him just fine. Most of the time, by the time he finished his rounds he was so drunk he could not sit up right in the seat of the buggy. He simply fell backwards and that mule took him home.

Granny, my great-grandmother (Charlotte Hicks-Reid-Bush), was another very strong woman in our family who had a baby by a white man. She died in 1921, three years before I was born. The father of her first child was her slave master. She was his property and that included her body. A Black woman was made a more valuable slave if she was fertile. And as her master, he improved her value by raping her several times and impregnating her with his child. She gave birth to Emma at the age of 15.

Granny's father, Jack Hicks, also a slave, witnessed his daughter's sexual abuse by his slave master first-hand and could do nothing about it without forfeiting his life to protect her.

Great-Great-Grandpa Jack Hicks got the last laugh though. He outlived his slave masters after serving them for more than 75 years. After Abraham Lincoln freed him in 1863, he regularly went to the cemetery at night to piss on their graves until he died in 1872.

My Great-Great-Grandpa Jack was born in 1791, in North Carolina, when George Washington was in his first term as President of the United States. His slave masters moved the family from North Carolina to Sumter County, Georgia. Here, his slave masters bought some of the cheap land that the U.S. government stole from the local Creek Indians. His slave masters freed several of his grandchildren before the Civil War broke out. It was their backward way of recognizing that they were the slave master's blood.

Charlotte Hicks went on to marry Green Reid and conceived five children by him. Upon his death, she married Walker Bush and conceived an additional eight children, of which Victoria (Ma Babe) was their first. She outlived both of her husbands and three of her children. I have a lot of respect for these women. What they suffered was unimaginable. They survived so I could arrive here and continue to take on the challenges of moving our family forward. But I'm different. *I am Mother Nature.* And I refuse to jump through hoops or suffer abuse from anyone - Black or white, man or woman. I made my own rules. But, unlike most, I was willing to live and die by mine. *Prophet or Pariah?*

976 383 675 624

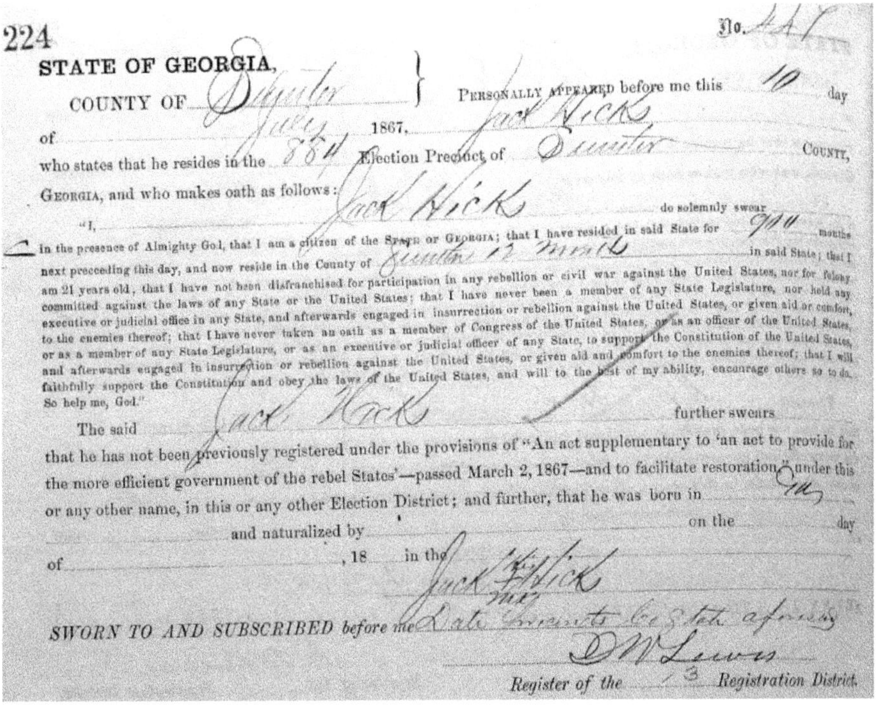

Jack Hicks Voter Registration

State of Georgia, Sumter County:　　159

TO ANY JUDGE, JUSTICE OF THE PEACE OR MINISTER OF THE GOSPEL:

YOU ARE HEREBY AUTHORIZED TO JOIN

Walker Bush & Charlott Read

In the Holy State of Matrimony, according to the Constitution and Laws of this State: and for so doing, this shall be your sufficient License.

And you are hereby required to return this License to me, with your Certificate hereon of the fact and date of the Marriage.

Given under my hand and seal, this *1st* day of *October* 187 *8*

Tho. H. Stewart　　**L.S.**

Ordinary.

Georgia, Sumter County.

I Certify, That *Walker Bush* and *Charlott Read* were joined in MATRIMONY by me, this *22nd* day of *October* Eighteen Hundred and Seventy- *Eight*

J. R. Littlejohn McG

RECORDED :

Ordinary.

Walker Bush and Charlotte Hicks-Reid Marriage Certificate

Walker Bush and Charlotte Hicks-Reid
Marriage Certificate

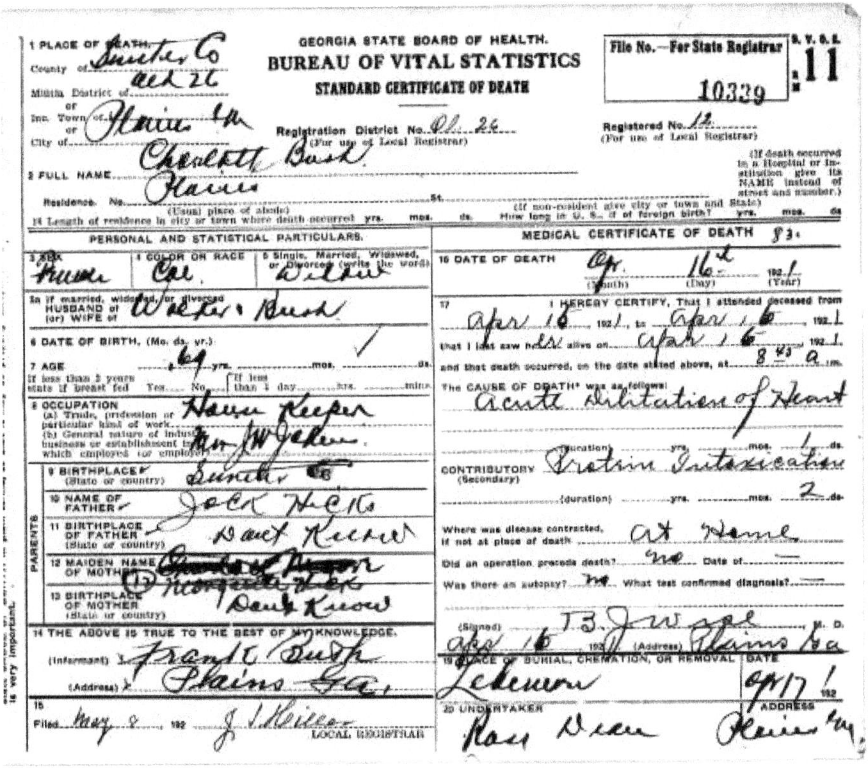

GEORGIA STATE BOARD OF HEALTH.
BUREAU OF VITAL STATISTICS
STANDARD CERTIFICATE OF DEATH

File No.—For State Registrar 10339

S. V. S. 11

1 PLACE OF DEATH.
County of Sumter Co
Militia District of
or Inc. Town of Plains Ga
or City of

Registration District No. Dl. 26 (For use of Local Registrar)

Registered No. 12 (For use of Local Registrar)

2 FULL NAME Charlott Bush

Residence. No. Plains St. (Usual place of abode) (If non-resident give city or town and State)

(If death occurred in a Hospital or Institution give its NAME instead of street and number.)

18 Length of residence in city or town where death occurred yrs. mos. ds. How long in U. S., if of foreign birth? yrs. mos. ds.

PERSONAL AND STATISTICAL PARTICULARS.

3 SEX Female

4 COLOR OR RACE Col.

5 Single, Married, Widowed, or Divorced (write the word) Widow

5a If married, widowed, or divorced HUSBAND of (or) WIFE of Walter Bush

6 DATE OF BIRTH, (Mo. da. yr.)

7 AGE 69 yrs. mos. ds.

If less than 2 years state if breast fed Yes No If less than 1 day hrs. mins.

8 OCCUPATION
(a) Trade, profession or particular kind of work House Keeper
(b) General nature of industry, business or establishment in which employed (or employer) Mr. J W Jackson

PARENTS

9 BIRTHPLACE (State or country) Sumter Co

10 NAME OF FATHER Jack Hicks

11 BIRTHPLACE OF FATHER (State or country) Dont Know

12 MAIDEN NAME OF MOTHER Margaret Hicks

13 BIRTHPLACE OF MOTHER (State or country) Dont Know

14 THE ABOVE IS TRUE TO THE BEST OF MY KNOWLEDGE.
(Informant) Frank Bush
(Address) Plains Ga.

15 Filed May 8, 192 J. I. [illegible] LOCAL REGISTRAR

MEDICAL CERTIFICATE OF DEATH

16 DATE OF DEATH Ap. 16 (Month) (Day) 1921 (Year)

17 I HEREBY CERTIFY, That I attended deceased from Apr 16 1921, to Apr 16 1921
that I last saw her alive on Apr 16 1921,
and that death occurred, on the date stated above, at 8 45 a.m.
The CAUSE OF DEATH* was as follows:
Acute Dilitation of Heart
(duration) yrs. mos. 1 ds.
CONTRIBUTORY (Secondary) Protein Intoxication
(duration) yrs. mos. 2 ds.

Where was disease contracted, if not at place of death At Home

Did an operation precede death? no Date of —

Was there an autopsy? no What test confirmed diagnosis? —

(Signed) T. B. J. Wise M. D.
Apr 16 1921 (Address) Plains Ga

19 PLACE OF BURIAL, CREMATION, OR REMOVAL Lebanon DATE Ap 17 1921

20 UNDERTAKER Ross Dean ADDRESS Plains Ga.

Charlotte Bush Death Certificate,
April 16, 1921

Chapter II

Bullets In The Fire

Mama Daught gave birth to me at the age of 13 in 1924. Believe me, there was no coercion involved in that conception. As I said, I was the oldest and it was my dreaded job to take care of my younger brothers and sisters while Ma Babe was at work and Mama was looking for work out of town. All of this was Daught's fault. Every time she left home, she returned pregnant or carrying an- other one in her arms for me to take care of. Ma Babe always complained that Mama started having sex too early.

Ma Babe told her, "If you are grown enough to have children, then you are grown enough to work, feed 'em, and take care of 'em."

Ma Babe always cautioned me, "Do not be like your mama. Keep your dress down, Kitty."

Well, she should have told her daughter the same thing. "Keep your dress down, Daught, and your legs closed."

I often asked, "When did you start having sex, Ma Babe?"

When I asked, she stopped talking and shied away from the conversation.

I had very little time for myself. Most girls my age had boyfriends—plenty of them. They were out dating and everything. I had to take care of these coon heads! And I was an attractive girl. *I was Mother Nature.*

I had many guys interested in me—too many, really—but no time to date them. I had to find ways to make up for lost time. I would sneak out of the house as much as possible. Once, I went as far as Americus, the Sumter County seat with Roger Brown, to the picture show. Americus had the only picture show and ice cream parlor. They served colored folks through the side door. My money was as good as anyone else's, but I was not going to jump through hoops for an ice cream cone. Instead, we went and hung out at his father's funeral parlor.

Whenever I would sneak out of the house to date or meet a guy, my younger sister Freddie Mae would tell Ma Babe, who punished me. I often took my youngest sister, Elizabeth, along with me because she could keep her mouth shut.

Either way, I always stayed too long. When I arrived back home, Ma Babe made me go out in the front yard to the large pomegranate bush and break off a switch. You learned not to fetch a long thin switch because those stung the worst. Instead, you picked one that did not bend much; those did not sting as much. She beat my behind until I cried bloody murder.

It didn't stop me though. I loved me some Roger Brown, the undertaker's son from Americus, Georgia. He looked so good driving his father's Cadillac. Yes, he was married. So what? *I was Mother Nature*, and I did as I pleased.

I had to make up for lost time anyway, and he would take me for a ride in that Cadillac every chance he could. He even let me drive it by myself—only once though— because I stripped the gears and he had to lie to his father about how it happened. The first time I ever "did it" was with him in the back of his daddy's hearse. He rocked me so hard that one of the tires went flat. He rubbed a lot of Vaseline "up there" so I would not get pregnant. It sure felt good. My girlfriends always said that Vaseline was an excellent birth control fix. I figured they must be right because Ma Babe always made you wash your hands before handling chicken eggs.

She said, "Grease on an egg would prevent it from hatching."

After Uncle Fass heard that I stripped Mr. Brown's Cadillac gears, he promised my teacher, Mrs. Etta Mae Frazier, that he would teach me how to drive, if I graduated from the seventh grade. I was about to graduate, even though I was a year behind in age in school. I had to work in the fields a few years back because times were very tough. I was almost there. I would be the first one in the family to get that far in school.

Mrs. Frazier encouraged me to learn how to drive more than I encouraged myself. She wanted to show me off to the entire community because she said girls could do anything boys could do. She said that good things come to those who worked hard and who could drive. What she was really saying was that there was little future here in Plains, Georgia for women with any talent and who could drive a car.

My teacher was very proud of me. She was the best teacher in Sumter County, Georgia, and in the rest of the world. I loved me some Mrs. Frazier and I was her best student. She always made sure I knew my lessons and that made me feel great. I was especially good at math. I really was a math whiz. I even helped tutor the other children in class who were having problems keeping up. I could add and subtract numbers three digits across in my head.

Uncle Fass was now teaching me how to drive in his 1934 Model A Ford Truck. My mind was not on the road and I could still hear him screaming!

"Hot-damn Kitty, stop daydreaming. I told you to watch the road! Your mind has been in a fog for the past two miles. Slow down Kitty, slow down girl, or your whole life will come to a crashing halt. Slow down now and change the gears. That's it, Kitty. Now release the clutch and give her some gas. Hot damn girl, you got it now!" Boy, I was trucking along now.

My brothers and sisters had taken over my mind. They were all a royal pain in the ass. They were always fussing and fighting about something. I never had any time for myself. I often hid in a corner trying to read, but I never finished one book because of those ninnies. I read very well also, and I liked to read those sexy dime store novels—the spicy ones that Mama and Ma Babe said I couldn't read. They said they were heathen stories. When she asked me what I was reading, I told Ma Babe they were religious books. Neither Ma Babe nor Daught could read well because they never really went to school.

Instead, they had to work in the fields. So, I wrapped the book covers with brown paper or took the covers off completely so they would not see the pictures.

Daught almost caught me red-handed once. She asked me to read a bit to her and I made as if I was reading a Bible story. She sort of hated me for that when she found out what I was really reading. She said I was mocking her. And I was. The truth was, Mama could not read because she partied all the time, especially when she wasn't working in the fields. Oh yes, and maybe she did something else too because she turned up pregnant almost every year like clockwork.

You could find fieldwork for about a dollar a day back then, but we ate that much food in a day. Somehow, Ma Babe managed to keep us fed, clothed and healthy after cursing and screaming at Daught about spending all her money in roadhouses before she could get it home.

I washed and ironed the kids' school clothes and fed them in the mornings before school. That was whenever the boys were not working in the fields and decided to go to school. In the evenings, I helped them with their homework. On Saturday nights, I had the boys pull water up from the well so I could bathe all of them. This made little sense because the boys peed in the bed almost every night. It was always a smelly mess to clean up in the mornings, which forever made me late for school.

Even with that, the boys were not as much of a problem as the girls. The girls fussed and fought all the time over small things, about anything and everything. They fought over who should use the crayons first, who Santa Claus brought the doll to, and whose turn it was to feed the chickens or clean the kitchen.

Ma Babe cooked and left food on her wood burning stove before she went to work at the hospital. At dinnertime, I heated the food, but those greedy boys would sneak into the food behind my back.

They would holler out, "There's a snake in the hen house!"
I would run out to the hen house with the hoe in my hand, but the snake would have disappeared...there was no snake. Then they would laugh, saying Jesus appeared and chased the snake away. When I returned to the kitchen, four pieces of chicken would be missing from the covered pot on the stove.

They did not fight over or steal food that I cooked though because they didn't like my cooking. When Ma Babe caught on to the fact they were feeding my food to the hogs, she stopped me from cooking for them. I learned to watch the boys like a hawk so the girls and I would have something to eat.

We kept two to three hogs. Keeping more than that on our small plot of land was too difficult. I collected food-slops from our table and from our neighbor, Mrs. Pie's table, to feed them. Hog feed was too expensive to buy. By the time I finished feeding the hogs in the evenings and fighting off a phalanx of gnats and flies, I smelled worse than the hogs. Have you tried to catch a loose hog running through a briar patch in the middle of the night with a flashlight and a stick? I cut up my arms and legs worse than a pecan pie at a Baptist church picnic! How was I going to catch a man with scratched up legs? And I had pretty legs too! *This was no way to treat Mother Nature...*

We also kept quite a few chickens. They ran free in a large fenced area and were easy to keep. Most of the time, I fed the animals myself because my younger brothers and sisters played with the animals while they fed them, and they escaped from their pens.

We also had a large garden. We grew much of our food and canned it for the winter in quart mason jars. We canned speckled butter beans, corn, green peas, string beans, tomatoes, beets, apples for applesauce, peaches, and strawberry and blackberry preserves. The only enjoyable time I had with my siblings was when we gathered the green beans together and sat down on the front porch pulling the strings and snapping them for canning. It was the only time that no one was fighting.

The collard greens and potatoes grew into the cold weather. We dug a pit in the back of the house, lined it with straw, and buried the white and sweet potatoes to keep them cool and preserve them. They would keep for most of the winter. But I really loved those canned speckled butter beans. I also tended the garden myself because my younger brothers and sisters stepped on the young plants, killing them.

Often, Uncle Fass took the older boys wild fruit gathering, hunting, and fishing in the woods. But because of his bad leg he stayed with the truck as they gathered and hunted. When they hunted rabbits and other small game, the boys went up-wind of the open fields and set the fields afire. Then they ran down-wind hollering and shouting, scaring the game into running. Then two of them would shoot the rabbits and other small game as they ran fleeing the fire.

They brought home wild birds, possums, raccoons, rabbits, and squirrels. I hated cleaning those possums. They stunk up a storm. Most of the boys were good shots. Some of us girls were too. It was a family custom to teach the Hill family women how to shoot.

Uncle Fass often said, "Any man, smart or stupid, should think twice about putting his hands on a Hill woman knowing how well she can handle a gun."

He also told the boys, "I taught your mama how to shoot, but I do not know who taught her how to use a razor. She is one dangerous woman with it. One Sunday, your father, George Mac, went to church in his newly bought suit. He thought he was the toast of Plains, Georgia! He stayed at church all day eating, drinking shine in the parking lot, and pulling on the young girls until he found one that would go into the woods with him. Your mama was at home sitting on the porch nursing your newborn sister, Elizabeth. After frolicking with the young girls and getting half drunk, he decided to walk to Ma Babe's house, where we lived. As he approached the house, he noticed your mama sitting on the porch. He called out, "Daught, what in the hell are you doing?" She looked at him silently trying to figure him out.

He called out again, "What in hell are you doing on that porch nursing that baby? You should be in the house!"

Daught replied, "Go on about your business, Mac."

"Woman, I told you to get into that house!"

"Go on now, Mac," she repeated calmly but firmly.

Then he came up and slapped her. Like a bolt of lightning, quicker than I ever seen anybody move, she reached inside her bosom, and pulled out her straight razor with her right hand while still holding your newborn sister, Elizabeth, with her left hand. She started slashing him about his arms as he held them up to protect his face. He swung and hit her in her left jaw and knocked her down. But she refused to drop your baby sister. She got back up on her feet, slashing the left side of his body. As he held his hands up again to protect his face, she started cutting him on the right side of his body.

Seeing little result for her efforts, she hit him on top of his head with the butt of the razor. He sobered up quickly! You should have seen the way panic filled his eyes as he saw his newly purchased suit coming apart in shreds. Little blood was evident as he ran for Sheriff Phillip Martin's house on the backside of Ma Babe's property fence. He leaped over the back fence hollering for the sheriff. Hearing the commotion in his backyard, Sheriff Martin came running to his backdoor. Before he opened the backdoor, he retrieved his pistol lying on the table and holstered it.

"Who's out there hollering for me?"

"It's me, Sheriff! George Mac Wilson, and oh Lord, she has cut me to pieces."

"Are you still living George Mac?"

"Yes sir, I think so, sir."

"Then whoever cut you to pieces didn't kill you."

"It was Daught."

Seeing Daught standing by her back fence with the baby in one hand and her razor in the other Sheriff Martin replied, "What do you want me to do, George Mac?"

"I want you to lock her up."

"For what? She has your baby in her arms and she is standing on her own property."

Not seeing much blood, he asked, "Daught, does that razor of yours need to be sharpened?"

Your mama replied, "No, it does not, Sheriff. He has a silk lining in his new suit and no razor will cut through silk." The Sheriff laughed his ass off.

Uncle Fass loved telling the boys that story. I may have heard it 10 times. I believe it was to teach them how to treat and respect women. *Prophet or Pariah?*

To add insult to injury, every Sunday afternoon after church, Reverend Foster Jobarr came by the house for dinner with the deacons from Lebanon Baptist Church. They ate all the best pieces of chicken while we kids huddled outside sitting on the kitchen steps, watching, waiting and hungry. By the time they finished, all they left us kids were the chicken backs, butts, gizzards, necks, and feet. They ate their fill and they did not move from the table until Uncle Fass sent Old Satchmo, our dog who was part bloodhound, out into the cotton fields to find and dig up some moonshine. Once they had a few good swigs, they would stumble out to Uncle Fass's 1934 Model-A Ford Truck, and he drove them home. Sometimes, it would be 6:00 or 7:00 in the evening before they left. We kids would be in an evil mood, tired, hungry, and crying. One Sunday, I got tired of it because we had all had enough.

I told Ma Babe, "The Bible says, feed first the children of Israel."

I thought I was going to get my behind beat, but she smiled and said to me, "I am surprised you know the Bible so well, Kitty."

The next Sunday, she fed us first. There was no such Bible verse.
Prophet or Pariah?

There were eight of us now: Earnest, Homer, Willie, Fred and Freddie Mae (the twins), Elizabeth, Alfred, and me, Erma the oldest. I loved them all, but I was damn tired of taking care of them. The last time Mama left home, she returned with a new one, my newest brother Alfred. Then she left again. I had to make his formula, change his diapers, and rock him back to sleep at 2:00 a.m. One day, I was so tired that I fell asleep in class during my poetry lesson, and I loved poetry. My teacher, Mrs. Frazier, scolded me for it. This really hurt my feelings and made me very angry.

I told Ma Babe, "I am going to kill all of them."

She replied, "I will beat the hell out of you, if you do."

She thought I was joking. She kept a .38 caliber pistol under her pillow, although she hid the bullets. I knew where she hid the bullets, but she didn't know I knew. As soon as she went to work, I went to the cupboard in the kitchen. I stood on a chair so I could reach the top shelf and I searched with my hand for the bullets that Ma Babe kept for her .38. I found six bullets in a matchbox.

I climbed down and told all of my brothers and sisters to gather around the chimney fire in the living room. When I seated them all in front of the fire, I threw all the bullets into the flames. I refused to let 'em move. As the bullets started to fire, scream, and ricochet out of the fireplace, they tried to run screaming and crying. I pushed them back down. I was going to kill them all. A bullet ricocheted a few inches from my head. Then there was quiet—not a sound, except for the crackling fire. I looked at them and they all looked at me. No one was hurt, not a one, not a one. If Mother Nature wanted us to die, she would have taken them and me too. I decided she must have put us all here for a reason after all.

I got the beating of my life when Ma Babe arrived home. But this beating was different. She made me break off the thinnest Pomegranate branch I could find. I received seven licks: one for each child. Six licks: one for each bullet, and one for good measure. This is when the numbers 761 became one of my favorite number combinations.

> *Prophet or Pariah*
> *I threw bullets into fire.*
> *Only to cement my desire*
> *To commit my soul to aspire*
> *By committing this feverous deed*
> *I succumbed*
> *To my selfish foolish needs*
> *That would not heed.*
> *Yet, I did not yield*
> *To Mother Nature's speed*
> *That one's life purpose*
> *Must be righteous and true*
> *For their soul to reap.*

Now, Ma Babe was very concerned about me continuing to care for my brothers and sisters. She tried to talk to Mama trying to make her turn her "ways" around. She didn't tell her what I did because she would have beaten the life out of me too. Ma Babe asked Mrs. Pie, who lived across the road, to write a letter to her oldest daughter, Nora, who was living in New York City, asking for her help with my situation of Daught's dumping her children on me.

After Ma Babe told her about the bullets in the fire incident, Aunt Nora sent for me in the summer of 1939 to give me a break from my brothers and sisters. The Ramses, her employers, gave me a summer job helping Aunt Nora care for their children. A few years earlier, Aunt

Nora had moved to New York City from Plains to work for them. They were a prominent Jewish family living in Forest Hills, Queens. They were part owners of a major department store chain. Years before, she worked for a Jewish family here in Plains and she was highly recommended by them. She was an excellent Nanny and the Plains family hated to lose her. But they wanted her to be successful in her profession. Based on that recommendation, the Ramses asked that she come to Queens, New York, to take care of their young children. They doubled her salary to $30 a week at the time.

The scourge of the Hill Family was that many of our women were barren. I often wondered if I had the same condition. None of Ma Babe's four sisters had any children. Either they were barren, could not carry children long term, or would lose them in their early years. Aunt Nora loved children but could not have any.

I went to New York City that summer and had a ball. I learned how to prepare kosher meals as well as how to set a table, and clean and dress a house for holidays. I was already an expert at taking care of kids, and I did a good job taking care of Bill and Sarah.

On our days off, Aunt Nora would take me shopping downtown to all the fabulous department stores on 34th Street. I spent most of my earnings on clothes, shoes, and whatever else Aunt Nora wanted to spend on me.

761 874 058 393

Hill Family Home, 185 Bonds Trail Road
Plains, GeorgiaPlains, Georgia

Hill Family Home Ma Babe's Wood Stove

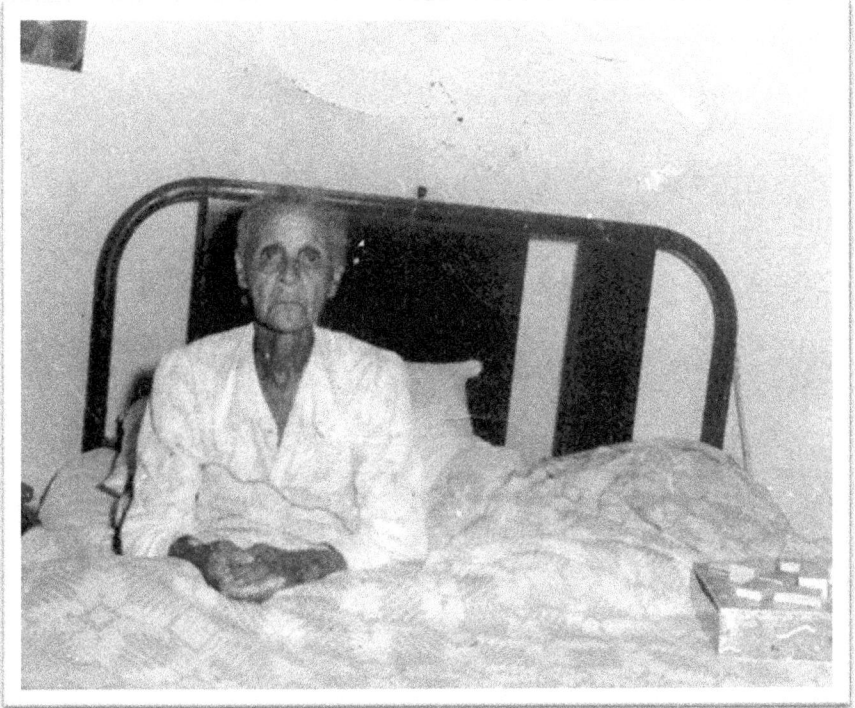

Ma Babe, 1950

Chapter III

Red Dirt and Moonshine

Uncle Fass hauled peanuts for the Carter family and other farmers between Plains and Americus, Georgia during the week. On the weekends, he ran his Roadhouse. He was a real 'card.' And he was stingy as hell! He refused to pay us much for working at his Roadhouse. He said we loved him so much that we should work for free. About a nickel a day was all we could squeeze out of him, and we worked most weekends.

He never spent more than he should for anything, and he saved his money in a large steamer trunk that Ma Babe kept an eye on under her bed. It was so heavy with nickels and dimes that we kids couldn't pull it out from under the bed if we wanted to. He even had difficulty pulling it out himself because of an injury to his right leg he had since he was a child. He had a wound that became infected and never healed. It caused his left leg to grow longer than his right leg, and he walked with a severe limp.

Bad leg or not, Uncle Fass felt like he was the slickest guy in Plains, Georgia. Mr. Carter's white supervisor loaded extra bags of peanuts on Uncle Fass's truck for him to take to market. When Mr. Carter caught his supervisor red-handed stealing, his foreman snitched on Uncle Fass.

He said, "It was Fass who stole the extra bags of peanuts."

Since no Black man could challenge the word of a white man, no matter how white he looked, the judge sentenced Uncle Fass to two years on the Sumter County Chain Gang. Mr. Carter's white supervisor got three months. Uncle Fass told us that he did not know anything about the extra bags of peanuts, but we knew he was lying.

Ma Babe begged the Carters to ask the judge to reduce his sentence to one year. But he still got two years on the Chain Gang for it. This destroyed the long relationship our family had with the Carters.

Often in the past, Mrs. Lillian invited my brothers and family over to her home for playdates. On one date, the boys and Jimmy were out in the front yard playing while we sat on the porch drinking sweet tea. The boys were playing with Jimmy's red wagon when all of a sudden Mrs. Lillian jumped up out of her chair and went running towards the boys screaming "No, no!"

We all stood up to see what was wrong. The boys were taking turns pulling one another in Jimmy's red wagon. My brothers would pull Jimmy, and then Jimmy would pull my brothers. When she saw Jimmy pulling Negro boys, she had a fit. It was okay for my brothers to pull Jimmy, but not the other way around. They were good people, generally without prejudice, but old habits die hard in the south.

Uncle Fass's bad leg had also kept him from being able to do road-work on the Chain Gang. But the county knew he was a good cook. Sheriff Martin knew our family because he lived directly behind us. So, he told the county to hire him as the Chain Gang's cook for $1.00 per day.

Uncle Fass did his time mostly at home. They let him come home every night because he needed to start really early in the mornings cooking for the prisoners and guards. They loved his cooking. When he finished preparing their meals, he delivered them to the inmates and guards on the road. Then he returned home to bed down with his family for the night. Now, you know he prepared extra for us to eat too. Uncle Fass served out his time on the Chain Gang at home and he made money doing it. *Prophet or Pariah?*

Uncle Fass did not have any children. So, he helped Ma Babe take care of us. We still missed a few meals—not many—but some. Even with the government's help, the Depression was very tough. To help make ends meet and to keep regular folks from starving, President Franklin D. Roosevelt gave us surplus food. When you added the Chain Gang's food with President Roosevelt's 'New Deal' food, like powdered milk, cheese, flour, canned vegetables and meat. Boy, did we eat well during those years. We really ate better than most white folks some of the time. I made a promise to myself that no child of mine would ever struggle to eat as I did during the Great Depression.

He knew he could 'cook it up good' too. It is what inspired him to open the Roadhouse on the back side of Main Street in Plains. It was the hit of Plains. Chute Cranford, South Georgia's best moonshiner, did time on the Chain Gang with Uncle Fass. He loaned Uncle Fass money to help open the Roadhouse and advanced him the moonshine to sell.

When the summer was over, I was one sad young lady going back home to Plains, Georgia. I traveled back to Plains with hopes of finishing high school at A.S. Staley High School in Americus, Georgia. On weekends, I still worked in Uncle Fass's Roadhouse selling five-cent pig ear sandwiches and pop through the front door and moonshine through the back door. Ma Babe still would not let me work there, officially. So, I lied to her, saying that I was going to Minifield's, my girlfriend's house, to visit. Then I would sneak over to the Roadhouse and beg Uncle Fass to let me work.

The only 'sparking' going on in Plains was at Uncle Fass's place. The jukebox was full of nickels by the end of the night although half of them were slugs. Fats Waller's "The Viper" was one of the top tunes played on the jukebox. Most white folks did not know what he was singing about. But it was about smoking marijuana. Fats wrote and recorded many popular songs. The federal government didn't like his songs. They said they were immoral. But they allowed him to be recorded anyway on something they called a V-Chip.

My Aunt Effie hung out a lot at Uncle Fass's Roadhouse and performed for free every chance she could. She could really sing and cut a rug too. When she was growing up, she sang in the Lebanon Baptist Church Choir every fourth Sunday. She had one son named Garrett, who she loved to death. Her mother-in-law took care of him while she was on the road. She was going to make it big in Vaudeville as the opening act for a well-known comedian named Pig Meat Markham. Vaudeville was a traveling variety show including song, dance, comedy, and freak acts like the smallest man on earth as well as the rubber lady who could tie herself up into a ball.

Once, Fats made a stop at Uncle Fass's Roadhouse on his way to Atlanta. Aunt Effie left town with him, headed for the bright lights of

Vaudeville in Atlanta. She was going to make it big in Vaudeville as the opening act for a well-known comedian named Pig Meat Markham. Vaudeville was a traveling variety show including song, dance, comedy, and freak acts like the smallest man on earth as well as the rubber lady who could tie herself up into a ball. Aunt Effie and her partner also filled in for a popular duo that everyone knew as "Butterbeans and Susie." They were going to sing, dance and laugh themselves into Vaudeville fame.

Ma Babe said Effie had to leave town with Fats in a hurry, they were just ahead of the local Sheriffs. Her boyfriend, Joe Mercer, had shot and killed Jimmy Lord's white son at his gas station on the road to Americus. Jimmy Lord's son tried to cheat him out of his money after filling his gas tank. The Plains Sheriff, Phillip Martin, learned Joe had moved in with Aunt Effie, but they were too afraid to go after him. They called the County Sheriff, Willis Perry McAndrews in Americus, but they only had one pistol between them for the whole police department. That was all Sumter County could afford at the time and they said it wouldn't shoot half the time. They had to wait until they got help from the Sheriff in Crisp County, the next county over.

They tried to sneak up on him at night at Aunt Effie's house in the Negro section of downtown Plains, which we called "The Bottom." But there were no electric lights there and Joe beat two deputies senseless in the dark before escaping.

The Sheriff then came knocking on Ma Babe's door hollering, "Open up, Babe!"

"Hold your horses! Who is it and what do you want, anyway?"

"Open up, Babe! It's Plains Sheriff Martin. We are looking for Joe. He killed Jimmy Lord's son!"

As Ma Babe opened the door, there were three police cars loaded with enough redneck crackers to have a Klan rally on her front porch.

"Well, he is not here and the children are asleep."

"We wanna come in to look for ourselves!"

"Well, you can come in, Phillip, but the rest of you have to stay put."

The Sheriff walked into the house and looked around. Then he stuck his billy club under the beds and into the closets. He then walked back out onto the porch, waking up the whole family saying,

"He ain't here, boys."

The Sheriff turned to Ma Babe and said, "Tell that nigger we are going to kill him, if he doesn't turn himself in."

Ma Babe replied, "That makes a lot of sense, Sheriff. You are going to kill him one way or another, anyway."

Half asleep and looking at three police cars full of rednecks, I said, "Sheriff, you're gonna need mo' help than that to kill him."

Ma Babe scolded, "Shut your mouth, Kitty."

"Babe, you had better teach that young'un how to talk to white folks. Let's go, boys."

Two weeks passed before someone snitched to the Sheriff that Joe was hiding in the attic of his sister's house in Tifton, Georgia. They found him there with his second girlfriend, Rosa Lee. They did not ask any questions. They just shot into the ceiling until they saw his blood dripping through the holes. Rosa Lee said there were more than 20 bullet holes in the ceiling of his sister's house. Rosa Lee escaped by removing boards in the roof and climbing down the side of the chimney.

As for Joe, they chained his body to the back bumper of a police car and dragged him back to Americus.

Deeds like this were supposed to scare Negro folks back to the white folk's 'straight-and-narrow.' But all they did were cause more Negroes to leave town for the 'War Factories' up north. In turn, this left no men for us young women who were left behind. What little remained of the planter's cotton and peanut crops were dying in the fields because there were not enough Negro farmhands left in Plains, Georgia to pick them. The poor white folks that remained were too few and they would not work for 'peanuts,' like Negroes.

As a businessman, Uncle Fass did a good liquor business, and the law knew it too. The revenuers would stop by the Roadhouse often to search his place for liquor. I remember one time this new revenuer came to the Roadhouse late one evening saying he was new in town, and Uncle Fass sold him a drink. He went into the bottom of the cooler, reaching through the hidden trapdoor for a fresh jar of shine. He pulled it up slowly as the revenuer sat there licking his lips, and poured him some. Before the night was over, the revenuer got good and drunk, and he tipped me well too.

Uncle Fass said to me, "Kitty, we haven't seen the last of him."

The next day the revenuer pulled up to the Roadhouse in a shiny new car, wearing a new suit with a shiny new badge hanging from his collar. He jumped out of his car with another revenuer in tow.

He pulled his gun on Uncle Fass saying, "I got you now boy, and I know where you are hiding the shine."

He went over to the cooler, opened it up, reached deep into the cold water and pulled out a jar.

Then he turned to his boss and said, "We got 'em now."

Then he handed the jar to his boss. His boss took a long slip and spit it all out, hollering, "You stupid ass! That is iced tea!"

They never found anything because Uncle Fass kept a few mason jars of iced tea on top of the trapdoor in the cooler. This worked fine if someone really wanted iced tea or if someone was trying to set him up to bust him, like those revenuers. And we kept our shine supply buried in Mr. Murry's cotton fields a short way from the Roadhouse.

They would have to dig up his entire 18 acres of cotton to find it. Uncle Fass only went out at night to dig it up. He would get to 'scat singing' like Ella Fitzgerald to his dog, "Old Satchmo." Then he would pour a little swig of shine in his bowl. That dog would lap it up, start to howl, chase his tail, and then take off into the cotton fields. When he found the right spot, he would start digging like a maniac. On cue, Uncle Fass came running behind him with his shovel to dig up the shine.

Everybody in Sumter County knew we were selling Chute Cranford's Shine. This was the best shine in Southern Georgia. We didn't have any problem out of Plains' Sheriff Martin with selling shine because we shared the same back yard. It was the county sheriff and federal revenuers that we had to be mindful of.

Uncle Fass could not read much either. But he sure knew how to count money in his head. You couldn't keep count on paper tabs while selling shine. I was getting to be as good as Uncle Fass was at keeping every customers' tab in my head. Some of the customers would try to confuse or fool me, but I never lost a nickel. Those who refused to pay were put out, and they could not come back until they paid up. The customers also shot dice out the back door under the new electric light.

Ma Babe warned me several times, "That's how your grandfather, Robert, got killed. It was in the same year that your Aunt Leila Mae (Touchy) was born. I told you, Kitty, to stop working there with your uncle."

The honky-tonk business was good in hard times, if you could stay ahead of the revenuers. Every Thursday night, about 11:00 p.m., we received a shipment of shine from Chute Cranford's still. Chute's youngest boy, Cory, came flying down the highway about 120 miles per hour in his 1936 souped-up Packard, with no headlights on and in pitch darkness.

Cory often said, "My Packard put the new Georgia State Police V8 Ford Deluxe to sleep by the side of the road. My Packard could outrun the devil, if it wanted to!"

He called it "The 120."

I thought it was because the vehicle could run 120 miles per hour. But that was not the reason. It was 120 inches long and had a souped-up, 282 cubic-inch inline 8cylinder engine. They made the Packard 120 the Indy Pace Car that same year.

When Cory was outrunning the police, he called it "dancing by the moonlight." He would brag, "Three whole police cars took after me last Tuesday night and they did not find anything but my tracks. There ain't a police car in Sumter County that can catch it, even when it is fully loaded with shine. That Packard knows it can run!"

All of Chute's cars had false compartments behind the back seat that hid the liquor. I was the only one thin enough to slide in back to fetch out the shine from boxes filled with quart mason jars. Cory was a few years ahead of me in school. He was a good student, but he said he wanted to drive racecars for a living.

His papa would say, "My boy is plumb crazy."

Uncle Fass said, "It is safer to drive on a professional racetrack with Cory than on these back roads in Georgia, hauling shine at night and with no lights on. Chute Cranford lost two drivers this year. One was his nephew, Samuel Beaver, whose souped-up Ford ran into a new electrical poll after he missed a high-speed turn in total darkness in Crisp County. The car exploded when the broken electrical line ignited the moonshine in his car and he burned to death." This was truly a very dangerous business.

On Friday and Saturday nights, the Roadhouse was hopping. Even the white folks snuck in. Boy, those five-cent pig ear sandwiches sold like hot cakes. Plains Sheriff Martin often stopped by to run the white folks off when the place became crowded. When he did, the white folks would drive down the road a bit, turn around, and come back before their drinks got warm.

Uncle Fass tried to make me go home early because he knew I had snuck out of the house to work. He also knew my youngest sister, Freddie Mae, would tell Ma Babe I was at the Roadhouse working. And when she heard, Ma Babe would beat the devil out of me when she came home from work. He also knew many of the men in the Roadhouse got very rowdy when they were drinking. The white boys from Americus, Georgia were the worst when they drank. When they got drunk, they tried to put their hands up my skirt as I served them shine. When they did, I slapped the natural born devil out of them. *They didn't realize—I was ice.*

Uncle Fass said that I had to be careful slapping those white boys because they had some evil parents and they would close him down. Some were the sons of the Sumter County judges, commissioners and sheriffs. Jason McAndrews was the son of Sumter County Sheriff Willis Perry McAndrews, and I could not stand him. When they were drunk, Jason and his friend Morse Smith would drive to my house after I got off work. Knowing no men were in the house, they called out, "We want Kitty! We want Kitty!"

This went on Saturday night after Saturday night, and Ma Babe put up with it. Finally, one Saturday night she grew tired of it and pulled me straight out of my bed in my nightclothes. She threw open the front door and hollered, "If you want her, come-on and get her!"

As my sister Freddie Mae held the kerosene lamp up behind me, Ma Babe hid behind the door with an axe held above her head. I must have been one sexy, enticing sight standing there half naked and half asleep in my nightclothes with my body's silhouette blending in with the moonlight. However, I do not think I was worth losing their lives over, and they didn't think so either. We did not have any more problems out of them after that for a long while.

And that Jason was nothing but trouble. He raped Mr. Murry's daughter, Beth, about six months back on her way from school in Americus. The white kids from Plains had a school bus to take them to and from high school in Americus, 10 miles away. The Negro kids did not. It was a prime example of our separate, but equal conditions. It would take you close to three hours to walk there one way. Some stretches of the road were long, heavily wooded, and deserted. Most Negro kids' families or friends drove them or they caught the Greyhound bus extremely early in the morning. The brave ones thumbed a ride back in the afternoon.

One day, Mr. Murry was late picking up his daughter, Beth. So, she started walking home alone. Jason McAndrews and his friend Morse Smith followed her in his pickup truck. About halfway between Americus and Plains, they pulled up beside her and asked if she wanted a ride home. She knew Jason from the white high school, which was nearby, and said yes. She got in the truck and sat between them in the front seat. They started driving down the road and Jason suddenly turned off the road. She asked them to let her out of the truck and she started fighting them. They beat her up really bad. Then they pulled the truck into the woods and raped her several times. They told her to keep quiet about it, or they would kill her.

Mr. Murry, coming from the opposite direction, saw her walking bloodied and dazed on the side of the road. He went crazy. He did not even ask her what happened. He placed her in his truck, drove her home, went into their house, and got his loaded shotgun. His wife, Maggie, begged him not to kill Jason. The whole town knew he had done this before. She grabbed the shotgun from him and shot out the tires on his truck. She knew they would kill him before he got within 10 feet of Jason McAndrews. He just bent over and cried as Maggie tended to Beth's wounds. *Now, I was Mother Nature and if I got the chance, I would rain thunder and lightning down on them both.*

God knows I would.

263 478 850 933

Leila Mae and Luther McGarrah, 1940

Erma Louise Hill,
Plains, GA, 1940

Arthur Bush Hill and Lilly Ann,
Detroit 1940

Chapter IV

Twin Spirits and Fred

Another reason you could say that Uncle Fass was teaching me how to drive was that it was his way of paying me for working at the Roadhouse. One thing was for sure: he loved fussing at me while I learned.

"Kitty, I told you to stop daydreaming while you drive! You had better pay attention, gal. Watch out for that truck, Kitty!"

"What truck, Uncle Fass?" I asked laughing as he grabbed the steering wheel.

"Be careful, Kitty, and slow down! There is a stop sign ahead! Now, push down on the clutch—that's it. Now, release it slowly and give her some gas as you release it. Make a left turn here. Hot damn,

Kitty, you got it now!"

"Kapow!" went the engine of Uncle Fass's 1934 Model A truck as it jerked its way down Georgia's dusty Highway 308.

"Boy Kitty, you kicked up a storm of red dirt behind us. That red Georgia dust is covering everything in sight."

The wind started blowing hard and in every direction at the same time. It was strange. The red dust prevented me from seeing where I was going. A man's figure appeared in the middle of the road. I veered right to avoid him. Uncle Fass had me pull over so we could see if I had hit someone. After I pulled over, a man walked out of the red dirt storm, raised his hand to say hello without saying a word, and handed Uncle Fass a container of salve.

It was Mother Nature's ambassador himself, Twin Spirits, who made the salve. He was an old Creek Indian medicine man who lived deep in the woods south of Plains. Some say he was about 80 years old. Some say he was over 100. And some say he did not know how old he was. His father was a Creek Indian medicine man, and his mother was also a Creek Indian medicine woman. They told him he was a special being, spiritually connected to the earth and to his ancestors who traveled the stars.

He often said, "I live with the Star People. They visit earth all the time. They move around with earthly people unnoticed. They are not pleased with the human caretakers of the earth, nor with how humans treat one another."

He could talk for hours telling his peoples' story. And what he said made you want to listen: "The Creek Nation was a large and powerful nation that controlled millions of acres of land in Georgia, Alabama, and Florida. The United States Government sent agents and land speculators, unsavory characters who made fraudulent land deals to scam and steal our rightful lands from the Creek Nation leaders.

Then internal civil war broke out, dividing our tribe and killing many. Taking advantage of our dissension, General Andrew Jackson led a military force at Horseshoe Bend in Alabama, killing 800 of my tribesmen in the so-called Red Stick War. The resulting treaty of Fort Jackson took 22 million acres of Creek native land from us.

The Creek Nation was soon relieved of their remaining land with the treaty of Indian Springs. For his treachery in illegally signing over our land, tribal members voted to kill William McIntosh, a Creek Nation tribal member. Several other worthless treaties followed, which brought about the complete removal of my people from Georgia. Remember Kitty, you must never trust your own people simply because you are of the same tribe."

He explained further: "My parents refused to go west in 1826 with the rest of the Creek Nation when President Andrew Jackson ordered their land be stolen from underneath them and ran them off to Oklahoma. In 1838, President Van Buren ordered the U.S. Army into Georgia to run off or kill the remaining Native Americans everywhere east of the Mississippi River. The U.S. Army found my parents' home deep in the Sumter County woods and burned it to the ground, forcing them out. Many of my people, including my parents, died on our 'forced marches' to Oklahoma.

My mother fell ill on an unknown, desolate, and snowy mountain pass. She could not go a step further and collapsed, falling into a ravine. My father could not reach her and he was forced to leave her there un-rescued and unburied.

Many women carried their dead babies in their arms for days, refusing to acknowledge their deaths or to leave them without a proper burial. My father made the 800-mile trek on foot; hungry, through the snow, rain, sleet, and tornados. There was little to nothing for them to eat on the trail and there was no food for them when they arrived in Oklahoma. He died of malnutrition two days after he made it.

We Native Americans called our forced move the "Trail of Tears." The U.S. government took our land and held corrupt auctions. They sold our land to white folks for almost nothing. That is how most of the counties in Western Georgia got started.

We traded with the white man along the Chattahoochee River. We welcomed white men into our huts and allowed them to marry our women. The whites convinced many of my tribesmen to become farmers and ranchers. Many of my tribesmen took up their trades. This caused a great deal of dissension among the tribal members.

The white man asked us to assimilate, and we did. He asked us to learn to speak his tongue, and we did. He asked us to accept his religion, and we did. He asked us to wear his clothes, and we did. He asked to live among us, and we allowed it. Then he stole our land by dividing our people against themselves and having us sign his papers. Our land cannot be sold, traded, abused, abandoned, or stolen. There is no word in our tongue for the ownership of personal land. The land is not ours. It belongs to our ancestors, our children, and our grandchildren, and must be protected and preserved. Kitty, please learn from our tragedy and from our discarded bones that were pounded into the dust."

We had many long conversations as we walked the red dirt roads of Plains, Georgia, in the evenings, when it was cool and easy for him to travel around without people noticing him.

He poured his wisdom into me regularly, saying things like: *"Kitty, you are Mother Nature.* You are a beautiful, young, intelligent woman, but you must not allow your beauty to become a vice that takes advantage of others: men or women.

It is your responsibility to protect the earth, your family, your way of life and most importantly your beliefs, no matter who speaks against them.

Always be your best self by setting and living by your own righteous rules and not the corrupt rules of others. You must reject the primitive instructs of men. Use your knowledge and skills for the benefit of all.

You must always show compassion and be kind and considerate of others, no matter their station in life, their physical or mental condition.

Discover your passions and live your own dreams. Dream big, follow your own heart, and cherish all of life's moments. Make no excuses for yourself, because you are responsible for creating your own happiness.

Embrace every possibility by making a wish and believing in miracles. Be spontaneous and fall in love, because today is the day your dreams will come true.

Always remember you are Mother Nature, the mother of the earth. The children from your loins will bring balance and harmony to our land, and rectify the sins committed against our peoples. One day we will lead again and we will do so with love, compassion, and respect for all."

"I respect everyone only if everyone respects me. I fall in love every week. The only problem is someone else may be in love with him also. It will take me a lifetime to understand the huge amount of knowledge that you have given me.

I have always dreamed that I was Lena Horne and Betty Davis rolled into one. They are beautiful, talented, intelligent, and successful women. But how can I really feel that way with my legs scratched up from chasing hogs through briar patches in the middle of the night?"

He looked at my legs, reached into his sack, pulled out a small container of salve and rubbed it on my battered legs. It looked similar to the salve he made for Uncle Fass. Uncle Fass used it to treat his leg that had not healed since he was a child. It prevented the infection from returning and his leg was fine as long as he treated it with the salve.

When it ran out, the infection returned and Twin Spirits always showed up in the nick of time with a new supply. Then he rubbed a sweet-smelling lemon oil on my forehead saying it would protect me from danger while he continued to tell me of his people's history.

He pounded the lessons of his people into my head until I thoroughly understood their history of having their bones pounded into the earth. Their discarded bones would be one of the foundations built of lessons I learned that I would build my dreams upon.

But I didn't understand many of the things he was saying, not yet at least. It seemed crazy to me that no one in the county, not the county sheriff nor anyone else could find where he lived—and many tried. He just showed up when he wanted to and he found you.

Twin Spirits was an outstanding medicine man. He knew things white doctors did not know about healing. He said his parents passed down all their knowledge to him as they were both greatly skilled in the ways of medicine men and women. He never went to a white school or a doctor in his life. His parents taught him how to make powerful medicine. He knew medical secrets of healing most humans would not understand. He said he had the gift to see into the future, but it was not permissible to reveal what he saw. He said we would meet again in the future.

He refused to leave Plains and said he would never leave Sumter County, Georgia. He maintained that one of his two souls, the earthly one, must remain connected to the earth in Sumter County, Georgia. The other one traveled the stars, racing back and forth through time. A glow emitted from his body when he walked the dirt roads at night. He walked the roads of Sumter County in total darkness, and he never moved from the middle of the road as cars approached. They slowed down and went around him without ever hitting him.

Fred, my younger brother, loved Twin Spirits. They talked for hours as they cut firewood in the forest. They would stack the cut wood high in cords so it could dry and be sold to the townsfolk and traveling gypsies. Twin Spirits would get very angry with Uncle Fass because he cheated customers by stacking the firewood in a cone shape in the basket, preventing it from filling properly, thereby shorting the customers of wood. He claimed Uncle Fass was teaching Fred bad habits, which he was. Uncle Fass was actually teaching us all his bad habits. Times were tough and we had to survive. *Prophet or Pariah?*

Fred was very smart, but he hated school. He felt learning to read and write were not necessary skills for earning a living. He worked in Uncle Fass's Roadhouse as a cook on weekends, and he was good at it. During the week, he worked with Twin Spirits cutting firewood in the forest that he and Uncle Fass sold.

Fred's biggest problem was the white girls in Plains. He was handsome as hell and they were always running after him. He just had a way with women, especially white women, which made Casanova look like a choir boy. The problem, he was deep in southern Georgia and that was a death sentence for any Negro male here; good looking or not. Although Plains, Georgia was not as segregated or racist as other towns in Georgia, you still had to be very careful.

Twin Spirits also talked to Fred about his women and the concerns we all had that too many of his girlfriends were white. Once again, he had a way with women, period. Black or white. I knew he was screwing at least two. One was C.L. Walker, the grocery store owner's daughter, Cookie. They would sit and talk for hours on the back porch of C.L. Walker's Grocery Store. When they got hungry, she would go and get food from the store and Fred would cook it for her at the Roadhouse. Her favorite was his smothered pork chops and Spanish rice with red eye gravy. I could see why the women loved him so. The key to a woman's heart is the same as a man's, through her stomach.

They packed up deliveries together in Uncle Fass's truck. When he left to deliver them, they snuck into the storage room at the back of the store and they went at it like rabbits. He must have been doing a good job because she would moan and holler like a sow in heat. I begged him to stop because you could hear them a block away. If he got caught, they would hang him for sure. The first thing white girls do when they get caught in the act with a Negro man is lie and say "He raped me!" I even told

Cookie that she was trying to get my brother killed. She just claimed that she loved him so much she could not leave him alone. I asked Uncle Fass to tell him to stop, but Fred still wouldn't listen.

One evening, I was mopping the floor of the Roadhouse. I could hear them going at it through the alleyway that connected the back of the Roadhouse with the store. They were really moaning and groaning in the storage room. I saw Mr. Walker walk though his back door heading for the storage room.

I hollered out, "Fred, I told you to ask Cookie for some Crisco cooking grease. Where is it, Fred?" The storage room door opened and he walked out. Then Mr. Walkers' sister, Flo, walked out behind him saying they could not find any. My mouth dropped to the floor. This was outrageous. He was now banging Mr. Walker's sister, and she was married. He was a dead man walking. I could tell by Mr. Walker's facial expression that he did not believe a word of it. His sister's reputation was well known in Plains and he told Fred he was not welcome in his store anymore. I know how these things work. All of a sudden, a group of hooded rednecks would show up at your doorstep late at night with guns and a rope in their hands.

Twin Spirits also begged him to stop. Then miraculously out of the blue, a few days later, a white Tennessee racehorse breeder by the name of Richard Baughan stopped by the Roadhouse for a drink. He was visiting Plains to purchase a race horse. He was very impressed with my younger brother, Fred, who hated Georgia and Georgia peanuts. And he refused to serve Georgia peanuts to customers in the Roadhouse, even though they were free.

Mr. Baughan, laughing his behind off, asked Fred, "Why do you refuse to serve me free peanuts?"

Fred replied, "I would leave Plains, Georgia today if God gave me wings. And I would destroy every peanut stalk in Sumter County before I left. Venomous snakes love to make nests in drying peanut stalks. When you lift them up, after they dry to place them on the wagon, the snakes strike by biting you in the neck. A good friend of mine was killed after being bitten in the neck in these damn Georgia peanut fields. The snakes hunt field mice, who are attracted to the drying peanuts."

Mr. Baughan asked, "Do you like horses?" "I like everything, but peanuts," he said.

"Fred, ask your Uncle Fass for permission to go to Tennessee with me to train racehorses."

Uncle Fass, overhearing the conversation, immediately replied, "Fred, if you are old enough to work, then you are old enough to take care of yourself."

The breeder drove Fred home and waited in his car while he packed his clothes. He kissed Ma Babe and me goodbye. I wished him well for Mama because she was out of town. And I waved him bye as they drove away on the dusty road, into the red sunset.

God knows, I was happy to see him leaving sitting upright in the front seat of a car instead of lying in the back of a hearse.

My Aunt Anny Lord Reid, Ma Babe's sister by Granny's first marriage, had several white boy friends, but she didn't care who knew it. She had them scheduled like doctor's visits. Sam Jacobs was one who visited her late on Friday nights after stopping by Uncle Fass's to pick up his "medicine." He stayed at her place all night. He told his wife she could sleep in their car all night in Anny Lord's front yard because she did not want to stay in their house alone. I just think she wanted to be close to him, even though he was with another woman. At least she could be close and keep an eye on him. Anny gave birth to a son fathered by him. But she did not tell him that Billy was his son until he was going off to college on a scholarship. He had a fit when he found out about it.

As I said, in Plains, Negroes and white people generally got along.

Some even got married, although marriage between the races was illegal in the state. You still had some white folks who lived in the same neighborhoods with Black folks and vice versa. Some even had children together. The Jim Crow segregation laws did not come about until the late 1800s, many years after the Civil War. Then slaves lived in the same houses with their masters. In fact, if you let white men tell it, the only miscegenation going on was between white men and Black women. I know for a fact that is not true. During the Civil War, there were not many white men available at home. Most of them were off fighting those "damned Yankees." Well, what do you think Old Nigger Jim was doing with lily white Mrs. Ann? He was earning his keep. I am willing to bet that the Census recorded a sharp increase in births, and all of them were not Black. This was even happening despite many white midwives' ugly practices of not tying off the umbilical cords of mixed-race babies of white mothers.

Every now and then, the white churchwomen would get riled up and they would hold a prayer vigil in front of a mixed couple's home. They said the devil's work was going on inside and they asked the Lord to clean-up the miscegenation. Every Friday and Saturday night at Uncle Fass's Roadhouse, you found most of their husbands here chasing after Negro women. Many said you could also hear Twin Spirits' Indian war drums beating in the forest late on Friday nights from the Roadhouse, but no one, drunk or sober, could ever find him or his drums.

In Europe, the world war drums were also beating loudly again. Life here at home was still recovering from the 1929 stock market crash. I read in the newspaper that those fancy fellows on Wall Street in New York City flushed the U.S. economy down the toilet. Now, we poor folks were trying to figure out how to fish it out and pay for it, and we had no money. Germany was scaring the devil out of everybody and the Europeans were killing one another. The U.S. government began talking softly about the peacetime draft once more. Suddenly, on September 18, 1940, they started it.

We had heard it all before. World War I was to be the war to end all wars. But here we go again. Uncle Frank Bush, Ma Babe's brother, started smoking marijuana to get out of the draft during WWI. When he went to take his physical, he told the draft board that he was hooked on the drug. But it didn't work. They marked him ready, but never called him. Uncle Fass's bad leg disqualified him for active duty and of no use to Uncle Sam. And my brothers were too young to fight.

Mrs. Frazier, my teacher, showed us a map of where Germany was. It was all the way on the other side of the world in Europe. It was a place that did not have many colored folks— just white folks. I had never been anywhere where there were no colored folks, which I could not even imagine. Boy, I thought I would like to visit that place someday.

And this Adolf fellow, the German leader, was saying all kinds of nasty things about Jewish people. I helped my Aunt Nora mind kids and clean the house for a Jewish family here in Plains. They paid her well for it. Also, a rich Jewish man from up north gave a lot of money to our colored school here in Plains to keep it open. They were nice, caring people to me. They were not the greedy, evil, domineering people this Adolf man said they were. It also did not seem to me that Jewish people were running the world because a white Christian family, the Walkers, owned the grocery store and regular southern white folks like the Carters owned just about everything else in town.

However, the "Tan Coyote," Jesse Owens, really showed that Adolf fellow a thing or two in 1936 when he won four gold medals over there in Germany and Negroes won a total of 13. Too bad these white folks down here in Georgia were not watching, listening, or paying attention.

On December 7, 1941, the colour of everything changed overnight from beautiful hues of yellow, blue, pink, and white dresses to ugly, drab olive. On this day the gray, painted bombs dropped from Japanese planes at Pearl Harbor. The bombs did not segregate, discriminate, nor distinguish in any fashion between the Black and white Americans they killed. They killed and wounded all Americans equally.

The newspapers were full of heroic stories of young Americans fighting to the death in defense of our nation. A young Negro Sailor Messman named Doris "Dorie" Miller was stationed on the battleship USS West Virginia in Pearl Harbor. His job was to serve white sailors. During the attack, he left the kitchen below deck, came up to the gun deck, and shot down several Japanese planes while his ship was on fire and under attack by Japanese torpedo bombers. The Japanese killed him later in the war. Once again, America's enemies did not discriminate, but Americans do.

The war and the attack on Pearl Harbor had an effect on us all. Most of my aunts and uncles had no children, except Aunt Effie. She was traveling and performing in a Vaudeville Show Her only son, Garrett, was living with his grandmother, on his father's side. Aunt Nora had been taking care of kids in New York City for a while, now. Uncle

Roy wanted to leave Plains, but his wife Lucille would not allow it. So, he helped Uncle Fass with the Roadhouse on the weekends. Aunt Touchy got married to Luther McGarrah, and they moved to Hartford, Connecticut for jobs at the steel mills. Why on earth was I begging my younger brothers to stay in Plains, Georgia? All of my family, including myself, were rethinking our lives.

913 483 819 532

State of Georgia
DEPARTMENT OF EDUCATION

Certificate

SUMTER _____ County _____ Plains Colored _____ School

This Certifies

That _Erma Louise Hill_ _____ has satisfactorily completed the __7th__ Grade Course of Study of _Sumter_ County, Georgia, and has passed the examination issued by the County Superintendent of Schools. **In Testimony of this fact** the signature of the school officials and of the principal of said school are attached hereto, this _____3rd_____ day of _____June_____ One Thousand Nine Hundred and _Thirty Eight_

State Superintendent of Schools

Teacher

Principal

SEAL
Date

County Superintendent of Schools

President County Board of Education

Erma Louise Hill Diploma, 1938

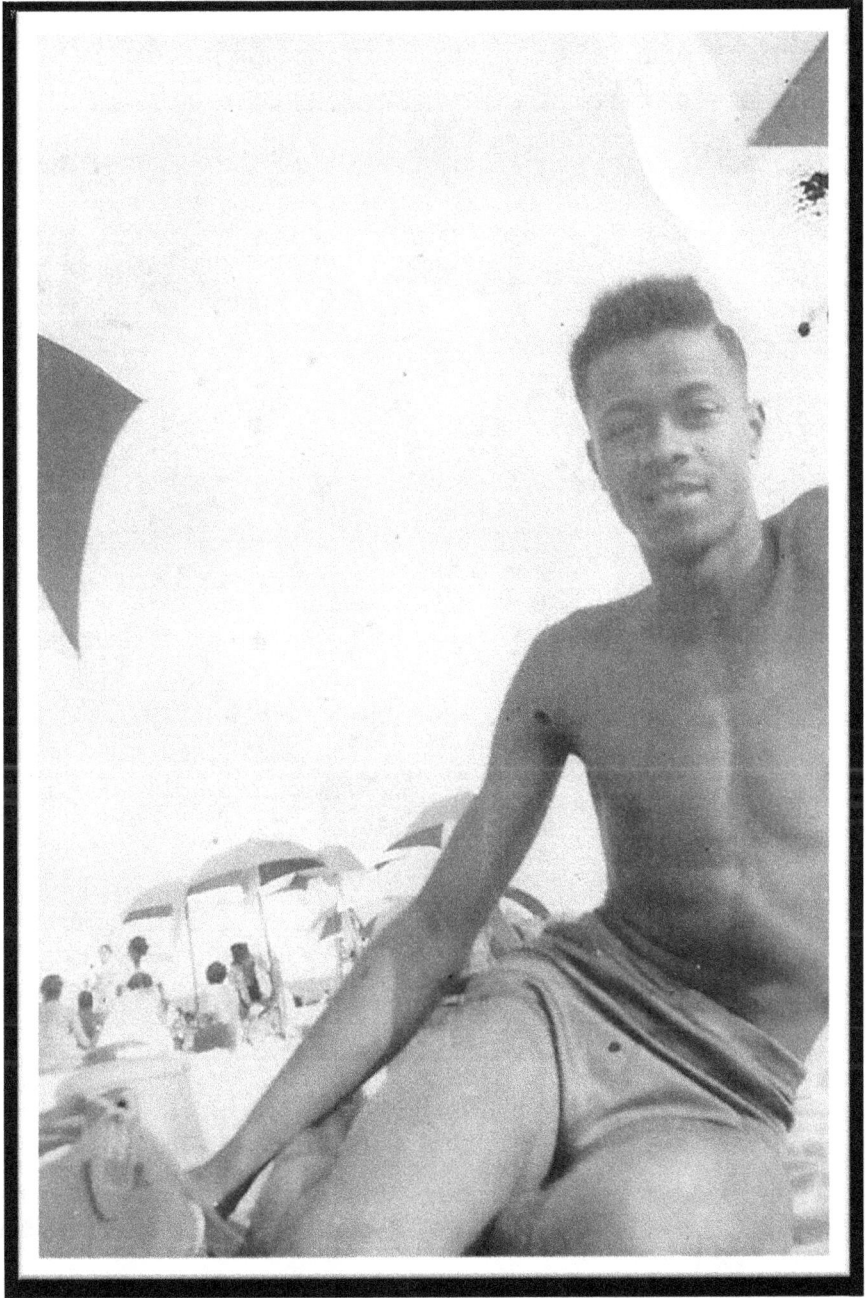

Fred P. Wilson, Coney Island, 1950

Fred P. Wilson in his Riding Outfit

Fred P. Wilson 1955

Chapter V

The Second Rape

Mother Nature sure knows how to take care of herself. Ma Babe told Uncle Fass to drive to Americus and pick me up from A.S. Staley High School.

But I refused to let him pick me up in the afternoons. Uncle Fass became really upset with me because I let Roger Brown, the undertaker's son, drive me home from high school in his father's Cadillac. He did not like Roger Brown because he was married, and all the girls in Sumter County wanted to ride in that car. He was cute as could be and very polite. I told Roger I knew he was married and that he had children by another woman other than his wife.

His only reply was, "Kitty, never mind all that. I like you a lot."

"Roger, you like too many other girls a lot. I am no cheap thrill just because I gave you a little bit. I am special. *I am Mother Nature and I deserve to be pampered and respected. You never want to cross Mother Nature because she neither forgets nor forgives.*"

He laughed, "You are the only true one, Kitty."

"What about your wife? Is she truly number two? And what does she have to say about it?"

"But she ain't here now to speak. Look what I got for you the last time I was in Atlanta."

"Are those real pearls?"

"Sure, I bought 'em from a real jewelry store. Try 'em on, Kitty.

After I tried them on, he just smiled and said, "Boy, they sho' look good on you."

"I know you men don't give up something without wanting something back, Roger," I protested.

"Naw Kitty, you and I are just real good friends. Go on, take 'em. I will stop by your uncle's place after I make my rounds on Saturday night. Have one of those pig ear sandwiches ready for me."

"How do you know I will be there?"

"You'll be there."

Beth, Mr. Murry's daughter walked over to the car saying "My father missed picking me up again."

"Beth, you can ride home with us."

"No, I will start walking and meet his car on the road."

"Roger, I will walk home with her," I said.

Roger said he had to retrieve the hearse to pick up a body and take it back to his father's funeral home. Then he would take us home. So, Beth and I started the 10mile walk to Plains together with the hope that we would meet Beth's father coming for her or Roger Brown following us.

We had walked about four miles when we noticed a blue pickup truck following us. Beth started to tremble and cry because she recognized the truck. I looked at her. She couldn't speak. The truck pulled up beside us. It was the Sumter County Sheriff's son, Jason McAndrews, driving, and his friend Morse Smith in the front seat.

"You nigger gals sure look like you need some tender loving care! Heh, heh, heh! Kitty, I noticed you have the hots for that nigger boy, Brown! You ain't the only nigger gal that have the hots for him. Too bad you will have to stand in line behind his wife and others. If you were my nigger gal, you would not have to stand in line for me."

Morse said, "You need another ride, Beth?" They both laughed and repeated together, "Another ride!"

He stopped the truck and opened the door. Shaking like a leaf, I grabbed Beth's hand and we took off running through the woods. The white boys took off after us. Chasing after those hogs had taught me how to run through a briar patch, but Beth couldn't keep up with me. She tripped and Morse caught her. I kept running; Jason was gaining on me. I heard Beth scream. I knew I wasn't going to outrun Jason. I stopped, picked up a tree branch, and leaned it out of sight against a tree.

As he grabbed me, I pulled up my dress and said "OK Jason, you want it, I will give it to you." He released me smiling with his eyes bulging at the sight of my panties covering my well-proportioned body. He unzipped his fly, dropped his pants, and pulled out his erect penis. I reached for the tree branch and hit him across his head. It startled him as he fell backwards with his pants binding his legs. Now mad as hell, he kicked off one of his pants legs, and came charging at me screaming "You nigger bitch!"

I rammed that tree branch as hard as I could between his legs. He let out a yell, that the devil could have heard in hell. I finished him off with several blows to the neck and head, breaking the tree branch in several places in the process. He fell to the ground unconscious.

I heard Beth crying in the distance and followed her crying to a clearing in the woods. Morse had mounted her from the rear. He was yipping and yelling as if he was riding a wild bronco. I picked up another tree branch and rammed the point of that branch straight up his naked ass. As I did so, I tripped and fell, and the branch broke off in his ass. It hurt him so bad that he started to speak in tongues. We both beat heaven and hell out of him. He had ripped Beth's dress and torn off her panties. I stuffed her bleeding panties in his mouth to keep him from hollering aloud. We continued to beat him, breaking both of his legs, so he could not chase after us.

"You good ole boys wanted it so bad! Now you can tell the rest of your friends how good it tasted!"

I grabbed Beth by the hand and we took flight like two new robins fleeing the nest for the first time. We ran out of the woods onto the highway. I went over to their truck, opened the hood and pulled out the distributor wires. Uncle Fass replaced them on his truck many times, and I knew the engine would not start without them.

About that time, Uncle Fass came driving down the road looking for us. Roger Brown told him we were walking home. He knew immediately whose truck we had disabled and the sight of us told him what had happened.

"You gals jump into the back of the truck! Hurry up!" He drove Beth home first. When Beth's mother saw her condition for the second time, she was inconsolable.

She screamed "No more!"

She went into the house and grabbed the shotgun. Mr. Murry ran for his truck, opened the driver's side door, and took the keys out of the ignition. She walked around to the front of the truck with her shotgun in one hand, opened the hood, reached inside, and pulled a spare set of keys from behind the battery.

Mr. Murry was now begging and pleading with his wife not to kill Jason. Beth told her parents what we had done to the boys. Hearing how we beat them helped her calm down just a bit. Then her parents told her to get into their truck so they could take her to the hospital in Americus.

Uncle Fass drove me home next, and I told Ma Babe what happened. She immediately told me to pack a suitcase full of clothes. As soon as I finished packing, Old Satchmo started to bark. A police car pulled into the front yard. County Sheriff Willis McAndrews got out of one door and his son stumbled out of the other. Through the curtains, we could see Beth was handcuffed, severely beaten and trembling in the back seat. He pulled his pistol from his holster and walked onto the porch. We all looked at one another because we were uncertain what to do.

Ma Babe whispered to Uncle Fass, "Get her out of here."

He replied, "My truck is blocked in front of the police car."

"I will hold them as long as I can. You get her out of here," she ordered.

Old Satchmo would not allow the Sheriff on the porch.

Ma Babe went to the front door and asked, "Who is it?"

"County Sheriff! Open up and you better call off your dog, or I will shoot the S.O.B.!"

She yelled out, "Satchmo, go into the backyard. Sheriff, I do not have any clothes on."

"We want that gal named Kitty!"

"What do you want her for?"

"Open up, or we will kick the damn door in!"

"Hold your horses. Let me put some clothes on."

There was only a speck of daylight left as Uncle Fass ran into the kitchen, grabbed a flashlight, and handed it to me.

He said, "Chute's grandson Cory is due to make a shine drop off nearby, in about 10 minutes. He will be low level flying on the road behind the house. When you hear that V8 rumbling, you jump onto the road and flash two short and one long. Be careful, he may run you over. Have him drive you over to Crisp County. There you will take the first bus to Atlanta and go to Ma Babe's youngest sister, your Aunt Sarah's house on Old Wheat Street. When you get to the bus station, put on Ma Babe's gloves and hat. The hat has a net that covers your face. Here is $20. Sit in the white section of the bus."

Uncle Fass was an old hand at passing for white. The sheriff continued to bang on the front door. I climbed out of the back window as Old Satchmo's barking kept the sheriff from coming into the backyard.

I took off running across those same briar-patched and snake-infested peanut fields that I ran after loose hogs on so many other nights. I did not realize this would be the last time in my life that I would run through these fields. I didn't need my flashlight, just that beautiful Georgia moonlight was enough. My legs had grown numb from the attacking weeds by the time I reached the back road and hid. A few minutes passed, and right on time, like Uncle Fass said, I heard this thundering noise from Cory's souped-up Packard. I saw his taillights sparkling through the trees like Christmas ornaments. As the car whistled around the curve, I jumped out into the road and flashed the signal with my flashlight. The car did not slow down and just in time, I jumped off the road before he ran me over. Quicker than a flash, Cory did a 180 degree turn in the middle of the road and stopped. He flashed his lights back at me and I flashed back.

Walking over to the car, I asked Cory, "What in the hell is wrong with you? You almost ran me over!"

"Kitty, I have to be careful. I have been robbed twice this year because too many people know the signal to stop me. Why did you stop me?"

"We beat the hell out of Jason McAndrews, the county sheriff's son, and his friend Morse Smith for raping Beth and trying to rape me. Now they are at my house looking for me and I need to get to the bus station over in Crisp County!"

Without asking any questions, he said, "The whole county knows those two have been doing that to Negro girls for years and getting away with it. Kitty, I just made a delivery and the "shine hole" behind the back seat is almost empty. Get in there quickly and pull the back seat up behind you."

Before I was seated well, he took off like a lightning strike. I bounced around like a bag of black-eyed peas in a grocery cart while moonshine spilled all over me. He flew through the back roads of Sumter County, Georgia with no headlights on, driving by the moonlight like we were being chased by a mad demon in the dark.

When we arrived at the bus station in Crisp County, he told me to stay in the 'shine hole' of the car while he entered the café that served as the bus station. He returned from the café with a bus ticket he bought for me to Atlanta. He told me the bus schedule said it would arrive in 20 minutes, but there were two Crisp County sheriff deputies in the café.

"When the bus arrives, I will distract the deputies so you can get on the bus."

I tried to give him the $4.00 he spent for the ticket, but he refused to take the money.

"Cory, boy, I have to pee badly."

He groaned, "Damn, Kitty."

He pulled his last full jar of shine from the trunk. He opened it, shook his head in disgust, poured it out on the ground and handed me the empty jar. He turned his back as I filled that empty shine jar halfway up, placed the top back on it, and handed it back to him to get rid of.

"I hope you don't sell it to somebody. They will get the surprise of their life."

A few moments later, the Greyhound bus pulled in front of the café. The driver stepped off the bus, calling all white passengers to produce their tickets to board first. I exited the car, dusted off my skirt, and turned its front with the small tears around to the back. With the hat-net covering my face, and gloves covering my hands, I walked over and got into the front of the boarding line with the other white passengers. No one noticed a thing. I placed my suitcase down by the bus's door and the driver said, "Pick it up."

I froze as my eyes opened wide. He told a Negro passenger standing at the back of the line to pick up my bag and place it in the bus's baggage storage compartment. As I stepped up to board the bus, one of the sheriff deputies who Cory was talking to came out of the café and walked straight towards me. I almost shit in my panties. He then made an abrupt left turn and walked to the men's room behind the café. I took a seat in the second row behind the driver.

After the driver seated the white passengers, he instructed the Negro passengers to board. The sheriff deputies came out of the café and checked each Negro passenger before allowing them to board the bus. The driver then took his seat, released the brake, and went ahead to Atlanta. Then unexpectedly, the white passenger seated next to me jumped up in disgust. She looked at me, then the driver as he slowed the bus, and mumbled, "Drunkard" softly. She then changed her seat to one in the back of the bus next to a Negro passenger. I smelled like a moonshine still. The driver smiled, shaking his head, and continued towards Atlanta.

Plains, Georgia is about 160 miles from Atlanta, a four-hour trip with one stop. The cultural difference between the two towns is like the Earth vs. Mars—two separate planets. I had the second row behind the driver to myself. The bus made one stop in Macon, Georgia and I had to pee so badly. But I stayed on the bus because the station was crawling with sheriff deputies. The trip was uneventful, except for me crossing and uncrossing my legs trying to hold my pee.

When we finally arrived in Atlanta, I flew straight off the bus into the white restroom. I still smelled like a jar of moonshine, so I tried to take a birdbath and change clothes, all to no avail. A white passenger took a double take at me as I washed in the bathroom. She said nothing. She was unsure whether I was white or a Negro after I replaced my hat-net covering on my face. Anyway, this was Atlanta and there were more Negroes passing for white here than Carter had liver pills.

The bus terminal was on Cain Street, just north of Auburn Avenue This was an area better known to the Negro locals as "Sweet Auburn

Avenue." The Negro taxicabs lined up across the street from the white ones at the bus station. I walked across the street and took the first cab in the line. The driver was an older guy, short in stature about 5'6", and well spoken. Anyone older than 30 was old to me. He was good looking, with light skin and hazel eyes.

"What is your name, driver?"

"Roy. Roy Wiley."

"Wow, those hazel eyes. Wow. There are so many transplants here in Atlanta. Roy, where are you from?"

"I am from Opelika, Alabama. What about you?"

"Ummm, I am headed to my girlfriend's house on 495 Gary Drive, North West."

I decided on the bus not to go to Aunt Sarah's house because people in Plains knew we had family here.

"Are you all right?" he asked, looking at the condition of my clothes and smelling the moonshine that had spilled all over me.

I teased him saying, "You wouldn't take advantage of a girl who had one too many, would you?"

Laughing, he replied, "I would lose too many customers if I did."

He threw my well-tortured suitcase in the trunk of his cab and drove to Gary Drive.

My friend Minifield and I were so excited to see one another that I forgot to pay Roy. He was so patient and polite, he stood there smiling at me jumping and hugging my girlfriend. Finally, I reached into my well-traveled bag and gave him $2.00 for the ride.

As he turned to give me change, I said, "It's yours, Roy. Roy is your name, right?"

He replied, "Yes, I didn't get yours."

"They call me Kitty. Boy, I bet those hazel eyes have broken many hearts."

"Not as many hearts as yours. An intelligent, good looking young lady like you will do well here in Atlanta. My cabstand is across the street from the Royal Theatre on Auburn Avenue. They are looking for a cashier to sell movie tickets. Tell Mark, the manager, that I sent you. That is if you are really looking for a good job."

My friend, Minifield did not ask me any questions about why I showed up on her doorstep unannounced and late at night. She had left Plains about a year ago and we were very good friends before she left. She was a hairdresser in a beauty shop on Auburn Avenue.

Minifield revealed, "I have heard of Roy and his cab business on Auburn Avenue. He is well known in the community as a good person.

But girlfriend, those beautiful hazel eyes are married."

She said that Mark, the Royal Theatre's manager, got in about 10:00 a.m. I arrived at 9:30 a.m. and yes, he needed a cashier to sell tickets from the ticket booth in the front of the theater. Mark put me through several practice ticket sales to see if I could handle making change accurately. After he realized I could count change in my head, he hired me on the spot. There was only one problem. I had to work the evening shift, which I did not like.

Roy Wiley's "Car for Hire" cab service was about a block away from the theater. Roy Wiley was a part owner of the service. At least 40 to 50 cab drivers paid him a fee to receive telephone calls for cab service in Atlanta. The cab service was not a colored only business. Whatever customer called for service got service. Some white cab services refused to pick up in Negro neighborhoods, and they did so at their own economic peril. The color of money is green, not Black, or white. Roy Wiley was Head Operator/Manager. He managed the telephone calls, priced the rides, and dispatched the cabs to the different locations three days a week. And he drove his own cab the other three days.

We became good friends. He picked me up regularly from work and drove me home late at night after the picture show closed. Often, he brought me lunch, which I took at 6:00 p.m. In between runs and calls, with so much happening on Auburn Avenue,

Roy always looked in on me. He was losing about one cab a week due to shootings. On Friday and Saturday nights, customers being chased and shot at by disgruntled lovers and spouses ran all the way from the Top Hat Club on Auburn Avenue to the cabstand four long blocks away. The escaping customers jumped into the first cab they could find before the driver could say no. Bullets rained through the back windows and trunks. The drivers either hauled ass or were shot.

Often the drivers welded steel plates behind their rear seats to stay alive.

One evening, my girlfriend Minifield ran out of the Top Hat Club with her lover being chased by her former disgruntled boyfriend, Sam. She took off her high heels and was running for her life right past my ticket booth when shots rang out from behind her. She cried out "Oh God, I'm hit!"

Her lover looked down at her waist and saw blood covering her new dress. He pushed her into Roy's cab and they sped off to Grady Hospital. They rushed her into the emergency room, cut open her new dress, and started to look for the wound.

The doctor said, "Something smells strange," as he examined the wound.

He found nail polish all over her midsection. The bullet had gone through her handbag, struck the nail polish and splattered it all over her dress. She was fine. She had a few glass cuts from the bottle, but no bullet wounds at all. You would have thought it would have taught us a lesson about men, but it didn't.

The knowledge and skills I learned in school, from Twin Spirits and working in Uncle Fass's Roadhouse came in handy at the movie theater. I was always on time for work, I was never short with my cash receipts, and I always treated my customers with dignity and respect.

Almost a year after I arrived in Atlanta, on one rainy night at about 11:30 p.m., and after the last show let out, Roy was late picking me up. He had a fare across town. I grabbed an umbrella from the booth and went ahead to walk home. Suddenly, this tall figure appeared out of an alleyway and began following me. Due to the darkness of the night, I could not make out who it was, except for his slight limp. At that instant, I knew who it was. There was not another person in sight for me to cry out to. I started to run as fast as I could. As I turned the corner, I slipped and fell on the wet pavement, hitting my head on the curb.

I was dazed as the pursuer took off his belt, threw it over my head and around my neck saying, "You can run, nigger bitch, but you can't hide. I am gonna send your yellow, nigger ass back to Plains in a pine box in the back of a Brown's Funeral Service hearse."

I began to fight for my life. I stuck my fingernails into his eyes and he let out a scream louder than mine. But he would not let go of the belt no matter where I hit or kicked him. He was choking the life out of me. My consciousness began to fade and I began to see Twin Spirits standing in a dirt road in the middle of a bright light.

Then shots rang out, "Bam, bam!" one of them striking him in the side of his head, shattering it in large pieces. Blood and brain parts exploded all over me, my new dress, and the rain-soaked sidewalk. Then a friendly, familiar voice quietly yelled, "Who in the fuck was he?"

"The rapist from Plains that I told you about."

It was Roy, "Sorry I'm late, Kitty."

"Better late than never."

"Hand me his wallet."

He took his money out and scattered it all over the wet sidewalk.

Then he took his ID, ripped it up, and put the fragments in his pocket.

"The police will think he was just another white guy trying to pick up Negro prostitutes on a rainy night in a Negro neighborhood and got robbed. Leave him. Let's go."

"Go where? I am not going home. I may lead the police to my friend, Minifield."

I was scared to death and I refused to go back to Auburn Avenue. I had just gotten paid and I had enough money to buy a one-way ticket to New York City on the Silver Meteor that left the next afternoon. I asked Roy to drive me to the train station. I bought a newspaper and used it to cover my face, trying to hide as best as I could.

182 195 279 493

Chapter VI

Burning It At Both Ends

I sat in the train station all night talking to an elderly white woman. I did not ask her name because I did not want to give her mine. She sensed that I was nervous and upset.

She held my hand and said, "We are all sinners, but what is most important is what we do with our sins. Do we add to them by not learning anything from them? Or do we seek forgiveness by simply not repeating them again?"

We sat there and talked for hours. As the morning light began to rise through the station's stained-glass windows, she hugged me and said, *"Always remember child, you are Mother Nature."*

I almost fainted. She quickly got up, saying she had to catch her train, and then she wished me well but there was no train arrival announcement.

Twin Spirits' words began to ring in my ears. I remember him saying, "You can't run nor hide from your fate."

I made up my mind that I was not going to run from anything again. I was tired of running. I walked out of the train station to hail a cab, to where I didn't know. Then suddenly Roy's cab pulled up to the curb.

He said, "Get in; I will take you anywhere you wish to go."

I replied, "I do not know where I wish to go. But that was the nicest woman in the world that I talked to all night."

"What woman? I sat here all night watching you, making sure you were safe, and you did not talk to anyone all night. I have a friend with a very nice, vacant apartment on the north side, and the rent is cheap."

"Roy, I like you a lot, but I can see where this is going. The reason I am here in Atlanta is the married man I was dating could not keep his fucking mouth shut. I am not going to date another married man and

I am not ready to get married either. I do not know much about you other than you are married and own a cab company."

"Well, the only thing you need to know about me, Kitty, is I am a decent man, I never beat or raped a woman, and I know how to use a pistol. I once served time in the Fulton County Jail for it and I am willing to serve time again for you, if necessary. I know you are very confused now. So, let me introduce you to Mrs. Carrie Cunningham, a friend of mine. She owns the Royal Hotel and Restaurant on Auburn Avenue. She will rent you a room for a couple of days until we can figure this thing out together."

Mrs. Carrie Cunningham was well known in the community for being an outstanding person and ready to help anyone in need. He started the cab and then proceeded back to Auburn Avenue to the Royal Hotel. I was still trembling from head to toe and still in total confusion. Who was the nice elderly woman that I talked to all night?

Mrs. Cunningham met us at the hotel's front door. She was a beautiful, athletic looking woman, very pleasant, and made me feel right at home. She was immaculately dressed and made it very clear to me that she was not running a house of prostitution. She asked that I pay upfront in cash and I paid for two days.

Once Roy left, she invited me into the restaurant's kitchen for a cup of tea. She sensed that I was very tense and nervous. I told her I was living with my girlfriend in Atlanta. I also said I could not stay with friends or family anymore because of some personal issues I was having. I needed to be alone for a while, collect my thoughts, and then find my own place to stay.

Then she began to tell me her story. I was dead tired and began to fall asleep while she talked.

She said, "My mother and father were freed Negroes from Fitzgerald, Georgia. I left home very young to join the Silas Green Show as a circus rider."

I said half asleep, "My younger brother was in Tennessee learning to train racehorses."

She lit up squealing, "I love horses!"

I hadn't heard of the Silas Green Show, but that was nothing new for a country girl from Plains, Georgia. But that night I learned that it was one of the largest circuses in the country. She performed in front of a 16-piece band in a main tent that seated 1,400 people. She performed with top entertainers such as Bessie Smith and Muddy Waters.

She started her business life with a rooming house in Decatur, Georgia. Through it, she saved her money, and bought this hotel and restaurant, which sat on top of the Citizens Trust Bank on Auburn Avenue. She showed me the Jet Magazine article that said, "The Silas Green Show was as much a part of southern culture as collard greens and cornbread."

I was dead asleep by this time.

She said, "Come on, Kitty. I will show you to your room."

The next morning, Roy took me to look at several rooms. Most were too expensive for my pocketbook, but I settled on a place on 63 Hilliard. While Roy and I had breakfast, I bought a copy of the newspaper. In a bottom corner appeared a small article about an unidentified white man with half his face blown off found in an alley off Auburn Avenue. It said he was possibly drunk and became the victim of a robbery.

I finally told Minifield why I had to move. But these events didn't slow me or her down. We partied hard every weekend, all weekend. We attended all the clubs from Club Beautiful—The Top Hat Club to no name holes in the wall. By the time I got off work the clubs were just getting hot. The next day I could sleep late and still be on time for work. This work schedule was working out just fine after all.

Neither of us was a heavy drinker, but we knew all the bartenders and did not pay for most of our drinks.

We would nurse a glass of wine or champagne most of the night and we never accepted drinks from men we didn't know. That was a recipe for trouble. Men wanted to see where those drinks went down to and came out of before the night was over. We made a point to never do drugs or leave our drinks unattended. One of us would stay seated watching our drinks while the other danced or went to the restroom.

We always had to keep our wits about us. Our limit was two to three drinks because our storied past could rise up and bite us in the ass anytime. We saw all the big-name bands and acts that came through Atlanta like Count Basie, Lionel Hampton, Bessie Smith, Ella Fitzgerald and Duke Ellington. Duke's "Jungle Music" was hot and we loved those "Cutting Contests," during which two bands battled it out for top applause to win the top prize.

Mrs. Cunningham introduced me to her son, Red McAllister. He was a saxophone player and bandleader. He was not well known outside of the south, but he was a good musician. He told me about the unreported killings of Negro entertainers that were taking place all through the back roads and by ways in the south.

The Chitlin' Circuit was the Negro entertainment circuit that stretched from Texas to Chicago to New York City to Florida, and all points in between. Bandleaders and band members driving from gig to gig often fell prey to racist, corrupt police officers in rural counties. If you didn't have $25.00 bribe money to pay the local sheriff on some dark, desolate back road, you could lose your life and no one would find your body. He always carried extra cash to feed those 'redneck egos,' but many times he did not have enough. His mother sent bail money several times to get him and his band members out of backwoods jails.

I mentioned to Red that I had just received bad news from my grandmother concerning my Aunt Effie. She and her partner once opened for Butterbeans and Suzy. They traveled the treacherous Chitlin' Circuit trying to make a living in Vaudeville, and it was no joke. Ma Babe sent word that Aunt Effie died in Los Angles, California. She was working as a dance extra while they were making the movie Stormy Weather, starring Lena Horn. The director did retake after retake while he sprayed water-simulating rain on the cast. She caught pneumonia and died. Her only son Garrett died a month later after falling off a logging truck working at the local lumber mill in Plains. The driver of the truck brought his broken body to Ma Babe's house and laid him on the porch. They said his final words were, "Now I can go and be with my Mama."

Ma Babe said, "He didn't die from his injuries. He died from a broken heart."

World War II was in full swing in 1943. I could not believe the patriotism sweeping over the Negro community in Atlanta. I believe there were more Negroes signing up to buy war bonds than white folks. I even bought a few bonds myself. Young Negro men were signing up for the army in droves. I complained about the slim pickings of Negro men in Plains. Well hallelujah, that was not the case here, especially now in Atlanta.

There was an old Hill family saying, *"Be careful what you ask for. You may get it."*

Trains carrying colored troops were stopping and traveling through Atlanta headed for Fort Benning, Georgia, and all points south, two or three times a day. There were Negro men everywhere. There were tall ones, short ones, dark ones, light ones, fat ones, and skinny ones. There were straight-haired ones, kinky-haired ones, and curly-haired ones. There were hazel-eyed ones, brown-eyed ones, and gray-eyed ones. There was even a blue-eyed one—yes, a blue-eyed Negro. There were Baptists, Methodists, Catholics, Jews, and Adventists. I didn't have to make up for lost time now. Uncle Sam took care of that for me.

Almost everyone I dated fell in love with me in five seconds and proposed to marry me in 10. I received so many gifts, jewelry, flowers, and pictures that I gave most of them away to Big Bethel A.M.E Church on the corner.

The Royal Theatre was the first place they stopped on Auburn Avenue. And who was perched in the middle of Auburn Avenue sitting in the ticket booth to be the first to greet them? Yours truly.

There was Morris from Oklahoma, Charles from Arkansas, Scotty from Connecticut, Camden from Michigan, and many more. All were provided by Uncle Sam and I loved them all. Frankly, many were afraid of the war and the new killing skills that Uncle Sam taught them. Most of the men I met were young virgins, immature, lonely, and homesick. I made love to Marion Overstreet, a home sick devout Seventh Day Adventist. He returned a week later saying that his mother told him he had to marry me, or he would go to hell. I took him to the local jewelry store, where he bought rings for both of us. I told him to show his mother the receipt and tell her we were engaged.

Many were married and a long way from home. Most of the time, good company was all that was necessary to lift their spirits. I went shopping for pots and tableware for Charles because his wife never left the small town in Arkansas where they lived. The town was without a department store. The fancy gift-wrapped box I sent her pots and plates in was the most fantastic gift she ever received. She liked the box more than the pots.

I was having so much fun. But it was all without a purpose. Twin Spirit's words continued to ring in my ears, and those of the elderly lady in the train station that night. I lit the candle from both ends and I was burning it from the middle as well. I always used protection, but the condoms often broke and sex was like shooting dice.

For the first time, I began to understand Mother Nature's sexuality, and what she really liked and wanted in men. She liked intelligent, well-traveled and well-groomed men. She liked being catered to and men who were not overly aggressive. She preferred the low-key and quiet types. Her men did not have to spend lots of money or buy expensive things for her. A simple, thoughtful gift was pleasing enough. She was making more money than most of them, anyway.

Her desires were true to the words of Little Esther's blues song, "I like my men like I like my whiskey, aged and mellow."

But she was burning me out. And this much sexual activity quickly became unhealthy and boring.

Uncle Fass sent word to me through Aunt Sarah that my brothers were on their way north to Detroit, Michigan, and they wanted to stop and see me in Atlanta before they left Georgia for good.

When they arrived, Ernest, the oldest, said, "Uncle Fass finally found a wife. Her name is Lilly Ann and his wife's sister, Delmar, visited Plains from her home in Detroit. She told Uncle Fass that the owner of the Greek diner in her neighborhood wanted to open a new 24-hour diner located a few blocks from the Chrysler Tank Plant in Warren, Michigan."

He was also looking for a business partner to help him run the new restaurant. She mentioned Uncle Fass to him and he invited Uncle Fass to come to Detroit. Uncle Fass took the next train to Detroit to check out the new business opportunity, and he did not return to Plains. After you left, the county sheriff began to harass him and the business. It was getting too dangerous to continue."

Uncle Fass requested the boys to continue their trip to Detroit. Chrysler, General Motors, and Ford all were hiring young men on the spot to work in their war factories. Plus, the Black men made the same money as the white men.

My brothers were now old and strong enough to work, but not old enough to fight in the U.S. Army. They all were very excited that Uncle Fass finally was married and had moved to Detroit and sent for them. Even though he was too cheap to pay us much, he always encouraged us to save our money in case we ever wanted to leave Plains, Georgia.

He told us, "Always pay yourself first before you pay anyone else. That amount should be 10% of what you earn. You put that money away. God helps those who help themselves."

Ernest went on, "Uncle Fass sent word to Ma Babe to pull his trunk loaded with nickels and dimes from under her bed and take it to Walker's Grocery Store and exchange it for paper money. This was all the money he earned in his entire life, including from his Roadhouse. He told Ma Babe to put the money in a money belt and strap it to me. I was carrying over $1,800 cash hidden under my clothes. I was nervous. It was Uncle Fass's life savings and I had never carried that much money in my life.

When I got off the bus in Atlanta, I had to go bad. So, I went into the restroom and took the money belt off inside the toilet stall. When I finished, I pulled up my pants and walked out of the bathroom without it. I was in a cab coming here when I remembered I left the $1,800 in the toilet. I told the cab driver to turn around because I had to go to the bathroom. The cab driver could not believe it.

He laughed, saying, "Didn't you country boys just come from the bathroom. I get it. You've never seen a real toilet before—just an Outhouse!"

All I said was, "I have to go again."

I rushed back into the bus station's bathroom, but someone was in the locked toilet stall where I left the money. I crawled under the stall's door and I scared the shit out of the man sitting on the toilet. Luckily, the money belt was still hanging on the back of the door." I laughed my behind off at his story.

He also updated me that our brother, Fred, was also on his way to Detroit from Tennessee. He'd gotten tired of shoveling horseshit. Fred was also too young to work in the war factories. He was going to work with Uncle Fass at the new restaurant. But Uncle Fass told him he had to go to school in the daytime.

Suddenly, Ernest stopped talking, took a long pause and looked me in the eyes, "Uncle

Fass wants you to come to Detroit to help him manage the new restaurant."

I paused and I told him to tell Uncle Fass, "I am doing well here in Atlanta."

I didn't tell him what 'well' meant. Working in the "cat bird's seat" at the Royal Theater on Auburn Avenue allowed me to get to know all the hustlers, players and con-men working the street. All I had to do was to keep my mouth shut and I got paid. I made more money keeping my mouth shut than I made selling movie tickets at the Royal Theater. I saw anything and everything that went down in the evening on Auburn Avenue, I saw, and I was the first person the police asked about it.

"No sir, Officer, I didn't see anything, sir," was my standard line.

But if I was not paid in the next day or two, the police got an anonymous call.

I also knew most of the business people on Auburn Avenue and they knew me. New arrivals in Atlanta asked me as I sat in the ticket booth where to find a good place to stay, or a good barber, hairdresser, shoe shop, cleaners, or place to get a good meal. I answered their questions with a smile and finished by saying, "Tell them Kitty sent you and they will take good care of you."

Well, the business people on Sweet Auburn Avenue also took good care of me. Yes, they made it very sweet indeed.

I showed my brothers around Atlanta in Roy's cab, making sure they didn't get into any trouble. Then I took them clubbing with Minifield and me, all while they fought off a flock of young women looking to prey on some fresh meat. The next day I put them on a train to Detroit, money belt and all.

Then my 'tattle-tale' younger sister, Freddie Mae, walked up to my ticket booth exactly two days after my brothers left. My brothers did not say anything so she could surprise me, and boy was I surprised! She had gotten married very quickly and moved to Atlanta. I thought she was pregnant, but she wasn't. She did it her way. She waited until she got married before she tried to have children. She married David Grimes, who was from a large, industrious family in Americus. He really loved Freddie and she loved him. They had been secretly dating and he was sending her money each week before they got married. Ma Babe didn't like Freddie accepting money from him. She asked Freddie Mae not to accept the money because guys always looked for something in return.

But it turned out well. He asked Daught if he could marry her, but she demanded he ask Freddie's father, George Mac Wilson, for permission first. Mac was in very ill health and barely understood what David was asking, but he gave his permission, whether he understood David or not. They were married in a heartbeat and moved to Atlanta in a flash. The only siblings I had left in Plains were Elizabeth and Alfred. I had forgotten that our mama had come home with a new boyfriend, Abe Jackson, and a new one in her arms, Lizzie Mae.

David and Freddie Mae made their way to Old Wheat Street, the same bunch of old tenements off Auburn Avenue where Aunt Sarah lived. Aunt Sarah said they had burned down twice, but she still found them a one-bedroom apartment a few doors down the hall from her room on the second floor. Aunt Sarah was Ma Babe's youngest sister, whose only daughter Sarah died when she was 10 months old. She did not have any more children after that. The Hill family 'barren curse' had bitten her, and it caused her to lose her first husband, Joseph Smith, after their daughter died. Freddie Mae and David had been married for more than nine months and she wasn't pregnant yet. I hoped the Hill family barren curse would not raise its ugly head and bite her. I was very afraid for her.

The Boys from Fort Benning, 1940

The Troop Train, 1942

Marion Overstreet, 1942

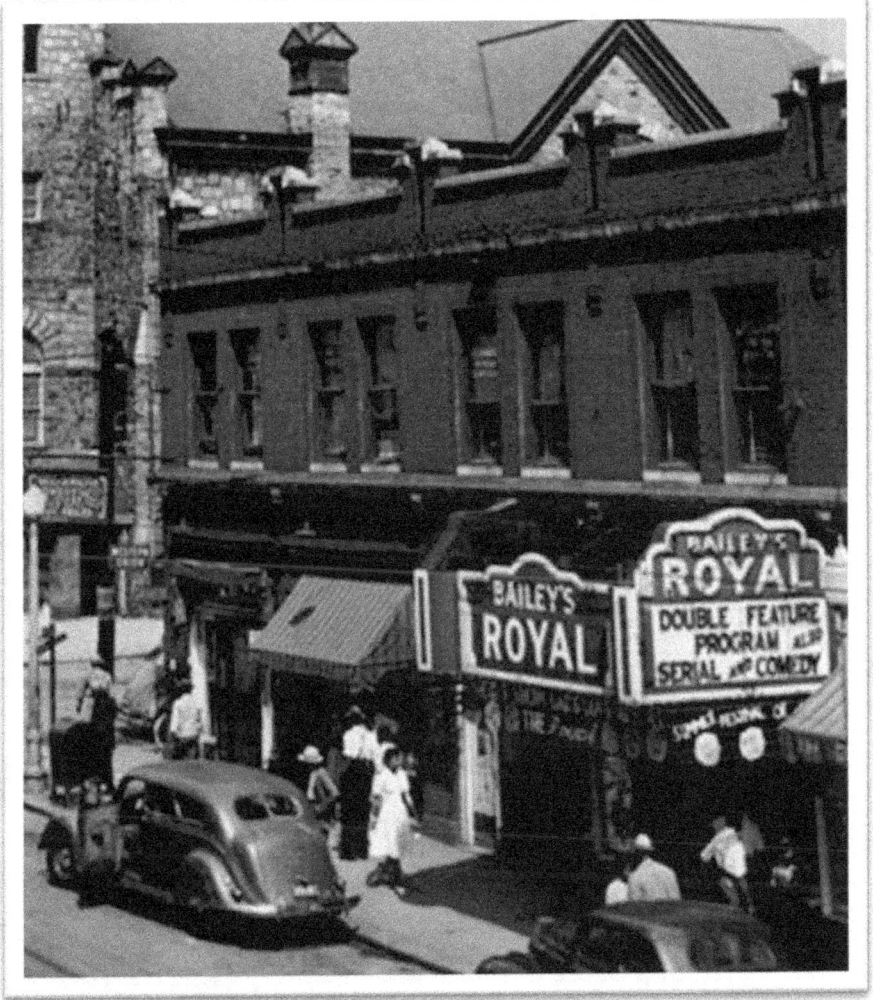

Royal Theater, Auburn Avenue, 1945

David and Freddie Mae Wilson-Grimes, 1945

Freddie Mae Hill-White (Mama Daught)

Chapter VII

The Royal Peacock

At the end of 1943, Roy and his wife had an ugly fight. His wife heard rumors about the affair he was having with me and told him to get the hell out of their house. Roy moved in with me after she threw him out. I felt very bad for him. How this happened I can't explain.

I was partying my ass off. Roy, as a friend, was concerned about me partying too much with too many different men. Then suddenly, I told him I was getting tired of it also and our relationship just happened.

Roy Wiley was much older than me by 21 years. Roy was always respectful, never raised his voice, or became overly excited about anything. He was always there for me. He was on time almost every evening to take me home with his pistol ready, if necessary, within reach underneath the driver's seat of his cab. I preferred tall, dark men. He was shorter than I and light skinned. However, those eyes, those hazel eyes drove me insane.

When we were having sex, he was always attentive to my every wish. He was experienced and careful not to get me pregnant. We were fine for a year and I became overconfident that the Hill family barren curse had possibly struck me. We became sloppy about using protection.

Then on D-Day, June 8, 1944, I told Roy, "I think I missed my period."

There were more fireworks exploding between us in Atlanta on that day than in Western Europe. This was the first time he became angry with me. He was angrier, though, with himself. I cut the conversation at this point because I really didn't know if I was truly pregnant.

When he and I calmed down I told him we needed to take a break. I believed our separation would allow us to think about our individual situations.

Roy and his wife had separated, and were still having drama. I did not want my child and me to be the reason for his marriage to end.

I made it clear to him when I said, "Roy, I am going to have your child and I am not going to marry you." When I confirmed that I was pregnant, I stopped partying at the clubs and began thinking about preparing for a child. I did not want to be like my mother. I was going to raise my child like royalty, not a servant.

Eddie Roy Hill was born on Wednesday, March 28, 1945, at 11:00 a.m. at Grady Memorial Hospital. Yes, he was a "Grady Baby." Grady Hospital was known to be one of the finest maternity hospitals in the country. It was a badge of honor to be born there.

World War II ended a few months later and there was much to be celebrating. He was a beautiful, healthy baby with the same hazel eyes as his father. He was perfect with the exception of his right eye being cockeyed. We both loved him to death and we could tell that he was very special. When he started walking, Roy took Eddie Roy on long rides in his cab while he picked up customers.

When they asked, "Whose kid is that?" he proudly replied, "My son."

He even took Eddie Roy with him to his Elks Club meetings, showing him off to all his fellow Elks Brothers. All of this just made it harder for me to leave Roy. Roy did not drink much, but he loved to chew on a good cigar. He chewed it more than he smoked it. It stunk and that was his only vice that I couldn't stand. Roy was a good, kindhearted man and he needed a good kindhearted woman, neither his wife nor me. *I was Mother Nature.*

He had three children with Mayme, his wife, and two of his sons were around my age. Roy introduced his oldest son, Addis, to Eddie Roy and me. He was the same age as I. Roy loved his children, but they all were having difficult times with life. They were basically drunks, constantly out of work and in trouble with the law. Mayme was always begging Roy for money to buy food for their grandchildren.

The word on the street was she was one mean bitch to live with, although Roy never discussed it with me or anybody.

I guess I would be a mean bitch also, if someone had stolen my husband. I never gave it much thought because I never worried much about other women stealing a guy from me. If that happened, maybe they would be doing me a favor.

Eddie Roy, who Aunt Nora nicknamed Butch, developed into an outgoing, wellspoken kid, who was not afraid of anything. When people asked his name, he would forcefully respond, "I am Eddie Roy Wiley Hill Jr., Kit, Cowboy, and Butch."

We moved from 63 Hilliard Street, off Auburn Avenue, to the edge of a white and Negro neighborhood on Cary Street in Atlanta. He played with the little white kids more than he played with the little Negro kids, and I wondered why? One evening, I was sitting on the porch watching him play with a small group of white kids and I noticed that the little Negro kids were off playing by themselves and were very upset. So, I snuck up on him talking to the little white kids and listened to their conversation.

He said to a little white kid joining the group, "Don't play with them over there. They ain't like us."

The white kids would not play with other Negro kids because he told them not too. The Negro kids would not challenge him and their right to play with the white kids, as he did. There wasn't much color difference between him and some of the other Negro kids.

He learned very early that Negroes developed an inferiority complex about themselves as children. He also learned early on that capitalizing on a Negro's inferiority complex was just as easy for light-skinned Negroes as it was for whites to do.

He learned how to use the white kid's superiority complex to manipulate them as well. One of the Negro kids was the little white kid's best friend before Eddie Roy started to play with him. When he did not allow Eddie Roy to play with the toy he wanted, he questioned his whiteness to his white friends and the fact that his best friend was a Negro. Just like that, the other white kids stopped playing with him.

Surprisingly, none of the white or Negro kids ever questioned who or what he was. Although many members of our family were dark, he was what he wanted to be, when he wanted to be it. He didn't even know what he was himself because I never told him until he was almost school aged.

When I thought about it, I was not making fun of the fact that he learned to mistreat others. I was making fun of the fact that he learned, at an early age, how to be cunning, manipulative, and devious. These traits were generally considered sinful. But in my family, they were skills passed down from one generation to the next and considered "necessary evils," and "good survival skills" in a hostile America.

His eye was diagnosed as a lazy eye. The ophthalmologist placed a patch over his left eye in hopes that it would strengthen the vision in the right one. That did not work. Later on, a plant burr hit him in his right eye during a dust storm while he was visiting Plains, and it became infected. This made the vision in his right eye deteriorate even more.

I asked my sister Freddie Mae and David Grimes, who were thank God, now expecting their first child to take care of him while I worked. Eddie Roy gave them a run for their money. When they put him to sleep at night he would not go to sleep unless his Uncle David took him to see me "one more time" while I worked late in my ticket booth on Auburn Avenue.

"Uncle David, please, if you take me to see my mother just one more time, I will go to sleep."

Naturally, one more time was never enough for him to go to sleep.

Mrs. Cunningham loved to talk with Eddie Roy and tease him about the long name that he gave himself. She was very involved in supporting community institutions, churches, and businesses. She did very well with the hotel and her other enterprises. She also loaned money to entrepreneurs who wanted to start businesses that served the community, like barbershops, dry cleaners, nail salons, and hairdressers.

But the Georgia lynching of July 25, 1946, rocked her very soul. George W. and Mae Murray Dorsey, together with Roger and Dorothy

6

Malcom, were pulled out of their car in Walton County, Georgia, and shot to death execution style by a racist white mob. Mae was seven months pregnant and her baby was cut out of her.

Mrs. Cunningham was not afraid of these white racists. She organized a special trip for visiting ministers to the site during the National Baptist Convention that year and held a prayer vigil to honor these Black martyrs. These events heightened her concern for her bandleader son Red McAllister, who still traveled these same treacherous back roads of the south, often at night, trying to make it to the next gig on the Chitlin' Circuit.

When the Top Hat Club, also known as "Club Beautiful" on Sweet Auburn Avenue, became available, she negotiated with the owners and purchased the club for $31,000. She said the purchase would provide a home for her son, Red, and his band to entertain in. It would also keep them off those racist back roads. Red was also promoting other bands and acts traveling the Chitlin' Circuit.

She renamed The Top Hat Club to the "Royal Peacock." Its opening was a fabulous event on Auburn Avenue and the best ever in Atlanta. She draped the entire front of the club in Peacock feathers for the opening. She decorated the interior walls with hand painted motifs of an Egyptian palace. The lines to get in always stretched from 186 Auburn Avenue, around the corner, and up Piedmont Avenue. White folks' performances were on Wednesdays and Saturdays. This was really something. Red charged more than $3 to get in, but he didn't charge Minifield and me on opening night or any night after that. Now, that was the woman I wanted to be: unattached, self-sufficient, and unafraid.

Mrs. Cunningham treated me very well and never allowed me to return any favors. She turned down every attempt, except one. She always accepted the free movie passes I gave her to see movies she liked at the Royal Theatre. When big name acts staying at her Royal Hotel came to Atlanta and they did not know how to get around town or get things done, she called me. She trusted me. I was available in the daytime, and she told them to tip me well.

I remember a time when Mahalia Jackson came to Atlanta. It was not her first trip to Atlanta, but she arrived late for a performance and needed help. She needed her gown cleaned, and her hair and her nails done. She also needed someone to drive her around town to take care of her personal business and to shop for shoes to match her gown.

The first person I called was Roy. We drove her to the best cleaners on Auburn Avenue. Then we took her to the Minifield's to do her hair and nails. Finally, we drove her downtown to Regal's Shoe Store to pick out a pair of shoes. The Regal's sales clerk would not allow her to try on the shoes in the store.

I told the clerk, "Do you know who this is?"

The clerk replied, "I do not care who she is. We do not allow Negros to try on shoes in our store."

I was about to escort Mahalia out of the store when she said to me, "These shoes are a perfect match for my gown."

Looking down at the feet of a white lady sitting across the room from us, I asked, "Madame, what is your shoe size?"

She looked at the shoes and replied, "The same size as Mahalia's. I know who she is."

"Madame, I will give you $10.00 to try on these shoes," I said to her.

The other white customers looked at me as if I was crazy. The lady took the money and tried on the shoes. Then she got up, walked around the store, and said the shoes fit great.

Mahalia laughed and said, "A white test drive is better than no test drive at all. I can't return them anyway after I walk out the door!"

She paid for the shoes, put them on, and we walked out of the store. Roy chauffeured us around town for most of the day and we completed all of her requests. She tipped me $200 and I gave Roy half. That was more money than I made in two weeks.

Mrs. Cunningham sent me on errands like this at least twice a week. She knew I was always well-groomed, well-dressed, and well-spoken. She said I was her 'concierge,' whatever that meant.

Aunt Nora sent word to me that Ma Babe's health was starting to fail. But I could not return to Plains. So, she sent for Mama, who was now "married" to Abe Jackson and living in Moultrie, Georgia with my two-year-old sister, Lizzy Mae.

Mama asked Abe, "Can I go home to see about my mother?"

He said "No."

So, she packed up her belongings and what belonged to her daughter, and prepared to catch the next bus to Plains.

Abe said to her as she walked out the door, "Don't come back, if you let that door hit you in the ass."

She simply replied, "Well, it just did."

Ma Babe was no longer working at the hospital. She had started her own business as a washerwoman. She washed clothes for the nurses and doctors at the hospital. She was very familiar with cleaning the surgical gowns, uniforms, and sheets properly. She was so good most of the employees wouldn't let anyone else clean their clothes but Ma Babe. She did a good job and her business had immediately expanded to local business people's shirts, dresses, and uniforms. It was a miracle how she cleaned clothes in a large cast-iron pot, fired by wood, sitting in the front yard using homemade potash soap.

When Mama returned home, she helped Ma Babe with the business, and they were doing quite well. So well, that Mama didn't have to leave Plains to look for work anymore. This took a large load off Ma Babe, which really helped her get back to better health.

I communicated with the family through Aunt Nora because I did not want anyone in the Plains Post Office to see a letter from me with an Atlanta return address. She gave me all the family news including the word that the county sheriff's son had up and disappeared without a trace.

In Detroit in 1947, my oldest brother, Earnest met Dorothy, a beautiful Mexican woman, who worked at Uncle Fass's restaurant. The relationship was getting hot and heavy between them. She had one small son already and Ernest didn't have any problem being a stepfather. That was another trait of our Hill family. Strong Black women raise, love and nurture strong Black men. Our family's men did not have any problem raising other men's children as well as their own. They taught their sons at an early age not to abandon their children under any circumstances. Whether they are born before wedlock, during wedlock, or after wedlock.

Roy would not say it aloud, but he began to question whether Eddie Roy was his son. If anyone asked him, "Is that your son?" he replied firmly "Yes, he is my son."

I appreciated that he was a strong, honest man who knew our relationship didn't conform to normal social or Christian standards. He was like me. *I was Mother Nature and I did as I pleased within my own ethical code.*

But once the rumors started, they persisted. Roy eventually started making veiled suggestions to me that our child might not be his; that our child could be Red McAllister's, Mrs. Cunningham's son.

I said to Roy, "Both Mrs. Cunningham and Red are very close friends of ours, both mine and yours. In fact, it was you, Roy, who introduced me to Red's mother. Now I understand— when Red and I became close friends, Roy, you became jealous and didn't like it. I did not pick that up at the time. I know you, and you didn't dream up this nigger shit by yourself. Where did you come up with Red being Eddie Roy's father?"

Unable to look me in the eye, he said, "One of my cab drivers started the rumors behind my back that Eddie Roy was Red McAllister's son. The driver said that he took Red and you to his mother's hotel one night before Eddie Roy was born."

"Roy, you are too old and wise to fall for nigger shit and repeat it. I am not even going to dignify that shit with a response or ask which cab driver."

I told Roy they were all lies. He accepted what I said as the truth, or at least he appeared to at the time. But my scolding had a depressive effect on him. I felt at the time that the issue of who fathered Eddie Roy was not resolved on Auburn Avenue. When Eddie Roy's third birthday approached, I had my friend Charles, who was a professional photographer with a studio on Auburn Avenue, take a wonderful photograph of Eddie Roy.

I placed his picture in the Society Column of the Atlanta Daily World, the local Negro newspaper, announcing birthday wishes for Eddie Roy Wiley Hill. He looked just like his father. This blew up Auburn Avenue. In turn, Roy's wife Mayme stormed into the cabstand in her nightgown, hair undone, and house slippers on her feet, and confronted Roy with her pistol sticking out of her pocketbook.

Roy was there and she said to him, "If I ever catch you and your bastard son in the same room, I will kill both of you!"

Mayme stopped the rumors in their tracks. She confirmed who Eddie Roy's father was to the world and in a more dramatic way than I could have ever accomplished. But I knew then that I was a junkie for married men. I was addicted. I never wanted to get married or be like Mayme. She was pitiful.

I was not without morals. I just had my own set. Some fit social norms. Some did not. Ma Babe taught all of us to obey the Bible's Ten Commandments. But I added my own twists.

1. Thou shalt not commit adultery: Yet, Ma Babe was coerced into being an adulterer.
2. Thou shalt not to lie: "However, there may come a time you will have to lie to protect yourself, your children, and the people you love."
3. Thou shalt not kill: "In this world, it is kill or be killed. I know that first hand."
4. Thou shalt not steal: "I would steal to eat and survive."
5. Thou shalt honor thy Mother and Father: "Only if they honor me."

It is easy for religious people to point their fingers at someone else's doorstep but not their own. I have found some religious people to be the biggest hypocrites in the world. I learned first-hand in Georgia that people who live in glass houses should not throw stones.

Mrs. Cunningham, along with other business and civic leaders, formed the Atlanta Negro Voters League. I helped as they registered large numbers of Negro voters in Atlanta, which started to turn Atlanta's elections in their favor. They negotiated with Mayor Hartsfield to hire the first Negro police officers in Atlanta's history. In exchange for their support, he hired eight Negro police officers and stationed them in the basement of the YMCA on Butler Street, off Auburn Avenue.

Guess what? *Be careful of what you ask for because you may just get it.* Most of the shady activities on Auburn Avenue dried up and my hush money dried up with it.

Roy Wiley would have done me a favor by denying Eddie Roy was his son. It would have made it easier for me to leave him and leave town. However, he was a good father and he spent a lot of time with Eddie Roy and me.

I had a line of attractive, well-educated single men who wanted to marry me. But as soon as they popped the question our relationship ended. I was not going to be dependent on or tied to anyone, especially a man, to take care of my children and me. I didn't care if I was called a hoe, whore, harlot, or bitch.

I promised myself that I would stop running from my fears. However, I was living for more than me, myself, and I, now. Roy's wife Mayme was for real. I believed she meant what she said and Eddie Roy needed protection. It was time to leave Atlanta. I was not running from something. I was running to protect something.

976 103 287 429

Minifield Bryant, 1945

Erma L. Hill and Minifield at The Peacock Club, 1945

Minifield Bryant, 1945

HOWARD CALLENDER and His Orchestra
"The Band That Plays The Blues"

Exclusive Management
RED McALLISTER AGENCY
214 Auburn Ave.   Atlanta, Ga.

Howard Callender, Band Leader, 1945

Sincerely Yours
EMPRESS of GOSPEL SONG
MAHALIA JACKSON

Mahalia Jackson, 1945

Aunt Effie and Partner, 1940

Chapter VIII

The Silver Meteor

I called Aunt Nora and told her I was ready to come back to New York City to live. It was difficult for me to say good-bye to everyone in Atlanta, with so many friends and acquaintances. Minifield, my 'Clubbing Partner,' Red McAllister, Mrs. Cunningham and my sister Freddie Mae, who cared for Eddie Roy, had all provided great support.

I saved my money, about $700, and I found out I had no warrants for my arrest in Plains. But it still was too dangerous for me to travel there to say goodbye to Ma Babe. The county sheriff had come down hard on Uncle Fass's business. I suspected that had a lot to do with his move to Detroit. I sent Eddie Roy down to see his great-grandmother and other family members before we left.

Roy Wiley did not want me to leave. He said he would leave Mayme. I reminded him that wasn't the reason I was leaving him. I loved his son now more than I loved him. I packed three steamer trunks full of clothes and shipped them ahead. We were going to arrive in New York City in style.

The trip on the Silver Meteor took about 24 hours, arriving in New York City on a cold and windy day in February 1950. The overnight trip gave me a lot of time to reflect on many aspects of my life. My party life was definitely over. There were many negative changes taking place on the Chitlin' Circuit and about clubbing in general.

Red and I had long talks about the direction of the music industry. The jazz bands no longer played dance music. Listening to jazz music was now a religious experience and needed your undivided attention. The bands had become smaller and the audiences had to work much harder to follow and understand the music.

Also, something very sinister was taking place inside of the music industry: heroin use. Many of the top musicians were addicted to it. It appeared as if they were marketing the drug to the Negro population by glorifying its use. Billie Holiday was arrested in a sting operation in 1947. She emerged from the ordeal an even bigger star than she had been. And the racist drug agents refused to arrest Judy Garland for the same crime. They maintained that Judy had a medical problem. Yet, they named Billie a criminal, which required her to do time in a West Virginia jail.

We had our first taste of this first-hand as we exited the train at Pennsylvania Station, in New York. Dressed to kill in our finest Sunday best we hailed a taxi. But before we climbed in, a panhandler bent over us in a heroin nod requesting money. His saxophone was lying on the curb; he was too high to play it. Even dressed to kill, it was difficult for Negroes to get a cab in New York City, especially with a white driver. Finally getting one, we took the cab to Harlem from Penn Station and 33rd Street, with snow on the ground, and the Christmas decorations still hanging up at Macy's.

Aunt Nora was very pleased to see us. She gave Butch a long, strong hug. She also loved hearing him say his long list of names including "Butch," the one she gave him. Aunt Nora was a beautiful, statuesque woman. She appeared mixed with Indian blood. Our family folklore said our women were all tall, intelligent, athletic, beautiful, and mixed with Native American blood.

Aunt Nora's first marriage to Reverend Argus Hightower in Plains failed after two years because she could not conceive a child. She was still working for the Ramses, who spent a lot of their time and fortune trying to help Jews escape Europe. Aunt Nora had her own room in their home and cared for their two children, Bill, and Sarah, alone for weeks at a time. She was actually the one who raised them. Through them, Aunt Nora met her boyfriend, Uncle Frank Perkins. He worked in an antique and second-hand clothing store on the Lower East Side that wealthy Jews supported. World events forced many Jews to sell their prized possessions to raise money to support their families and friends trying to escape from the war in Europe. There was a rumor that Uncle Frank found over $10,000 sewn into the lining of one of the coats donated to the store. Aunt Nora had two Cadillacs and she could not drive either of them. So, the story of Uncle Frank finding that money must have been true.

They also had their own place at 67-69 St. Nicholas Avenue in Harlem, in Apartment 4N. It was a large, well-kept apartment building between 113th and 114th Streets. Aunt Nora rented a room from Mrs. Marion Barnes. We called her Aunt Marion. She was a tall, attractive, light-skinned woman with a warm heart and welcoming soul. She had five bedrooms—four that she rented out.

Uncle Frank kept their room in Aunt Marion's apartment full of fur coats, expensive jewelry, and fine clothing. Aunt Nora loved beautiful clothes, shoes, and jewelry, and she was a meticulous dresser. I had a field day going through her stuff when she went to work. She was always very well-dressed, well-paid, and well-respected. Working in Forest Hills, Queens required you to walk through the neighborhood well-attired. The local police knew most of the servants, staff and employees that frequented the neighborhood, and they questioned ragamuffins often.

A new alcoholic rehabilitation hospital in Queens had recently released her, indicating all was not well in Dodge City. Uncle Frank was abusive because she could not have children, and he constantly scolded her for her condition. He was not physically abusive. She would not put up with that. But he was psychologically abusive. He knew her memory was going bad due to her drinking. So, he moved or hid her liquor bottles.

She loved Gordon's Gin. She would tear up the room knowing she had placed a gin bottle in a specific location and then discover it was not there. He also misplaced her jewelry and even her underwear. She would go nuts looking for these things. I saw him misplace her lipstick one day and I called him out on it. Aunt Nora heard me and scolded me for blaming him for something he didn't do. *He just did not know; I was Mother Nature and I was about to rain fire down on his behind.*

Then she started to show up for work with alcohol on her breath, which forced the Rameses to leave the children with her alone drunk. Uncle Frank became more mentally abusive and she continued to drink heavily. She started to have epileptic fits, and her drinking was causing problems within the Ramsey family. The Rameses' patience, pocket-book, and new hospitals available to treat her were all running low. The last hospital that treated her tried the new electric stock treatment. They strapped her down in a wooden chair, put a wooden stick in her mouth and sent electric current through her head. It is like being electrocuted. This made her epileptic fits worse and she was a mental wreck when they released her.

Uncle Frank's mental abuse got much worse, and I told him, " I am going to poison you with some herbs that Twin Spirits sent me if you don't leave Aunt Nora on your own accord."

She didn't have anyone in New York City to look after her, except me. Before her last hospital visit, she sent money home to Ma Babe to purchase the home we rented in Plains. That was a tremendous help because it eliminated Ma Babe's expense of paying rent.

Surprisingly, the Rameses still trusted her with their children, even with alcohol on her breath, and even after she started to have epileptic fits on a regular basis. Their children even learned to find a large table-spoon and place it in her mouth each time she had one. This prevented her from choking by swallowing her tongue or damaging her mouth and teeth. They refused to let her go, continued employing her for many years after her health failed, and retired her with a small pension. They even paid for her repeated treatment at expensive alcohol reha-bilitation centers in Forest Hills.

Fred was still in Detroit working at Uncle Fass's Restaurant. It was a hit from the day they opened up. They served all types of food from Mexican to Soul Food, and they stayed open 24 hours a day. Uncle Fass managed the restaurant from 4:00 in the evening to 4:00 in the morning.

He drilled into Fred regularly: "You must go to school when you finish working in the morning, then sleep in the afternoon."

Fred would only protest to Uncle Fass, "What for? They can't teach me anything I don't already know!"

He battled constantly with Uncle Fass about going to school.

When he finally became fed up with Uncle Fass, he told him "I am going to New York City to live with Aunt Nora and work."

I didn't want Fred to stop going to school either. But it was a relief for me because Aunt Nora would now have two family members to look after her. He arrived shortly after I did and at once got a good job working at a well-known delicatessen on Broadway in Manhattan. Aunt Marion rented him a room in her apartment, next to Aunt Nora's. And boy he at once started to work the women!

I asked for her help in finding me a job and a place to stay. She found me a wonderful place on Fifth Avenue. No, not that Fifth Avenue, the one in Harlem, 2056 Fifth Avenue. I would be renting a room from Irene Simmons. We called her Aunt Irene and she was a friend of Aunt Nora's. Fifth Avenue was an exclusive address in any part of Manhattan, and we were staying with her in her third-floor apartment.

She was a robust woman with a hardy laugh, who was renting us a room until I could find a job. Through Aunt Nora's boss, a friend of a friend, I found a job with Kent Cleaners. They needed a manager to run their Harlem store. Their cleaning plant was located downtown. I was surprised there were so many professional Negroes in Manhattan that needed to have their clothes professionally cleaned. I had helped Ma Babe clean my sibling's clothes, so cleaning clothes was not anything new to me.

Kent Cleaners had several stores for collecting customers' clothes, all to be sent to their cleaning plant on the Lower East Side of Manhattan. I was to manage the store on 138th Street and 8th Avenue in Manhattan. Mr. Goldman, the owner, had opened the store a few years before, but he was having problems keeping the store open because the employees' cash receipts came up short almost every night.

I immediately kept an eye on everyone in the store. I had three employees: Jane, Margaret, and Peggy. They all were good workers. I noticed they were not stealing any money from the store. Margaret and Peggy just could not add or subtract. I had to correct the amount of change they gave customers on several occasions. They could read well, but their counting skills were very bad. I began to help them with their figures, forcing them to use only their heads. I did not allow them to write anything down. They had to do all the figuring in their heads.

Mr. Goldman was very pleased. The store made a turnaround within two months after I arrived. Some of the customers had the nicest clothes. One person I really liked was a guy named Clifford Paul Bodie. He was from the Bahamas in the Caribbean. That Caribbean accent of his drove me crazy. I could not understand half of what he was saying, but I loved it. He was a chauffeur for a Jewish lawyer downtown. He was super clean in his black suits that we dry-cleaned for him. He always smelled good, wore the latest men's colognes, and his fingernails were always well manicured. He would drive up in his boss's limo and park it in front of the store. He always brought me flowers, chocolates, and cookies for the store each time he came.

He said his boss was a well-known lawyer downtown. He told me how his boss inspected him every morning, as if he was in the military. He was hard to please; his hands had to be super clean. He would go off like a rocket, if he found any dirt under his fingernails.

On my lunch hour, I loved him chauffeuring me around Manhattan in the limo. Once, we pulled over on Riverside Park Drive and had a picnic overlooking the Hudson River. I loved going to the movies and eating in fine restaurants. Saturday was his day off because it was the Sabbath Day for Jews. They were not to use any electrical or mechanical devices on the Sabbath. Therefore, he had the limo all to himself on Saturdays. I would leave the store early, asking Peggy and her husband Basil to watch Eddie Roy for me.

Was Clifford married? Yes, and I swore I was going to give up married men. His wife was still in the Bahamas. My fear of getting married was getting worse. Or on the other hand, was it just lust and greed?

Was I suicidal? *I didn't know.* Was it some kind of freakish fetish? *Possibly.* Did I enjoy the suspense of making love to a married man? Yes, I loved it. Was it a sense - some lewd sense of accomplishment? *Yes, it was.* Was I at war with myself, or was I just stupid? *Both!* Was I being used more than I used someone else? *Both!* Was this my safety net for preventing a long-term relationship or marriage, or was it tossing bullets in the fire?

It was tossing bullets in the fire.

Clifford had flawless dark skin, perfect teeth, was just a bit shorter than me, and had a body chiseled out of stone. He usually climaxed before me. But I would not let him up without him giving me full pleasure, and he didn't have far to travel. *I was Mother Nature and I had to be pleased, or all hell broke loose.*

I was asking Peggy to watch Eddie Roy more than I should have.

She and Basil were becoming very attached to him. Peggy and Basil had been together for five years. I never saw him go to work, although he said he had a job. He refused to marry her but told her he wanted to have kids with her. She told him she wanted to have kids also, but for some unknown reason she could not become pregnant. She requested something strange from me. She asked me to allow Basil to make love to me, impregnate me, and give her the child. I laughed thinking she was joking. She was not joking, so I said, "Hell no."

After I said no, our relationship started to go downhill. On the job, she started to become belligerent, uncooperative, and disrespectful. Then the hostilities started to quiet down a bit, or so I thought. Then one of the bullets hit me. I became pregnant by Clifford. Yes, Mother Nature rules. I told Clifford, and he wasn't too happy about it. He asked me what I wanted to do. I replied I wanted to keep the child. He said he would do the right thing and help as much as he could. Roy Wiley had said that same thing, but the road to hell is paved with good intentions. When it rains, it pours. Peggy overheard Clifford and me talking about my pregnancy. She boldly asked the both of us if she could have the child.

Clifford said, "It is alright with me." I looked at him as if he was a demon that escaped from hell. Seeing my expression, he changed his answer and said, "No."

She became very upset with me and said I would be the cause of her losing her boyfriend. I asked Peggy again to allow me to leave early because it was Friday. I turned over the daily receipts to her in a zippered bag for her to give to Mr. Goldstein when he arrived at closing time to pick it up. I placed $400 in the bag and left $20 in change in the register. When I returned Monday morning to open the store, Mr. Goldstein was waiting for me. He said that $200 was missing from Friday's bag.

He said, "Kitty, as manager it was your responsibility to make sure the daily receipts were transferred to me. I am firing you because $200 is missing from Friday's receipts. Peggy is now the new manager."

About this time, Peggy walked through the front door with a smirk on her face. I didn't say a word to her. About a month later, she got what she deserved. Basil left her for another woman. I thanked Twin Spirits in my prayers that night.

I moved to a small one-room that I sublet from the person who rented the apartment from the landlord on 138 West 123rd Street. It was small and cramped but clean. I started to look for another job, but my pregnancy started to show. I had morning sickness and I had to take care of Eddie Roy. He was entering the third grade and he was starting to be a royal pain in the ass. He was more interested in playing with toy soldiers than school.

True to his word, Clifford paid the rent on the room and brought a box of food up the four flights of stairs once a week. We had one refrigerator that was shared by the four families living in the apartment. Much of the food would disappear by Wednesday, whether you placed your name on it or not. I was always an independent woman and never dependent on a man to support me. It was difficult being told what to do and how to do it. On the other hand, I had children to think about, even though I was extremely uncomfortable with this situation.

121 597 908 084

Nora Hill holding Sarah Ramsey, 1945

Bill Ramsey, 1945

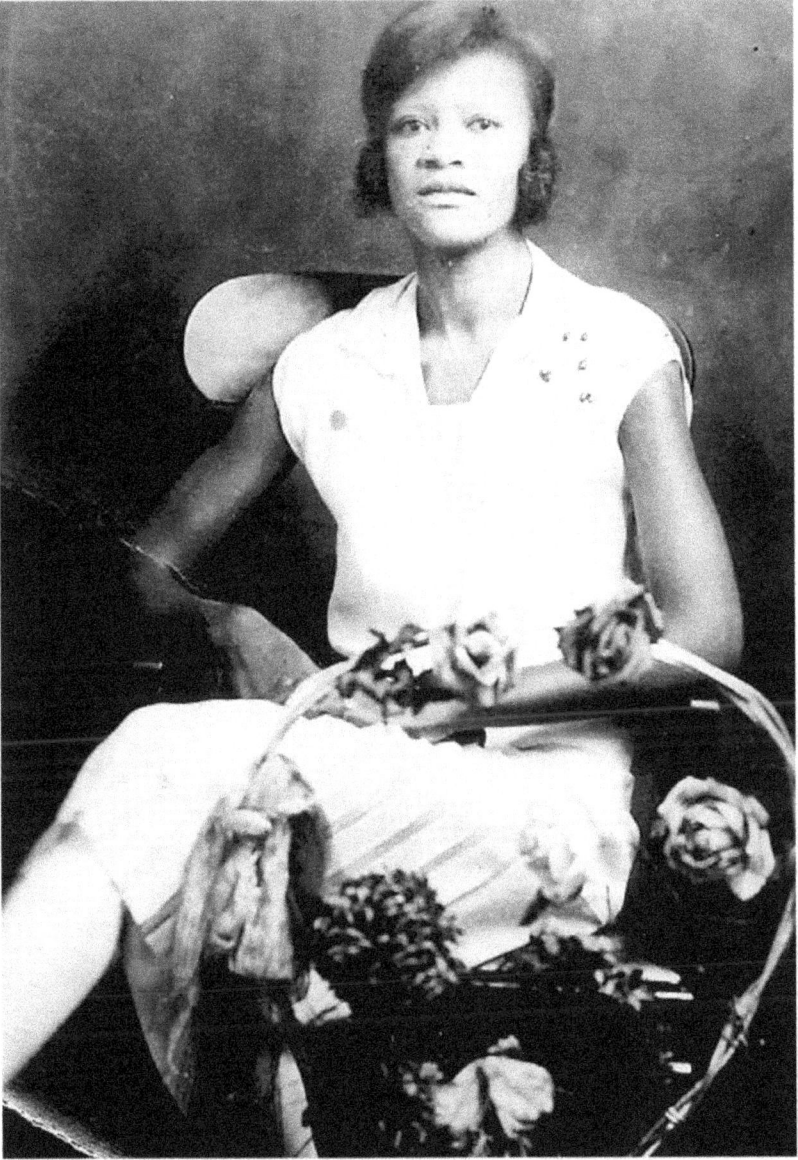

Nora Hill Hightower, 1945

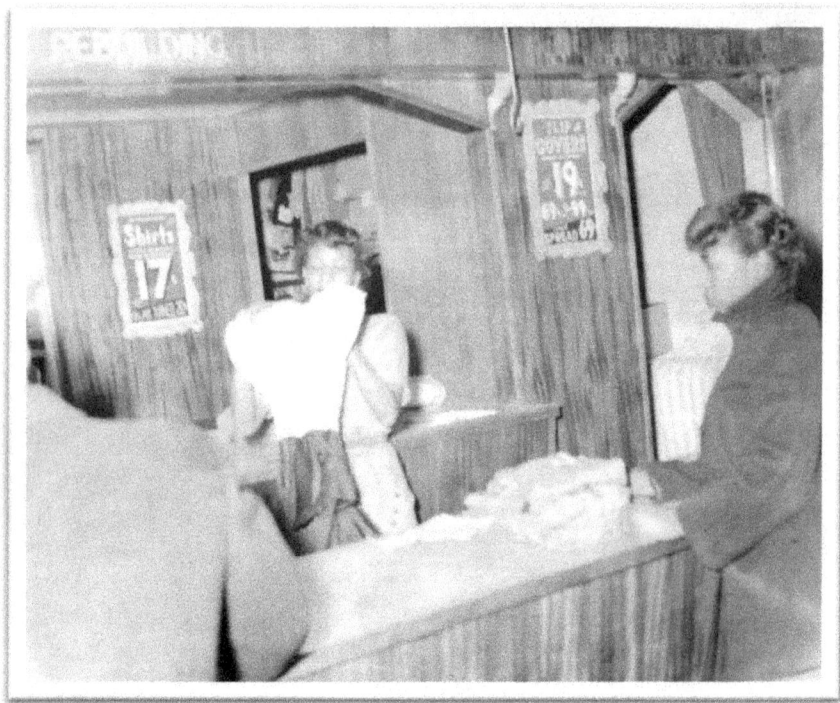

Erma Hill, Kent Cleaners, 1950

Erma L. Hill and Peggy, Kent Cleaners, 1950

Chapter IX

How Low Can I Go?

Paul Bernard Hill was born September 8, 1952. He was a beautiful, chubby, dark-skinned baby with blue eyes. Yes, blue eyes. Jane, my Kent Cleaners co-worker, told me about the NYC Department of Welfare. I have two kids now and I could get a check from them to help us out. I don't remember anyone in my family ever receiving welfare.

One of my neighbors in the building was an Assistant Pastor at the large Pentecostal Church on the corner at 40 West 123rd Street, about a half block away. He invited me to attend the church services with my two children, Eddie and Bernard.

He said, "God forgives all sins. He will take you into his bosom and give you the same peace, love, and blessings as all your brethren."

Believe me, Mother Nature needed a blessing. I will never forget that first Sunday. I dressed everyone in our Sunday best, which was not much, and we made the trek. From morning until evening, the boom of the drums and electric guitars pounded my head like a giant baseball bat. The noise was deafening. It was like attending a rock 'n' roll concert and sitting on the inside of the drum. Bernard cried for two hours straight. Eddie threw his toy plane into the air during the service and they asked him to leave. If this was Heaven, then I would have much preferred that God send me to hell.

After two Sundays of this torture, the unattractive wife of the Assistant Pastor approached me and said, "I am uncomfortable with you being around my husband and family. You and your bastard children are not welcome here anymore."

Although she shocked me, I came right back at her and said, "Mrs. Frankenstein, my children are not bastards. They have fathers and they were not conceived in hell, like you and yours. Please answer this: is it true that God treats everyone fairly? Is it true that he treats everyone with love, kindness, and compassion, although earthly men and women do not? Has God made man to be both cruel and caring but not at the same time? There lies your problem, Mrs. Frankenstein. Whatever happened to, 'Do unto others as you would have them do unto you?'"

That was the end of my spiritual awakening; it came to a screeching halt.

As I was saying earlier, my brother Fred started working the women as soon as he got to Harlem. Every Saturday morning, he got dressed up in his horseback riding suit and headed for the horse barn in Central Park, where you could rent horses for riding. A bridle path encircled most of Central Park. The young women from 114th to 110th Streets woke up early on Saturday mornings to watch Fred promenade his way to the park like some wealthy horse trainer. Some women even followed him to the park so they could pet his horse.

Since he discovered the secret of unlocking a woman's heart, he developed into an outstanding cook and he would cook for his girlfriends. Truthfully, his women talked more about his cooking than they talked about his sexual prowess.

Finally, a woman named Jean Foster slowed him down enough to catch him. She and Fred would talk for hours out of their respective apartment fire escape windows. She was a very attractive, nice young woman from 141 West 113th Street. They got married quickly because she became pregnant. They moved into a new apartment in the same building, one floor below her mother.

She gave birth to their first child, Fred Jr., which cut off the time he had to help look after Aunt Nora. He changed jobs and was now working with Hortense Spier, a well-known commercial baker on 90th Street and Central Park West. He met Mr. Spier on the bridle path, while riding one weekend, and Mr. Spier hired him on the spot.

Fred found me two adjoining rooms in another sublet apartment on the ground floor of 67 St. Nicholas Avenue. It was in the same building with Aunt Nora. Aunt Nora's fits were getting much worse, and her drinking was turning her into a violent person.

Eddie Roy was now as tall as I and giving me fits worse than Aunt Nora's. He was the class clown and was spending more time in the principal's office than he was in class. He managed to keep up with the rest of the kids academically because he was bright. I wouldn't have doubted that his teachers were simply passing him along so he would become someone else's problem next year.

Miss Schweda, his sixth-grade teacher, passed him into the seventh grade, but she placed him into an "opportunity class." This was really a class for mentally challenged children. This class just made him worse. His first week in Junior High School 88, he and his classmate Michael stole paint from the wood working shop, and they slung paint from the fourth floor down to the lunchroom in the basement. When they called me in to speak to the principal and to see his handiwork, I cried. The principal wanted to call in Children's Services, but I rubbed his hand and begged him not to.

Two weeks later Eddie Roy and Michael peed in front of his home room teacher, Mrs. Love's door and laughed at the students as they stepped in it exiting from class. Mrs. Love understood that this was his last straw. So, she didn't tell the principal what he had done. I do not know for sure the reason why she decided not to tell the principal. Instead, she worked extra hard with him to get him promoted out of her 'opportunity class' and into the eighth grade.

Within two months of moving into 67 St. Nicholas Avenue, Eddie Roy entered the the apartment owner's room, Mr. Willard, and stole two box cutters. He hid them in a potted plant by the door and forgot where he hid them. Mr. Willard walked into my room accusing him of stealing.

I asked Eddie Roy, "Did you take the box cutters?"

Eddie Roy said, "No Mommy, I didn't take them."

I then stood up for him against Mr. Willard's charges. Before long, Mr. Willard spotted the box cutters hidden in the plant. I apologized to Mr. Willard. I was very hurt that Eddie Roy lied to me.

Then, I realized that Eddie Roy had also lied about sneaking into my purse and taking money without my permission. I didn't like the crowd he was hanging out with. They were older boys, who played hooky from school a lot. *Education was my Holy Bible, and without it you could not get into Mother Nature's Heaven.*

The next day, I accidentally met the mail carrier placing the mail in my mailbox.

I stated, "I haven't received any mail in the last few days."

He said, "I gave your mail to your son the past two days."

I replied, "He doesn't get home from school that early."

He shrugged his shoulders, smiled, and continued his rounds. As I looked through the mail, I noticed that there was a postcard from his school saying that Eddie Roy had been absent from school for three days. He left the house in the mornings and returned home at his regular times in the afternoons. I walked over to the school, which was two blocks away, entered the principal's office, and spoke to the clerk.

She said, "Mrs. Hill, I double checked with his teachers and I sent three postcards home. He was definitely absent from school for three days. In fact, he was not here today."

Tears welled up in my eyes, "Not my son."

"Yes, your son," she said, disappointed for me.

He was playing hooky and meeting the mail carrier to intercept the postcards sent from the school. I cried all the way home. *Then I reminded myself who I was. I was; Mother Nature, and no one messes with Mother Nature.* I dried my tears, and when I got back home, I prepared him a very nice meal.

When he popped into the apartment, I casually asked him, "How was your day at school, Eddie Roy? What subjects did you study this week?"

He hammed it up, telling me things like, "I had a good time in science" and "The new gym teacher is a very nice guy!"

Then I told him, "It's time for you to take your bath. I will run the bath water for you."

Once I prepared his bath water, I asked him, "Is the water the temperature you like?" "Yes, Mommy," he replied happily.

He went ahead to remove his clothes and get into the tub. I started to walk out of the bathroom. Then I stopped at the bathroom door, locked it, and turned my back to the door so he could not get out.

Then I produced my steel braided ironing cord hidden under a towel, and I started to whip his behind, as if he was a slave.

"You liked school so much today, then you are going to like this lesson!" I pounded the words into him as I laid into him with the cord.

He hollered, "Please, Mommy, I won't do it again!"

"I know you won't! You catch more hell when you allow ass-whippings to accumulate," I reminded him.

And I continued to whip his naked, wet behind for a good five minutes. After I finished, he had welts from his head to his toes. I handed him a bottle of Witch Hazel and the towel that had hid my ironing cord. From that point, he got perfect attendance for the remainder of the school year, and all the way through high school. The only thing I regretted was saving up his ass whippings. If I had been on top of his misbehavior, I could have handled each incident much better.

He went to school, but his grades were horrible. He was still the 'Class Clown' on steroids and continued to hang out with the wrong crowd. It was difficult, but over time I stopped him from hanging out with his hardheaded friends. He was growing too old and too tall to beat anymore, but Eddie Roy still had self-control problems. The streets of Harlem were trying to consume him.

Mr. Willard did not have to ask us to leave. We moved to 120 West 114th Street, one- half block away, still near Aunt Nora. We only had to share the apartment with one other person this time, a guy named Joshua Woods. He wasn't home a lot. He was a traveling technician who repaired commercial sewing machines. He introduced me to my first sewing machine. I had always wanted to learn how to sew, but I messed up just about every pattern I purchased.

Joshua told me, "The patterns you are picking are too complicated for you to finish. You need to try much simpler patterns first."

Clifford stopped coming to see me as much as he had been, and I became very distressed and depressed about it. He was still coming by to bring his usual box of food on Saturdays. One Saturday, after he set the box down on the table and had something to eat, he told me, "My wife in the Bahamas is sick and I had to send a lot of money to her to pay her medical bills. I will not be able to help you out financially for a while."

Holding his son, Bernard, in my arms who had just turned two years of age, I asked him, "What in the hell is he supposed to eat, palm trees?"

He was unphased, replying only, "You're on welfare. You can make it without me."

With tears welling up in my eyes I told him, "Get the fuck out of my apartment."

I was really pissed off, but I quickly pulled myself together and moved on. I started to see other men—too many other men. I just did not care anymore. Many of the men who were once interested in me had disappeared. Now I had two kids, no husband, and was on welfare. The word on the street was I was a good ride, but nothing else.

About one month passed before I started dating Teddy Dorsey. Teddy was a friend of Joshua's. I made it very clear to Teddy that he had to be very generous with his money. He was a train conductor for the New York City Transit Department and he made good money. He was a short, brown skinned fellow, who was not very attractive. He said he wasn't married, but I really didn't believe him. At this point, I really did not care as long as the cash kept coming. I was a boat that had lost its rudder. My life was adrift, headed to no place in particular. His money was good and it was regular.

I didn't know at the time, but I was two months pregnant. Yes, I was pregnant again. And this time I did not know who the father was. I thought it was Clifford's, but I wasn't sure. I told Clifford I was pregnant and that the baby was his, but the truth was I was not sure. He did not believe me anyway. When Teddy found out I was pregnant he disappeared like a flash in the night.

My personal appearance started to wane. I stopped using Noxzema cream daily to clean my face or baby oil to keep my skin healthy looking and smooth. I stopped doing my hair, nails and pedicuring my feet. Some days I didn't even put on clothes. I stayed in my nightclothes and slippers all day. I was starting to look like Roy Wiley's wife, Mayme. Eddie Roy noticed the change and he called me out on it.

He said, "Mommy, you look like a bag lady, homeless and wandering the streets of New York City in a daze."

He could be rude at times, but he wasn't lying, and he was my only reliable redeeming feature. Bernard was too young to say much about my condition, and he did not require much attention. Eddie Roy, who was older, always expressed his opinion. He was always upbeat, honest, and never down about anything. He was always critical of the men I dated but was usually nonjudgmental of me. He never liked Clifford much. He loved his father and his father still sent money for his care, although it was not regular. He stopped in New York City to see him when he attended his Elk's Club conventions in Atlantic City. During the summers, he also sent money for Eddie Roy to visit our family in Atlanta and he paid for his keeping at my sister Freddie Mae's house.

I spent most of the few extra dollars I had on him. I made sure all my kids never missed a meal as I had. He had the latest sneakers, school clothes and roller skates. He was still not very interested in school, other than the social side of it, like playing basketball. And he enjoyed building model airplanes and ships. His reading level was off the charts because he had to read complicated and difficult instructions on how to build them. He had a quick temper, not bad, but quick. When other kids said ugly things about me, he responded quickly, usually leaving them in tears concerning their mothers and family members.

I remember another time when they called me to school concerning his behavior.

When I arrived, I asked the principal, "What did he do now?"

She said, "A girl jumped in front of him in the lunch line saying he wasn't moving fast enough."

He told the girl, "Your mama wears combat boots."

"The little girl cried the remainder of the school day until her mother picked her up."

I could not stop laughing. I told the principal that I wasn't going to chastise him for standing up for himself.

Vernetta Ruth Hill was born on May 28, 1955, in Sydenham Hospital located on 124th Street and St. Nicholas Avenue in Manhattan. You could tell she was going to be another feisty one, just like the other women in our family. She showed her intelligence and maturity at an early age and I gave her the nickname Miss Vee.

To add insult to injury, I received a stipend increase from the NYC Department of Welfare. I earned that increase by lying on my back. It was disgusting, but true. The more illegitimate kids you had the more money you got from New York City. My children were not illegitimate. I produced and loved every one of them, but I could not win for losing. I felt I was losing my sanity and my soul. I even called out for help from Twin Spirits, to no avail.

I had lost my way. *The chickens had finally come home to roost for Mother Nature.* To help turn my situation around, I started to visit the "Botanica Maria" on 116th Street, off Lenox Avenue, and I asked Maria to bless several candles to help me. For $20 more, she told me my fortune. She said my future was about to take a strange path from darkness to light, whatever that meant. I burned those candles day and night, without result.

Then the refrigerator broke down in the apartment and the escaping Freon gas almost killed my children and me in our sleep. The landlord took his damned time fixing it. The Department of Welfare threatened to have him placed in jail, if he didn't. It scared him so that in short order he found us a new, one-bedroom apartment around the corner at 112 West 115th Street Apt.1C. It was on the first floor and was small, but it was my first apartment that I did not share with anyone except my kids. *"Be careful what you ask for. You just may get it."*

I was so happy to get an apartment all to myself that I moved in without checking out the area. I had no clue that major drug dealing was taking place on the front stoop of the building. My children had to fight through drug dealing to go to school in the mornings and on the return home in the afternoons. I hated drug dealers with a passion, and I educated my children about the dangers and consequences of taking illegal drugs. They were not stupid kids, thank God. They could see all the hurt around them, the consequences and misery that resulted from taking drugs. I did not allow them to hang out on the stoop with their friends and would beat the hell out of them if they did. Ask Eddie Roy! I kept them all busy. I enrolled Eddie Roy in Boy Scouts of America and a number of the many after school centers in the neighborhood. On their own, all my kids became involved with All Souls Church around the corner on St. Nicholas Avenue. They had lots of children's programs and the best Catholic Youth Organization basketball team in the city. They also had a summer camp in upstate New York. It was expensive but worth it. The kids left the harsh New York City streets for the summer.

Our block was chosen as a Police Athletic League "PAL" summer camp block. The Police Department closed the block to all traffic between 8:00 a.m. to 4:00 pm. They painted the street to host all types of street games, basketball, loadies, hopscotch, and shuffleboard. During the day, a PAL counselor was present on the block and no illegal drug activities took place. The police department considered engaging in illegal activities on a PAL block the ultimate in disrespect. They arrested you, and while you were in police custody something very bad happened to you to teach you a lesson.

One afternoon, as I returned home from the Garden Market on 116th Street, I saw a brand-new Cadillac convertible parked in front of my building. A crowd of kids was standing around it. Morris, the head drug dealer on the block, was 'holding-court,' demonstrating the new features of his car to the crowd of kids. I paid little attention until I got close enough to see Eddie Roy slapping Morris 'five' in celebration of his new car.

I went off like a firecracker without a fuse. I placed my grocery bags on the stoop, went inside our apartment on the first floor into the kitchen, and I picked up the largest butcher knife I could find. I walked back outside, pushed my way through the crowd of kids, and grabbed Morris by the collar, pushing him up against his Cadillac, and sticking my butcher knife between his legs.

"Nigger, if I ever see or hear you utter a single word to my son again, so help me God, I will cut your balls off!"

When I let him go, he jumped into his Cadillac and sped off. I turned to pick up my groceries and they were gone. I thought someone had stolen them. After all, this was Harlem. I walked into the apartment and there was a peculiar smell coming out of the bathroom. I entered to investigate and all of a sudden, these four numbers appeared in my mind. 341, 576, 306 and 954. This was crazy. What's going on?

After a restless sleep that night in which I dreamed continuously about Twin Spirits. I could not wait to get into my numbers dream book looking up Native Americans, Indians, South Georgia and Medicine Man. Oh my God, the same numbers appeared in the dream book.

At that point the drug dealing seemed to stop on my front stoop. From then on, when Morris saw Eddie Roy coming home from school, he ran to his Cadillac and rocketed from the block.

A few months after we moved in, I started dating a guy who lived across the street from us. He went by the name of "W." He was a tall, heavy set, unattractive, lightskinned fellow with a fraction of a brain. He struggled to hold a coherent conversation by piecing together a half sentence at a time. His brothers got him a job in the same Brooklyn steel fabrication plant where they worked. He made serious money though. His brothers told him the only reason I liked him was for his money. And they were right. I had now stooped that low.

Eddie Roy was livid, saying to me, "This is the last straw, Mama. You might as well put a sign on your back that reads, "Highest Bidder."

I told "W" that I loved him and wanted to give him some, but I needed money to pay bills. He promptly gave me a few hundred dollars. He did not have anything to spend his money on anyway. He didn't have any clothes or a new car. And he was too stupid to pass the driving test. He lived with his brothers in their mother's large fourbedroom apartment and they refused to pay her rent.

Like Mother Nature said, there are two kinds of people in this world: those who are clever or shrewd, and those who are insensible, or stupid. Both have a place in her world. The clever are here to build their dreams on the missteps of the insensible. They achieve their dreams only when they please her. *Prophet or Pariah?*

As incompatible as we were, the sex was wild and we were going at it like crazed rabbits. Then he approached my children and told them he wanted to marry me. I cursed him from one end of 115th Street to the other. He had crossed the line, even before we got started.

I had rules: no men spent the night in my apartment, and they were to have no contact with my children, other than a polite hello and goodbye. Eddie Roy tried to be respectful and nice to him, but this was too much. Eddie Roy refused money that he tried to give to him and my kids.

He made it clear to "W" that their friendship was not up for sale.

I felt very sorry for "W" because he really tried to befriend my kids, but he did it the wrong way.

Then an NYC Department of Health Case Worker showed up at my door. They demanded that my children and I take a tuberculosis test. They tested all of us and found that we had been exposed to TB. However, the antibodies in our immune systems had fought it off. "W" had caught TB from one of his infected friends by drinking from the same liquor bottles.

I had told "W" just a few days earlier that I was pregnant with his child. He was as happy as a kid at an ice cream truck. But I realized I had fallen to a new low. I questioned if I was going to bring a mentally defective child into this world; one also defective from being exposed to TB? I had to make up my mind quickly, and I did.

I loved all my children, regardless of who their fathers were. But I was not going to bring this man's mentally and physically defective child into this world that had been exposed to TB. If it lived, that would be committing a child to a lifetime of fingerpointing, mistreatment, and poor health. It would be the cruelest and most irresponsible thing that I could do to a child.

A NYC Department of Health Case Worker secretly introduced me to a registered nurse who performed safe abortions in your home. She charged $75. I scheduled the procedure for the next week, even though abortions were illegal in the State of New York.

The nurse showed up at my door with a doctor's bag full of instruments, medicines and a long rod looking instrument with a light on the end. She was very nice and professional. She gave me a shot of Penicillin before she started the procedure.

About half-way through the procedure, Eddie Roy walked through the apartment door. I had forgotten that he had a half-day at school.

Luckily, he was looking in the direction of the kitchen as he walked in. I was lying on the bed with my legs spread open with the bedroom door open. She immediately shut off the spotlight she was using to look up my vagina. She got up, closed the bedroom door, and finished the procedure.

Later, Eddie Roy asked, "What is going on, Mama?"

"The nurse's visit was a follow up for our TB test." I don't think he believed me.

I always told Eddie Roy never to lie to me. "There are three people you never lie to: your mother, your priest, and your lawyer."

I had just lied to him for the first time. A few weeks later, I heard a loud banging on the apartment door. It was "W." He was drunk and crying, "You killed my baby! Bitch, you killed my baby!"

Earlier in the day I had told him, "I had a miscarriage. It is over between us."

I refused to open the door as Eddie Roy rolled his eyes at me. The neighbors called the police and yelled at "W" to go home. The relationship was finished.

341 576 306 954

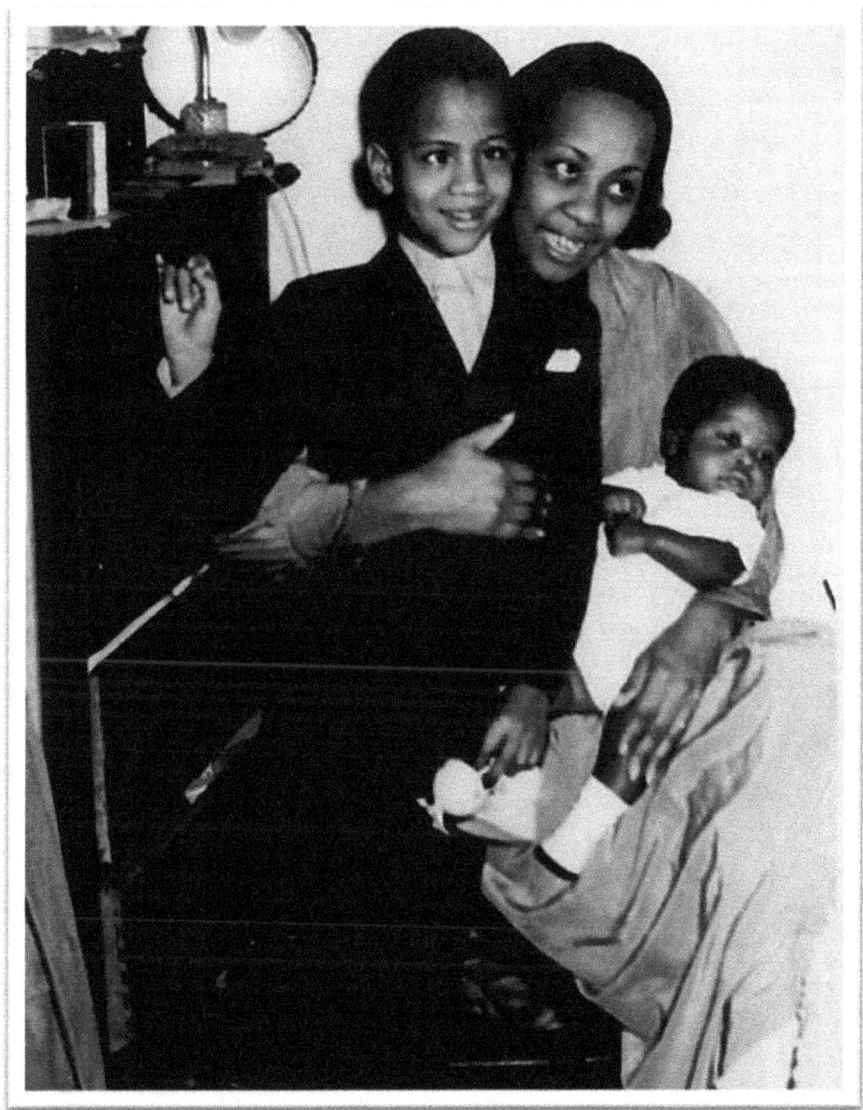

Eddie, Erma, and Bernard, 1952

Eddie, Erma, and Clifford, 1954

Eddie with Bernard, 1952

Vernetta, Clifford, and Bernard, 1958

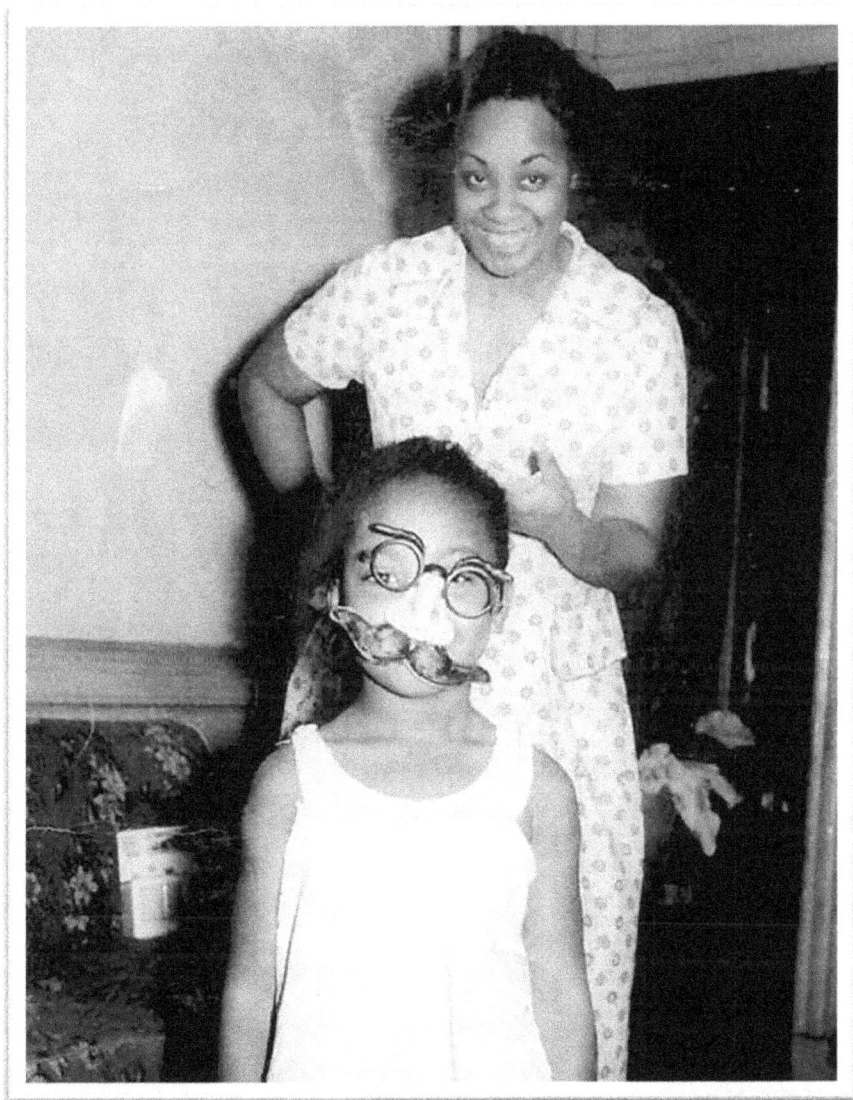

Erma and Vernetta, 1958

Eddie, Vernetta, and Bernard, 1958

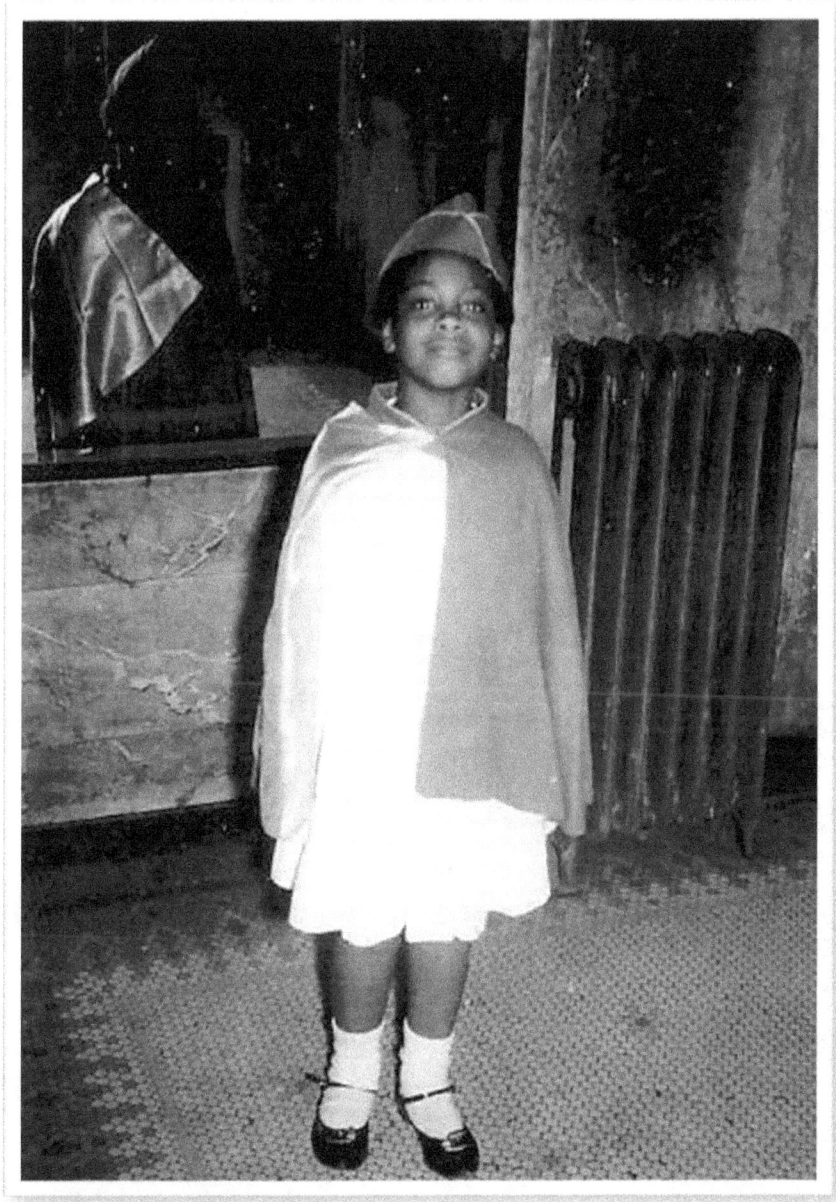

Vernetta in the Eastern Stars, 1964

Vernetta in her Sunday Best, 1964

Vernetta in the Girl Scouts, 1960

Chapter X

Single Action Number Money

I played all four of the numbers that appeared on the bathroom mirror for two weeks straight, and in multiple combinations. Three of them hit and the fourth hit three weeks later. I then started to play numbers on a regular basis. I fell in love with the digits and surprisingly I started to become good at it. I started hanging around the Number Hole on Lenox Avenue and 115th Street. It was not illegal to play numbers in New York State, just illegal to receive the bet. You figure that out. Most of the time, the police officers looked the other way concerning number playing.

I became a number playing regular. Steve Mitchell was the local Number Banker on the block. Steve was a tall, dark-skinned brother with a boisterous laugh and mean temper, if you got on the wrong side of it. Steve did a good business and had a good reputation of paying off when you hit, but he was not one of the top Number Bankers in Harlem.

I liked discussing the daily numbers with fellow players that I met in the Number Hole. One fellow I met was Aaron Cross. He was a tall dark-skinned guy from Trinidad with a polite laugh and strong back. We loved playing single action together, which is playing one number at a time. The payout was much lower, about 10 to 1. But, for some reason, I did very well playing single action and so did he. He was a Merchant Seaman and sailed for three months at a time all over the world. He was a Mechanic's Mate on the ships and he had a long and proud history in the Merchant Marines.

He was a good and decent man who only wanted someone who was kind and decent to love him. I was not that someone, but I did so anyway. His problem was that he stuttered. He was very interested in all my children, especially Eddie Roy. Eddie Roy liked him a lot, and he had the most interesting stories to tell him about his world travels. Eddie needed a male mentor. I felt it was what he was missing in his life. I asked him if he would consider being Eddie Roy's godfather, and he said yes without hesitation. When he was at sea, he sent Eddie raw gemstones, coins, souvenirs from everywhere he docked to unload and pick up cargo; the Middle East, South Africa, Europe, India, China, and Japan. Eddie and I would go to the library to read about each country he visited. He made those countries come alive.

When he returned home, it was Christmastime in July. He took us shopping at Macy's on 34th Street. We left with so many bags that we could not get the bags though the subway turnstiles; so, we took a cab home. We visited the circus at Madison Square Garden, the Yankee games at Yankee Stadium and the exhibits at the Museum of Natural History. We lived 'high on the hog' for a month or two, until he shipped out again.

In the summer of 1959, he returned to New York from a cruise and he called saying he had a surprise for us. He took us on a subway ride to the West Bronx. It was a beautiful neighborhood, just a few blocks from the aqueduct, in an outstanding apartment building with elevators that really worked and the halls didn't smell of urine. He opened the apartment door and I almost fainted. It was fully and immaculately furnished, with brand new furniture. There were three bedrooms and it was 'drop-dead boss, man!'

Then he took Eddie Roy into a room that was to be his bedroom. It was completely furnished with objects from all over the world that had taken him more than a year to collect and send back to the United States. Eddie was in seventh heaven.

Then he tapped Eddie on his shoulder and asked, "Eddie, I wish to marry your mother. I want you and your brother and sister to live here with me. May I have your permission to ask your mother to marry me?"

Eddie looked at him as if he was crazy for even asking the question. I was in total astonishment and started to cry.

Eddie turned to him and said, "Yes, yes, yes."

I turned to Aaron and gave him a big hug and kiss. Then I took him into the master bedroom and closed the door behind us. I cried for five minutes before I could get one word out. Then I held his hands in mine and shook my head. "No, and thank you."

I opened the bedroom door, walked out, and told the kids to get ready to go home.

Eddie said to me, "Home? Mommy, this is my home!"

Bernard and Miss Vee agreed with Eddie Roy, as I forcefully pulled all of them through the apartment's front door, leaving Aaron sitting on the bed crying. I didn't say a word to them as I dragged them down the subway steps. When the train arrived at the station, Eddie refused to get on. I held the door open pleading with him to get on the train. The conductor began to curse at us over the PA system for holding the train door open. At the last minute, Eddie jumped into the train heading back to 115th Street.

As the train pulled into 116th Street station, Eddie looked directly into my eyes and asked, "There was always something wrong with your boyfriends. I never liked most of them, but please tell me now, what is wrong with Aaron?"

I said, with a crooked smile on my face, "He stut...stut...stutters."

Eddie Roy placed both of his hands on his head with a sarcastic laugh asking, "He stut...stut...stut...stutters?"

We didn't see nor hear from Aaron Cross for about six months. Then one day he knocked on our apartment door with a young lady that he brought to meet the kids and me. She was his new girlfriend and was also from Trinidad. She was a tall, slim, good-looking woman and a schoolteacher from Queens. He wanted to get the kids' and my approval of his new girlfriend because he was going to ask her to marry him and move to Queens to live with her.

The kids liked her a lot and gave their approval. She appeared sneaky to me and the vibrations she was sending me were negative. I didn't approve of her, but he accepted the kid's recommendation to marry her. He invited us to the wedding, but we did not go.

Eddie Roy became more and more critical of my sex life and me as he grew older. Things continued to go downhill financially for us, except for the NYC Department of Welfare checks that kept us afloat. I traveled with Eddie Roy to the Stephen Foster Projects, across Lenox Avenue, to pick up the U.S. government surplus food from the distribution center. Everyone in the neighborhood could see how unfortunate we were by what we were carrying in our shopping cart. We had canned vegetables, fruit cocktail, applesauce, peanut butter, oatmeal, powdered milk, pasta, dried cereals, canned turkey, and a five-pound block of cheese. It was all marked U.S. Government Surplus. Eddie thought it was embarrassing to be seen carrying the surplus food from the distribution center, but all our neighbors asked us to share it with them.

I told him, "I picked up surplus food for the family during the depression in Plains, Georgia."

He replied, "The more things change the more they stay the same. Mommy, you have lost your personal ambition, your sense of self-reliance and your vision that you can make a better tomorrow for yourself. You are not taking care of yourself and you have gained a lot of weight. The doctor told you that your thyroid condition was getting worse and you refused to take your medicine like you should. Your ability to pick men is pitiful. You should take a break."

I was about to slap him, when he brought tears to my eyes by saying, "Mommy, the one thing that has not changed about you is your commitment to Miss Vee, Bernard, and me. We understand your motivation. You want nothing but the best for us, and you will do just about anything to get us the best. You know, Harlem will eat us alive, if you take your eye off us for one hot minute of time. You refused to allow us to become lazy and trifling. You never let me sleep late on Saturdays. I must go out into the streets and find a legal hustle, like carrying packages at the supermarkets, dropping off newspapers from the back of the *Daily News* trucks, and selling New York Age newspaper subscriptions. You enrolled us in every free program you could find from church programs to community centers in the evenings, to Boy Scouts, to Girl Scouts, and even the Eastern Stars. You even threatened to cut off the drug pusher's balls, if you ever saw him talking to us again."

It was wonderful to hear him say those things. I believed him, but I still mentioned to Eddie Roy's father that he was having growing pains on these very hostile New York City streets. He suggested that I send him to Atlanta, Georgia, for a year to go to school. It would get him out of the New York City streets and give him a break, the same as I did as a young woman. He had made up with his wife, Mayme, and Eddie Roy was no longer a threat to her. My sister, Freddie Mae, had just moved her family to their first home in the Collier Heights section of Atlanta. I asked if he could stay at her house while going to school, and she said yes. So, I sent all the kids down for the summer to spend time with my mother and sisters.

My relationship with my mother started to get much better. She only had my youngest sister Lizzie Mae to take care of now. Lizzie Mae was only two years older than Eddie Roy. Unfortunately, Ma Babe had died a few years earlier, and I was too distraught and too poor to attend the funeral. Daught was now living in Atlanta, and she sent for her sister Aunt Nora, who was finally out of the rehab hospital in Queens and retired from working for the Rameses.

Eddie Roy's behavior did calm down after the trip, but his grades did not get any better. He returned home the next summer from Atlanta about the same time that Bobby Thomas came into my life. I swore he was the last. At least he wasn't married. He was only about eight years older than Eddie Roy and much younger than I. He was an extremely good-looking guy, very bright, and a hardworking auto mechanic. He and I were madly in love. The one thing I loved about him was that he loved my kids. He would pack us all up in his Ford Thunderbird and take us on picnics in Central Park or drive us downtown to the movies. My kids, including my nephew Freddie Jr., would stuff themselves with all the popcorn and cotton candy they could eat and be sick as dogs before they arrived back home.

His parents were superintendents of a very large apartment building on Stebbins Avenue in the Bronx. Our relationship was going wild and hot for about six months. Then Bobby and I sat the kids down one evening at the kitchen table and told them we were going to get married. They all hit the ceiling because they had never been through this drill before.

Bernard and Miss Vee were ecstatic. Eddie Roy did not like Bobby. He was in the 'wait-and-see-if-this-pans-out' mode.

Bobby asked all of us to go with him to his parents' home that weekend to tell them the good news. We all put on our Sunday best and he drove us to the Bronx again. Bobby's parents asked the kids to sit in the hallway while Bobby and I went into the dining room to meet his family first. His family was very religious and extremely hostile. The meeting lasted about a hot two minutes. His parents had done their homework. They knew more about me than I knew about myself. Our conversation boiled down to one question.

"What are you going to contribute to this relationship, three children, all with different fathers?"

I could not answer their questions to my satisfaction, let alone theirs.

I flew out of the dining room, grabbed the kids' coats, and snatched them out of his parents' basement apartment. We all walked to the subway disgusted, as fast as we could, without Bobby.

Eddie Roy just looked at his brother and sister, smiled and said, "I told you so."

Bobby and I lasted about another six months. Maybe my kids were wiser than I thought. But I refused to let up on them.

Miss Vee was doing very well in school. Bernard and Eddie Roy were not. For some reason, they were not excited about school. Eddie was now in the eleventh grade at Charles Evans Hughes High School, located on 14th Street in downtown Manhattan.

This school was better than his district school, Benjamin Franklin High School on Pleasant Avenue on the East Side. His guidance counselor, Mr. Clarke, called me in for a visit.

I said to myself, "Oh my God, what in the hell has he done now?"

I walked into Mr. Clarke's office expecting to hear a list of foul deeds committed by Eddie Roy to flow from his mouth. Mr. Clarke, with a solemn expression on his face, simply showed me his report card. I almost hit the floor! He had earned all A's and B's, and he had earned placement on the Dean's List!

Mr. Clarke let me know that he had sat him down earlier in the school year and coached him, telling him, "It is time for you to grow up, Eddie. You are behind. If you want to graduate, you must get your ass in gear, improve your grades, and go to summer school to finish. Ms. Hill, he turned his attitude around overnight. His grades improved and he can graduate after summer school."

I think there was a little more to it than that. Mr. Clarke was three times his size and Eddie could not intimidate him. Eddie Roy had grown into a very smart, athletic, good-looking young man, and he could not wait to leave home. His biggest issue was sleeping with his brother, Bernard, on the living room sofa-bed, and Bernard peed in the bed almost every night. When he turned seventeen, he asked me if I would sign him up to enter the U.S. Army early. I said, yes, and Uncle Sam scheduled him to enter the Army in August of 1962. He finished high school after summer school just two months late. I was so proud of him. I knew he was on his way.

It really hurt all of us to see him leave, especially our dog, Spot, whom we patiently trained. Spot whined for two days after he walked out of the door headed for Army Boot Camp at Fort Dix, New Jersey. Spot was a Bull-Terrier mix and had a beautiful black coat with a white spot on his chest. He was very intelligent and very protective. He was the best dog we ever had. All we had to do was to give you a long stare and he would make a meal out of you. He was undersized, but loved to fight other dogs, especially the much larger Doberman Pinscher owned by one of Eddie's friends.

It was a smart thing Eddie did to enlist when he did. The war in Vietnam was getting hotter and they were drafting more and more young men, especially Black men. By volunteering, he was able to pick what he wanted to do in the Army and where he wanted to be stationed. He chose to become an Army Medic and he requested to be stationed in Europe. Uncle Sam gave him both.

After Medic school in Fort Sam Houston, Texas, and temporary duty in Fort Rucker, Alabama, he was sent to Europe and stationed at the Army's Hospital Kaserne in Bad Kreuznach, Germany, with the

517th Medical Clearing Company. He said, "Mommy, it is the safest unit to be in. If nuclear war breaks out, I would be among the very few that had the proper equipment to survive."

We communicated regularly by letter. He told me how much the European women loved Black GIs. So much so, that a young European woman he was persistently courting told him, "You are not Black enough for me. The blacker the berry, the sweeter the juice."

Responding quickly, he said laughing, "Baby, you must add a little cream and sugar to your coffee to make it sweet."

The welfare checks remained steady but were not enough to raise three kids on. Eddie was now on his own and sending me $25 per month out of his pay. Uncle Sam added another $25 to it to make it $50 per month. I opened a savings account and placed it all in there for him to go to school when he got out of the service.

The ugliest thoughts of desperation go through your mind when you are down on your knees money-wise. Just before he left, I started selling Gypsy Rose wine by the pint after the liquor store closed on the weekends. I had sold better moonshine in Plains, Georgia, which was better for you to drink than cheap wine. My children began to complain about drunks knocking on the door at 3 a.m. If you didn't open the door and sell it to them, they would piss in the hallway by your door. Little money was made from it, which is why that hustle did not last long.

I mentioned to Eddie Roy, in my letters, that I was getting good at playing numbers; especially single action. In fact, I loved playing 'Single Action' more than playing straight (three) numbers. I was now making a few dollars in winnings each week. I collected and studied a wide variety of dream books, like Black Cat, Lucky Lucille's and Rob's Number Guide, to name a few. I became an expert at analyzing dreams and the number(s) they predicted. I faithfully read and interpreted "Ching Chow," the Chinese cartoon character that appeared in the *Daily News*, to decipher any numbers I saw. I even developed a mathematical workout that predicted what number would fall on certain days, which was very difficult to do.

In his letters, Eddie always joked that I should consider writing numbers instead of playing them.

He would say, "Mommy, you make more money if you wrote numbers, rather than played numbers. No matter how well you gamble, you will never consistently beat the house. I learned about gambling in the Army. So, become the house."

Well, what did he say that for? I hadn't thought seriously about it until I had two losing weeks in a row. Steve, the Number Man, continued to tease me about "robbing" him.

Steve said to me, "You are hitting me so regular now that we should trade places."

I laughed saying, "Not in the last two weeks."

But Steve wasn't laughing and said, "I am not joking."

I walked away again not thinking seriously about it, but Steve just would not let it go. Every time I placed my bets, he made a comment about me working for him. To be honest, I was already spending a lot of time in the Number Hole anyway, and there was no better person at figures than me.

A month later, Steve asked me to have dinner with his wife and him. I made a dress for the occasion because my sewing skills had gotten much better. What I liked about him was that he was a dedicated husband, who loved his wife and didn't fool around. He said he had children, but I never saw any and I did not ask any further questions. He was also very dedicated to his number business and always paid his hits. He drove us to a Mafia-owned restaurant downtown in Little Italy. The food and service were outstanding. But I should have paid more attention to what was going on. I believe the owners were checking me out.

After dinner, Steve's wife, Mildred said to me, "That full time number writing job is still open."

Laughing, Steve replied, "Why do you think I invited you to dinner, your good looks?"

I replied, "Yes, I will take the job, but I want to start slowly."

Steve was in total shock. I had told him several times before that I was not interested in writing numbers.

Mildred smiled at me. I had met her several times before when she came to pick Steve up from work. I believe it was Mildred that was pushing Steve to hire me.

I told Steve upfront, "These are my conditions for the job:

1. I don't go to jail; I have children to care for.
2. No involvement with narcotics.
3. I will write out of one location; customers will come to me. No number- running for me."

Then I looked Mildred directly in her eyes and said "Steve, our relationship will be strictly business only. Now we can talk about salary."

Steve said, "First, I agree to your terms. Second, before we discuss salary, I have one request. You already know most of my customers. They like you, and you play one another's numbers. You will not give numbers to any of my customers anymore and you will not play numbers with me anymore. I know you will do great and bring in a lot of business. Therefore, I will start you at the top salary of my best Number Writers, $800.00 per week, plus tips."

I almost wet my pants, and I told him, "Thank you, Steve. That was more than I was going to ask for. I want to try the night number business very slowly at first, to get my feet wet."

I knew handling large sums of money on Harlem's streets could be dangerous. But I could use the extra money. Besides, Christmas of 1963 was approaching. Steve agreed with the suggestion that I start taking the night numbers. The traffic was usually very light and the police didn't raid Number Holes and runners at night. It was too easy for someone to turn out the lights. Police officers and civilians got hurt during night raids. I started taking the night numbers the following week.

The number business in Harlem has a long, tough, and proud history. The father of the most reliable "Daily Lottery" was Casper Holstein. He was born of Danish and Caribbean parents in St. Croix, U.S. Virgin Islands, on December 7, 1876. In 1920, in New York City, he devised a reliable way of picking a three-digit number that could not be fixed. He used the last three numbers of the Banking Clearing House daily totals that were published in major New York newspapers. In a few short years, he made millions in the number game. By the mid-1930s, after several arrests, being kidnapped, and having to compete with Stephanie St. Clair, Harlem's Number Queen, he left the Harlem number business and became a respected philanthropist until he died on April 5, 1944, in New York City.

When prohibition ended on December 5, 1933, the mob suffered a huge decline in revenues. But they discovered the nickels and dimes number game in Harlem was making a lot of money. So, Dutch Schultz, the notorious mobster of the prohibition era, tried to muscle in on Harlem's number businesses. He was successful except for one determined woman. She returned every favor, burnt-out store front for burntout store front and dead body for dead body. She once hid in a coal bin to hide from a Dutch Schultz hitman.

Stephanie St. Clair, better known as "Queenie" or Madame St. Clair, was one tough cookie. She was born of French and African descent on the Caribbean Island of Guadalupe. She had an abusive childhood, but she fought her way up into being one of the top and wealthiest Negro Number Banks in Harlem.

Finding good men who were willing to work for her was a difficult slog. But she found Ellsworth "Bumpy" Johnson—the infamous Bumpy Johnson. After several highprofile arrests and jail time, she promoted Bumpy, her top enforcer, to take over her business.

After taking over, Bumpy made a deal with Lucky Luciano of the Mafia to assassinate, or which the mob called giving a coup de grâce, to Dutch Schultz. In exchange, he divided up Harlem's number businesses 50/50 with the Mafia. As Dutch Schultz lay mortally wounded in the hospital, Madame St. Clair sent him a sarcastic telegram that read, "You live by the sword, you die by the sword."

Steve said, "In my younger hustling days, I once worked as a Number Runner for her. She is still alive today, about 80 years old and frail. She is still feisty, though, and wealthy as hell."

"I could see that she was one smart, tough woman, and Bumpy probably loved working for her. The word on the street was that they decided to move in with one another in their final years. She reminded me of Mrs. Cunningham, who I loved working for in Atlanta.

Within a month, I started writing day numbers in a brand-new location. It was a ground floor apartment at 103 West 115th Street. I had a new Number Runner and bodyguard by the name of Tom Bennett. A Number Banker on the Upper West Side of Harlem had fired him. However, Steve was shorthanded and gave him a shot at the new job aiding me. His job was to go and pick up numbers from my customers who were homebound or didn't want to visit the Number Hole. He was a decent looking guy, tall, dark skinned, heavy-set, with oversized eyes and a large head. He was very pleasant to work with, but constantly had problems proofing up each day. I usually did his proof at the end of the day to keep him from losing his job.

On my first day writing, I wrote more than $4,000 in numbers, and that was the lowest tally I ever had. Steve's number business and my number writing really grew rapidly. Within six months, I became one of Steve's top Number Writers.

He had four: Sylvester, Tyrone, May, and me. Sugar, Tom, and Nate were runners. Sylvester wrote across the street from me in a fake taxi stand office. Steve's office was there also. The word on the street was that Sylvester could not be trusted. That's why Steve wouldn't allow him to work alone. Steve handled all of Sylvester's 'hit' payouts himself to make sure his customers got paid and to keep an eye on him. This prevented him from stealing by writing late numbers for his friends.

Sylvester was Steve's top Number Writer before I was hired. He didn't like me much because I turned down his sexual advances and I hit a lot of numbers with him before I started to work for Steve. In addition, it became clear that he did not like females outperforming him. Within a few months, I caught up and surpassed him in my daily numbers tally.

In the evenings, he ran the local crap shooting games on 115th Street. Most crapshooters didn't like him much either because he was a cheat. He did anything and everything to win, from shaving the dice to having friends holler "Police!" in the middle of a large pot.

As my business grew, I told Steve to spruce up my Number Hole so it would look better and attract more customers. Steve purchased about $1,200 in new furniture for my customers to relax in while waiting to place their bets or to get paid. That was a big hit and it almost doubled my daily tally. I was now writing about $7,000 per day in bets.

But it was a struggle trying to keep Tom employed. Boy, I am a sucker for pitiful men. Yes, we started to sleep together, but I did not break my rule. We didn't move in together. Tom separated from his wife a few years earlier and had a small daughter that he wasn't taking care of. He never kept a regular job to make regular child support payments. I made sure when Steve paid him that he took money to his wife. She actually came by the Number Hole, introduced her daughter and herself, and thanked me on several occasions.

I loved kids, especially mine. You know, I never asked myself why I never took my children's fathers to court or demanded child support payments from them. I guess I felt my children were my responsibility. If their fathers wanted to help, fine. If not, fine.

437 391 615 524

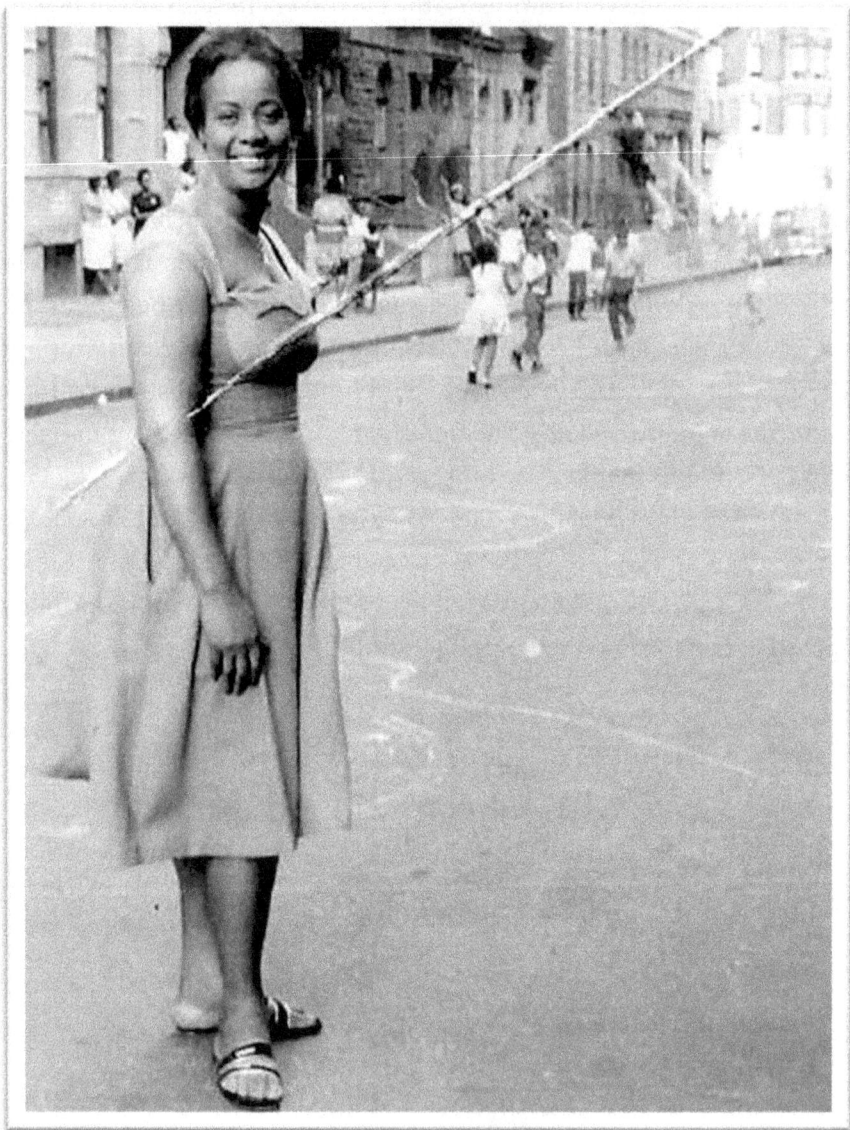

Erma Hill on 115th Street,
Harlem NYC

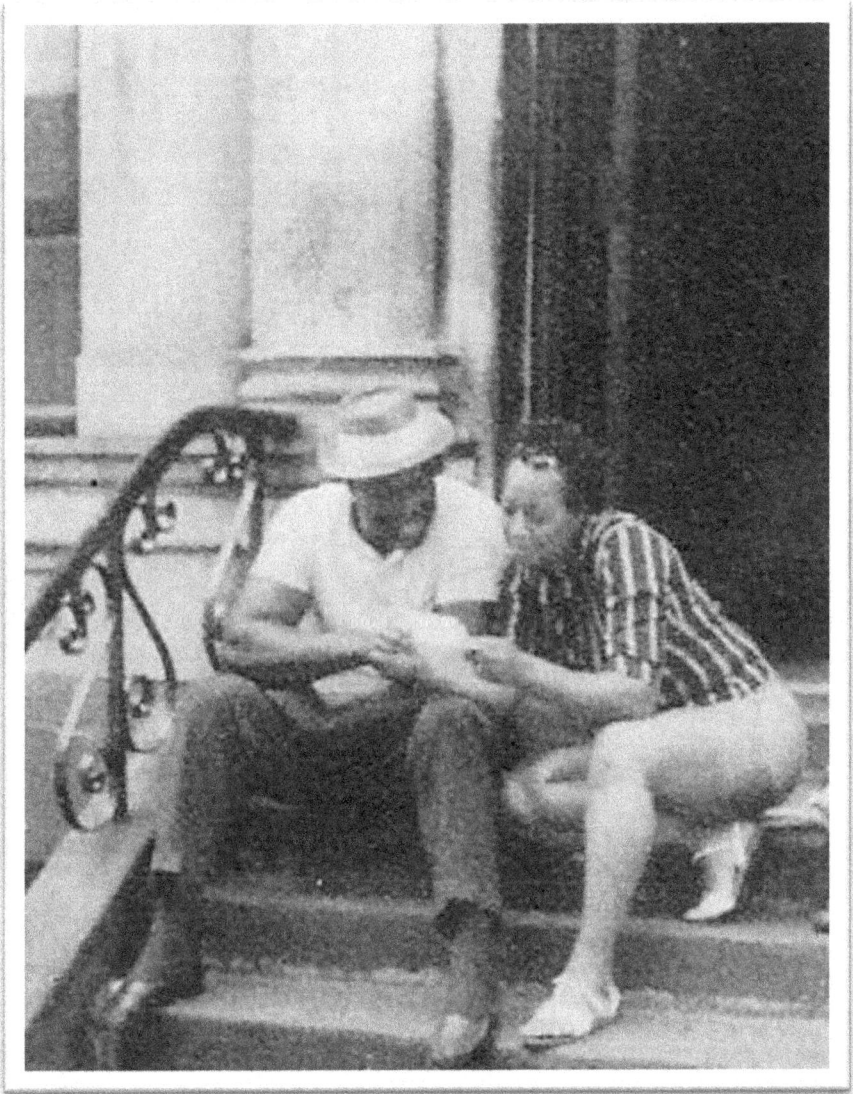

*Erma L. Hill with her number
playing friend on 115th Street*

Erma L. Hill and friends at
112 West 115th Street, 1962

Chapter XI

Dimes Make Millions

Steve always made himself available to his customers. If you were a good customer, he allowed you to run a tab, provided you paid up at the end of the week or when you hit. He also loaned money to his customers. They were basically 'payday loans.' The interest was high, but it was payable.

He even cashed customers' paychecks and welfare checks. On Thanksgiving, he bought a truckload of turkeys and I gave them out to our customers after the last number was drawn.

There were not many banks that provided service to the Harlem Community. Number Bankers filled the void by making small business loans as well. Steve did so just on a person's word and their relationship with him. He loaned money to businesses that were new start-ups, having cash flow problems, and fire victims.

On my say-so, he loaned $10,000 to Jeffery Smalls, one of my best customers, to open a liquor store on the corner of St. Nicholas Avenue and 116th Street. But six months passed and we hadn't received one payment from him. Steve was upset with me because I recommended him. One Saturday evening, I asked Sugar and Helen to go with me around the corner to 116th Street to check him out. Helen was a transgender person working as one of my runners now because she had taken too many busts for shoplifting. We stood across the street in a doorway for about an hour checking out his traffic flow in and out of the store. He was running a very good liquor business. So, we all walked across the street into Jeffery's liquor store and we exchanged polite greetings.

I stated, "Jeffery, we haven't heard from you in six months."

"Red, the liquor business is very slow and I couldn't make any payments on my loan." I looked at Sugar and Helen. Sugar went to the door, locked it, and turned over the open sign. Helen went into a corner and picked up a mop with its handle attached.

I said to Jeffrey, "Steve does not like liars, and I don't either. We watched your business for the past hour and you have a thriving business."

I looked over at Helen and she took the mop handle and smashed it into a large liquor display.

He said, "Oh God," and went running into his cash register, counted out $1,000, and handed it to me.

My reply was, "And?"

"I will pay Steve $1,000 per week until I repay him in total."

"Jeffery, I will not be back. If someone has to come back, it will be more painful than this. Thanks."

As a young Number Runner, Steve was often required to supply muscle to people his bosses loaned money to who refused to pay. His favorite weapon of choice was a baseball bat.

He would say, "If someone owes you money, the last thing you want to do is kill or maim them. You will not be paid. But putting them temporarily out of action generally does the job." I was a lot kinder to Jeffery.

Under my direction, Steve supported all neighborhood community institutions, causes and events, including paying for five buses for one of the Civil Rights Marches on Washington. Reverend Monroe of Memorial Baptist Church at 141 West 115th Street contacted me asking that Steve pay for the buses to take his parishioners to DC.

When I asked Steve, he replied right away, "No problem."

But it turned into a hair-raising situation the day the buses arrived. The local beat cops threatened to write the church tickets for parking buses in the church's no parking zone reserved for church vehicles, unless Steve paid them a bribe for the five buses. Steve cursed out the local beat cops publicly, to no end. One cop put his hand on his gun.

I calmed Steve down and told him to go to the corner street phone and call the 28th Precinct Watch Commander.

Then the cops said to Steve, "Forget about it, man," and left.

Two weeks later, when we had our monthly meeting with the Precinct Commander, we told him what happened and we gave him the officers' badge numbers. Within two weeks, the officers were transferred to some hell-hole precinct in Brooklyn on the night shift.

Malcolm X and his Fruit of Islam bodyguards from Elijah Mohamed's Temple #7, around the corner on 116th Street, were frequent visitors to my Number Hole. About once a week they "plowed-in" filling up their white donation buckets with cash donations from my customers and me. On one visit, while I was going into my purse for a donation Malcolm X said to me, "Red, do you feel bad working for whitey?"

I politely corrected him. "No Mr. X, I am not working for whitey. I am working for Eddie, Bernard, Vernetta, and self. One of your favorite phrases to Negroes is, "Do for self." Well, Mr. X, I am doing it for self. Also Mr. X, in your speeches you ask whitey to give you a piece of this country for your own and you will be satisfied, happy and willing to defend it. That's bullshit. First of all, this country doesn't belong to whitey. It belongs to Native Americans. And it is not his to give to you.

Furthermore, The U.S. government tried giving away large tracts of land to Civil War soldiers, both black and white, after the Civil War. The land was abandoned within five years because it was not farmable. So, Mr. X, if you can convince whitey to give you and me 40 acres and a mule, please make my 40 acres on the corner of 59th Street and Central Park West. And better yet, keep the damn mule.

Additionally, you suggest that Negroes are due reparations from whitey for the abuse and suffering they laid upon us. Well, when the check line for reparations forms, you and everyone else can get in front of me, but please don't hold your breath.

Finally, I do not want anything from whitey, except for him to get the hell out my way and I will get it myself."

"Sister, I could use you in the Nation. You mentioned Eddie, your son. Does he work at the Garden Market after school?"

"How do you know that?"

"I talk to him a lot when I shop. The market is very convenient, being found under Temple #7. I invited him into the Muslim bookstore to read material that will cleanse his mind."

"Yes, he told me. He did a book report for school on one of your favorite books, "World's Great Men of Color" by J.A. Rogers."

"Yes, I hope to bring him into the Nation also."

Handing him a $20 bill, I said, "Keep working on it, Mr. X. When you stop characterizing "All white folks are devils" and simply say, "Some white folks are devils;" you may get him into the Nation."

Another time, when Congressman Adam Clayton Powell, Jr.'s voter registration drive was going very poorly in the neighborhood, his campaign manager came hat-in-hand asking for help. I, along with my runners, set up voter registration tables in the morning on St. Nicholas Avenue and 115th Street before we started writing numbers. Within one hour, we signed up more than 400 new voters.

The independent Black number bankers in Harlem also had high profile help from Congressman Powell. The Congressman was constantly speaking to the New York Times, pointing his fingers at the police and judges who were working hand-in-hand with the Mafia to destroy independent Black number banks in Harlem. Many of his political donations came from the independent Black number bankers, and he was losing that revenue when the mob took over their banks.

The Harlem number wars had been going on for years between the Independent Number Bankers and the Mafia. The conflict had taken many lives in Harlem. Steve and I attended the funerals of several Number Runners and bankers that received the "coup de grâce" from one side or the other. This stuff was above our paygrade, and both he and I tried to avoid it.

The Italian Mafia took over much of Harlem's rackets just before WWII. This was after Bumpy Johnson made the deal with the Italian Mafia to divide up Harlem's lucrative number business in exchange for killing Dutch Schultz and peace. After killing Dutch Schultz, the mob started strong-arming many independent Black number bankers. This allowed them to keep some or most of their business, provided they sent a portion to the *East Side.*

Steve made peace with Fat Tony (Anthony) Salerno, head of the Genovese Mafia family. He paid Tony $20,000 for the 115th Street Block Franchise, plus 20% of the take from numbers he banked. Additionally, the arrangement called for his 116th Street, *East Side* crew to bank all number bets over $50. Fat Tony was not interested in the 'nickel and dime' players. He and his crew wanted the larger bets.

Fat Tony started out as a Mafia soldier in the 1930s under Capo (Captain) Michael Coppola. He advanced by controlling and developing profitable gambling and loansharking operations in Harlem and the South Bronx.

Many independent Black number bankers in Harlem felt Steve was a sellout. Most believed he was allowing white mobster outsiders to skim money off the top of Harlem's number playing public. This was true. But Steve felt he was too old and outgunned to fight a battle that was settled years ago by the infamous Bumpy Johnson. Steve responded to the criticism by saying, "The enemy of my enemy is my friend."

In exchange for Steve's partnership, the *East Side* provided bribed police protection, lawyers, bribed judges, and other officials, keeping his number runners and writers out of jail and working. But this arrangement was not working well. Tony was constantly complaining to Steve that he was shorting him and he was not getting his fair share of the business. Tony stopped paying the police, lawyers, and judges. When our runners and writers were arrested, sometimes it took a whole week to get them out of jail. The average waiting time would normally be overnight. To keep the police and judges off his back, Steve arranged to pay them directly.

On June 26, 1964, Steve brought a copy of the New York Times newspaper into my Number Hole between the first and second numbers saying "This article is going to cause big trouble for us."

After I read it, I replied to Steve, "Like my younger sister, Freddie, the NYT is the new tattle tale."

New York Times reporter, Charles Grutzner, wrote the article and he exposed everything, hands down. There were no more secrets about the number business in Harlem or New York City. He laid open chapter and verse the numbers rackets like an open wound. This is a portion of the article he wrote.

Dimes Make Millions for the Numbers Racket
June 26, 1964
An excerpt from a New York Times article by Charles Grutzner

"The numbers game, with its lure of a possible 600-to-1 payoff, has outpaced horse race betting with bookmakers as New York City's most popular form of illegal gambling. More than 500,000 daily players pour at least $200 million a year into this city's policy banks. About half of this sum comes back to the lucky ones who "hit the number," which varies from day to day. The rest becomes the booty of the policy bankers—after the payment of commissions to runners, controllers, salaries to accountants, security lookouts, fees to bail bondsmen, lawyers, and graft to police. The controllers keep track of the bets and make payoffs with money from the bank.

Police Commissioner Michael J. Murphy has conceded that some dishonest police officers are in the pay of the numbers bankers, but he denied that the graft "system" reached high into the Police Department, as it once did.

The money behind several policy banks comes from racketeers active in the thriving illegal narcotics trade. Some small banks must borrow from "shylocks" (usurers) when their players "score" heavily or when, as the gamblers say happened recently, the police increase their prices for promised protection. The borrowing brings even the so-called "independent" banks under the crime syndicate's influence...

The chart, adapted from one prepared by the Police Department, shows the organizational setup of a Brooklyn policy bank, doing business at an annual rate of $2,500,000, which was first raided last July...

In Harlem, which has the city's heaviest concentration of numbers players, a murderous war is in the making between a group known locally as the "Black Mafia" and a white syndicate, which has taken control from the Negro bankers who formerly ran the game.

The Negro racketeers accuse the police of having maneuvered the change in control by raiding the Negro-run banks and protecting Italian bankers in Harlem. Persons close to the Negro bankers predict that the "Black Mafia's" attempt to regain control will be marked, "by a few murders, maybe in the next week.."

Commissioner Murphy, in a report on February 27th to a legislative committee, said: "Syndicated crime, whether it be known as Cosa Nostra, Mafia or any other name, finds in the policy racket the ideal criminal activity.

"It [the numbers game] is easily organized; it is popular with the public; there is a guaranteed, built-in margin of profit; detection, because of the protection and security offered by the laws of search and seizure, and by recent court decisions, is difficult; and punishment is mild and hardly a deterrent."

The so-called "no-knock" and "stop-and-frisk" laws, which take effect July 1, are viewed by the police as potential weapons in their drive against the numbers racket. Both laws were passed at the 1964 state legislative session.

On most winning numbers, the bank pays off at 600 to 1. But the lucky player who has bet a dollar seldom wins more than $500 if he has a "hit." The runner receives a 25-cent commission from the bank on each dollar that is bet. But he usually gets what amounts to a compulsory "tip" of $100 from the lucky player.

Now the police aim at the top. The banker's profit comes to about 8 cents on every dollar played. On $200 million, this would be about $16 million a year. Some estimates put the annual volume of numbers play as high as $400 million.

Police officials, who have counted cash and slips seized in raids on policy drops and banks, regard $200 million as a conservative, "educated guess" of the annual amount bet here on numbers...

Actually, there is no law against playing the numbers, the player who gives only his own play to the numbers man cannot be arrested. Only the person who accepts wagers is liable to prosecution. This legal distinction resembles that of Prohibition. It was not illegal to buy a drink, but to sell one was...

But the cry for a local share of the profit from the racket has been taken up by others. James R. Lawson, president of the Harlem Council for Economic

Development, recently announced the group's program, including this plank: "BLACK control of the Numbers."

Mr. Lawson said in an interview, "A former controller, a Negro, who was put out of business just before a white racketeer took over the bank for which he was working, said that until that happened he "had the word" that two detective divisions were on the protection "pad" for payoffs along with the local precinct and plainclothes unit. He said the payments to the police were handled by the banker."

Numbers play enjoys such acceptance in Harlem that public figures like Representative Adam Clayton Powell make open demands that Negro racketeers get their share of the business. Four years ago, Mr. Powell first made the accusation that the police were driving out Negro number bankers to permit white operators to take over from the pulpit of the 10,000 member Abyssinian Baptist Church.

Mr. Powell said that white policy bankers were "pauperizing Harlem" by taking $50 million a year out of that community. He has been letting up on his charges of police graft since a Harlem woman he had named as "bagwoman" for the police won a suit against him for defamation of character...

While the runners and many of the controllers in Harlem are Negroes, it is a fact that most of the Harlem play is banked by white racketeers, several of whom have their headquarters in the Bronx...

In several high-level raids by the Police Commissioner's Confidential Investigating Unit, or policy bank teams set up by Commissioner Murphy, bolted steel doors have impeded police entry long enough to permit destruction of evidence...

The elaborate and costly precautions taken by the policy bankers in their attempts to foil high-level raids are cited by money in the numbers game goes Commissioner Murphy to rebut high into the department... charges that the protection

Steve said, "He must have

written the article from one of our Number Holes. Now we are going to have more problems from the police."

Steve and I agreed with most of the article's content. But we disagreed with some of Charles Grutzner's money assessments on the total dollar take in Harlem.

"The amount of money taken in numbers in Harlem is $50 million dollars per year." The real figure was over $1 million per day and over $250 million per year.

"That corruption only resides at the local police level," No, it reigns high in all law enforcement agencies.

"That narcotics money was bankrolling the numbers operation." No, it was the other way around.

I said to Steve, "I agree. Now we are going to have added problems from the police."

"Yeah, I am going to hire more lookouts. You can stop local police, but you can't stop the DA's office police unit from downtown."

512 982 429 126

Chapter XII

From Welfare To Wealth

As the money came rolling in from my salary, hits and tips, my children reaped the benefits, and they wanted for nothing. We had the best of everything and we ate little government or welfare food anymore. My brother, Fred, was doing well at the Hortense Spier Bakery and he had been promoted to Route Manager. He traded cakes and pies for lobster tails, steaks, and salmon from the best restaurants in New York City. Boy, did we love the goose liver pâté from the Jewish deli.

I bought my children the latest and best of everything - clothes, shoes, and toys. They were always dressed to kill. I took Bernard downtown to Barneys New York to buy his Sunday suits and alligator shoes. Miss Vee had the finest in patent leather shoes, leather, and rabbit skin coats. I was one of Helen's best customers before she started working for me. She was a professional booster (shoplifter) who measured the kids' and my sizes and boosted our exact request in clothes from the best stores in downtown Manhattan, like Saks Fifth Avenue, Bloomingdales, Bergdorf-Goodman, Macy's, and Gimbels.

Miss Vee's Easter outfit was so 'boss' that it turned heads at All Souls Episcopal Church on Easter. Father Lauder at All Souls Episcopal Church and Reverend Monroe at Memorial Baptist Church definitely opened my offering envelopes first. I had only one requirement for my children: that they must do well in school, and they did.

Miss Vee was the first young girl in the neighborhood to have a hair weave. My daughter and I both had a scalp problem called Alopecia. It was a very bad problem among the Hill family women. It caused our hair to go bald and only grow in spots. Sadly, the weave just made things worse for her. The kids picked on her, and she was afraid to go to school because of it. I was now making enough money to place all my children in private school, with the help of one of my top customers, Bert. She introduced me to the principal of the Seventh Day Adventist School, R.T. Hudson, in the Bronx, and I enrolled them immediately.

I returned to the hair salons, had a pedicure and my nails done twice a week. I had several custom wigs made on 3rd Avenue and 149th Street in the Bronx and at Wonder Weave on 125th Street in Harlem. My favorite style was called "Sassoon" in a burnt red henna tint that was especially prepared for me. I named it the "New York Red." It was a neck length cut and presented a sexy long bob across the upper face and left eye.

Red, New York Red, became my street name and the name I used to sign my number betting receipt slips. Like me, more often than not these days, this particular wig was a jaw dropper.

I started to have my clothes custom made by a Jewish seamstress/tailor on 125th Street, just off Fifth Avenue. She acquired the latest and best fabrics, leathers, suedes, and furs just for me. I had leathers and suedes in every color, with boots and pocketbooks to match. I preferred to work in pants suits and low heels, in case I had to move out quickly. I purchased most of my shoes from "Tall Girls" downtown on Fifth Avenue. I wore the best underclothes and bought the best bath oils, body powders and perfumes from Macy's. I stopped using facial soap again and returned to using Noxzema. I loved everything about Marilyn Monroe including her Chanel No.5. Boy, did you see her in that 'Subway Grate' picture? She had a set of legs on her that looked almost as good as mine.

"Being poor is not a fact of life. It is a state of mind." *Prophet or Pariah?*

On the flip side, I turned 40 in 1964, with three kids, and my Marilyn Monroe youthful figure was starting to fade a bit. It was a wakeup call. My thyroid condition started to get better after I started to work for Steve and the doctor recommended that I stop taking the medicine. I had to work hard to keep myself up and I received many compliments from my kids and customers. Also, the men started flirting again like drops of water in waterfalls. I got plenty of exercise because I stayed on my feet most of the day and my kids loved my new look from the weight loss.

Steve called a meeting with our 28th Precinct Commander, Timothy McGregor, to discuss the fallout from the NYT article. He repeated that I was not to be arrested under any circumstances.

Captain McGregor told Steve, "That is going to cost you an extra $200 per month, and that is half of my usual fee, to put "Red" on my no arrest list."

Usually, only the top Harlem number bankers who were large and well-connected enough were placed on his no arrest list. However, Captain McGregor also had his own reason to talk to Steve and for giving him a reduced rate. There was a well-known Jewish number banker, small but well known by the name of Bill Rosen, who was a friend of McGregor's. Bill was a problem for McGregor because Bill wrote numbers on 123rd Street, a block north of the 28th Precinct Station House. Internal affairs officers were taking pictures of police officers making bets there.

The new precinct captain felt the betting was too close to the precinct and told Bill he had to find another location. Bill told the captain he had been writing numbers for five years at this location and he didn't have the money to buy a new location from the Mafia's "116th Street Crew." This crew was the Genovese Crime Family, one of the Mafia's most powerful families in New York City. This group controlled much of the numbers business in Harlem and South Bronx, including our block.

The captain told him, "Move your Number Hole, or be shut down."

On McGregor's request and recommendation, Bill called Steve and asked if he would allow him to set up his franchise under him, on a percentage cut basis. Steve said yes, but he never discussed with me the details of Bill's partnership. I found out about the deal through the grapevine. Steve really wanted him because of his large customer base and contacts with the NYC Police Department.

The only problem was that Bill had a reputation of stealing money at the end of the day to feed his habit of betting on the ponies. He stole from himself to play the ponies. If a person didn't hit, their number slip and cash would disappear from the tally. That was also the reason his number business never took off as one of Harlem's largest.

However, understanding that, Steve hired Bill on July 16, 1964, the first day of the Harlem riots. Six days of rioting resulted when white police Lieutenant Thomas Gilligan shot and killed James Powell, a black youth, during an argument with a building superintendent. Steve slept in the Number Hole, armed, for three nights to prevent it from being vandalized.

Steve told McGregor, "Hiring Bill was a favor to you. And no charge for Red being added to your no arrest list settled the deal."

Steve set Bill up in a candy store a few doors down from my new location at 109 West 115th Street. Bill's business took off like a rocket. Many of his customers were white and traveled from all over Harlem and the Bronx to play numbers with him. Bill quickly overtook me in writing numbers. He was writing over $8,000 a day by the end of his second week. I learned something from this. Sometimes personal favors carry more weight than cash.

Bill also had a large number of well-to-do Negro customers who thought Steve worked for Bill now. Most of my customers thought it was that way also. Even the beat police officers on the pad thought that because he was Jewish and had once owned his own Number Bank. Many Negroes trust white folks with their money more than they do Negroes. Charles Grutzner in his NYT article said the same thing. And he was right.

At first, Steve took offense. But I convinced him it might be an advantage because the "Man," (the police) would give him less trouble if they thought he was working for Bill as a Number Writer. Based on my recommendation, Steve assigned Bill to handle paying off the local cops. They would think he was back in charge, and he knew most of the cops in the 28th personally. Following that change, we had fewer problems with the 'Bulls,' the police raiding squads that used sledge hammers to break down our doors. And it worked, especially in light of the NYT article.

The next reason was that Steve had a bad temper, and he knew it. He cursed the cops out at the drop of a hat.

The final reason was that the business was growing rapidly and Steve had to share the management workload.

But what really scared us to death about Bill was his customers. A shocking number of them were police officers. Sometimes there would be three or four uniformed police officers in Bill's Number Hole at one time. They liked Bill's Number Hole because it fronted as a candy store. They helped themselves to all the coffee, doughnuts, candy, and soda they could consume without paying. Steve didn't like the uniformed paying or non-paying traffic because it scared the regular customers away. They thought the Number Hole was being raided. If the police raided the Number Hole, the customers would lose their bets. Additionally, if the DA's office downtown got a whiff of it, they would close Bill and Steve down in a heartbeat.

He told Bill that "Downtown" sent word that, "If the police officers do not stop making their bets in uniform, they are going to lock up everyone, including them."

Bill put the word out on the street to his officers, and things calmed down. It was a 'white' lie, but it worked. *Prophet or Pariah?*

Steve paid the beat cops $100 per week, the sergeants $125, the watch commander $150, and 28th Precinct Captain McGregor got $250 per week. Bill handled the payoffs to the cops by dropping pay envelopes into the open passenger-side windows of the squad cars as they made their rounds. Sometimes he paid out more than $3,000 per month, total.

Because of the New York Times story, McGregor had to schedule more fake raids. Steve had to be careful in scheduling the fake raids with the police. To help with that, Steve placed Bill in charge of scheduling the fake raids. In doing so, Bill had to also make sure there were no police officers in the Number Hole during a raid.

Sometimes the fake raids did not go well. This happened mainly because of miscommunication. It was the case last month when my location was raided. The police liked to raid Number Holes just before the last number came out. That's when most of the cash receipts are available. We lost $9,000 in cash, plus the day's number receipts because the police raided the wrong location. The prearranged location was to have been Sylvester's location across the street.

The Bulls came with large sledge hammers and broke the door down in less than two minutes. It was just enough time for me to get most of the cash onto the "elevator." The elevator operator was stationed in an apartment a few floors above, with a rope dangling in the air shaft. I placed most of the cash in shopping bags, tied them to the rope and pulled hard on the rope. The elevator operator pulled most of the cash up two floors before the Bulls could break down the door. I left $9,000 behind on a table, plus some of the day's numbers receipts in this botched raid. I had to climb out of the back window of my Number Hole onto a fire escape leading to the roof to get away from them. This was an activity that I was familiar with from my youth, when I was living in Plains, Georgia. But I broke the heels off my suede pumps in the process, and I was pissed.

Steve was also pissed at Tom, McGregor, and me. When he got a chance, he gave the 28th Precinct Captain an ear full. But Steve mostly blamed Tom, our look-out, for letting the Bulls get past him, and he fired him.

Steve said, "This is the last straw, Tom. You can't go to the toilet and shit straight."

What happened was that the Bulls entered the apartment building two doors down, went up on the roof, crossed over the buildings, re-entered our building from the roof, and came down the stairs behind Tom, who was standing lookout on the stoop. When I heard them coming down the hallway, I slammed the door's vault lock system into the door's frame, like Fort Knox. The steel vault door we had custom installed in the apartment saved us. The banging sound of the sledge hammers on the door was deafening. But it bought me time. This prevented the Bulls from entering the Number Hole easily and confiscating more than $40,000 in the day's receipts.

Steve's Number Writers or Runners were not allowed to carry weapons. This was an unwritten rule that had been worked out with the police. One or two weapons were hidden in the Bank's apartment, and they were wiped clean daily to remove fingerprints. At least one was displayed openly on the accounting worktables. Our biggest fears were not of the Bulls. It was of the local hoods, who would rob the Bank. If the hoods got past the lookout on the stoop and past the reinforced steel vault door to the Number Bank, then we were not to put up a fight. It would do more harm to the business if a customer or Number Writer got killed in a robbery than the robbery itself.

Tom was a decent guy but was very inattentive and lazy. He started to run his mouth with a friend and the undercover Bulls walked right past him into the houses two doors over, unnoticed. He gave no warning, even when they started breaking the door down.

I loved Tom, but he was having a lot of trouble doing his job and was a danger to me. He could not proof his work at night and I tried to cover for him by adding money to his tally when he was short. Steve had moved him from number runner to lookout and bodyguard, but he couldn't do those well either. Now, Tom was without a job and I was six months pregnant with his child. This was definitely not planned. The sex was getting better, but I was getting very sloppy for a 40-year-old. Can you imagine me running up a six-story fire escape from the Bulls at six-months pregnant?

He claimed he got hurt during the police raid and never went back to work anywhere. Weeks later, he was still complaining about his arm, back, and his lack of strength.

I said to him, "Well nigger, you have enough strength to lift a fork to your mouth and hold your hand out for money. You should be strong enough to work."

Tom remained out of work for weeks. Luckily for him, his sister on 137th Street found space in her apartment for him. He could visit, but he could never move in with me because I refused to break my rule of not allowing my lover to move in with my children and me. I broke up with Tom Bennett a few weeks after that raid. Pandora Lavern Bennett was born November 14, 1964. She was my little princess, my Panzy, and another feisty one, even while in the womb. She kicked like hell when I was climbing that fire escape. I only took off a few days to give birth, and I was back in the street right away writing numbers.

Eddie Roy's enlistment in the Army was also just about up, and he would be returning home from Europe soon. I was on cloud nine. After three years, my son was on his way back home from Europe, and he had two jobs waiting for him when he arrived.

Steve was raking in well over $50,000 per day gross in numbers, and we paid out about half of that in winnings on normal days. On good days, it was less than 25%. When Steve promoted me to Controller, he increased my salary to $1,000 per week, plus tips. It became my job to proof the whole bank in the evenings.

Sylvester hit the ceiling when he heard about my promotion. I was faster at accounting than Sylvester or Bill. Both used an adding machine for running the ribbons that accounted for the winners, losers, and total take. I added figures three digits across in my head without using an adding machine.

As Controller, my new job was to account for all daily receipts, pay winners, and take Fat Tony of the 116th Street Crew on the *East Side* his 20% cut twice a week. Their cut included the large bets of $50 and more. If their take was only a few thousand dollars, Fat Tony wanted it to accumulate a few days before transporting it. It cut down the traffic on the *East Side*. Anything over $10,000, Steve assigned an armed bodyguard to go with me.

I always asked for Sugar to be my bodyguard. He did some amateur boxing, was very respectful of women, and was a good father to his three children that he supported, although they were all by different women. This was very important to me. The women in my family took no shit off men. Usually, we boarded the M116 crosstown bus that ran from the West Side of 116th Street and Manhattan Avenue to the East Side of 116th Street and Pleasant Avenue. We walked a block to 416 East 115th Street to the Palma Boys Social Club. Someone was always stationed on the corner to direct you to which building entrance to use. We never entered the same building entrance twice. Once we were inside, there were always two burly Italian guards at the door, neither of which spoke any English. There was an elaborate set of mazes for you to travel through before you arrived inside their Bank. They knew Sugar was armed, and they always made him stand in the doorway as

I walked into the Bank with their cut.

Even though I was scared to death, I didn't let them know I was about to shit in my pants. When I started writing numbers, I never figured I would advance this far in the number business. Also, I did not know at the time that the Genovese Mafia family, the 116th Street Crew, was the most vicious Mafia family in the country. None of this appeared very dangerous to me at the time. In fact, it was very exciting and profitable. *How naïve Mother Nature had grown.* I could disappear in this hell hole and they would throw me in the furnace alive and use my body as fuel to make steam.

I refused to allow Tony's bodyguards to hand search me. I simply opened the shopping bag, showing them the money. I always handed the money to Tony, per Steve's instructions. He was the head "Capo" of the 116th Street Crew. Tony was always very gracious, polite, and friendly, but you could feel that he was uncomfortable doing business with a woman, especially a strong black woman. Stephanie St. Clair, better known as "Queenie," refused to do business with the Mafia and gave them a royal headache. I engaged him in polite small talk as I waited until the money was counted and verified by his Controller. They never spoke in English to one another. And there were always plenty of Italian cold cuts and pastries on the table. I frequently boxed up a few delicacies for Sugar and me to eat on the way back to the Westside.

Every street hustler knows the story of Al Capone, who got locked up by the Feds, not for his crimes, but for tax evasion. Al could not document a valid job or valid source of income, but the Feds documented him to be raking in millions of dollars. I had a paper trail that was small but effective. I was still receiving welfare checks as a front for my lack of legal employment. I gave all the welfare money away, plus more, to my less fortunate customers. It would have been pure greed to do anything else. I gave to those who lost jobs, had kids in need of school clothes, or had sickness or death in their families. *Prophet or Pariah?*

After a few months on the job, Steve suggested that I move to 92 St. Nicholas Avenue, after he gave me a raise. I was making well over

$1,000 per week and could more than pay the $100 per month rent. What Steve really wanted was to use my current apartment at 112 West 115th Street as his Number Bank. It was in the back of the building and on the first floor. It also had a special feature, that made it ideal in case of police raids. It had an unseen air shaft in the middle of the apartment building that was accessible via a window in the living room. We used the air shafts as elevators on several occasions to save our Bank. I moved, and he paid the rent and gave me an additional $100 per week for the sublet.

Harlem was once a white upper-class bedroom community. That all changed when the subway lines were constructed in 1904. The landlords cut up the large apartments to half their size in order to double the number of people the apartments could accommodate and to double their rental income. After the white upper-class barnstormed to New Jersey and Long Island, the lower-class Irish went to West Harlem, the Blacks and Jews moved to Central Harlem, and the Italians and Spanish fled to East Harlem.

Moving into 92 St. Nicholas Avenue was a big deal. It was one of the premier apartment buildings in Harlem with large, still un-cut up, well-maintained apartments. It was also known for its lavish, exquisitely decorated lobby with an attendant that operated the elevator.

In my letters, I stopped talking about numbers altogether with Eddie Roy. I didn't tell him that I had already started writing numbers for Steve, and I didn't say much about my activities anymore. He said the Army randomly selected GI's letters to read. A lot of his activities in Europe were considered secret because he was stationed in a Medical Clearing Unit trained in Chemical, Biological and Radiological (nuclear) (CBR) Warfare. But when he noticed that my return address had changed to 92 St. Nicholas Avenue on my envelopes, he demanded answers. Well, he knew 92 was one of the most exclusive apartment buildings in Harlem.

He asked, "Mommy, why the move to 92 St. Nicholas Avenue? And how in the hell can you afford it?"

He should not have asked. I merely replied, "Do you still like sleeping with your brother and getting peed on every night?"

He was an excellent medic and a good soldier. He fired as an "Expert" with the M-14 rifle and was sent to The Seventh Army Advanced Marksmanship School in Landstuhl, Germany. Uncle Sam had taught him how to kill very well.

The Gulf of Tonkin incident in August 1964 caused President Johnson to increase the number of American troops in Vietnam by 500%. He felt remorseful that he was having a wonderful time in Europe while those poor grunts in Vietnam were losing their lives. Instead, Eddie lucked out. Uncle Sam flew him back to the states on Pan American Airlines while most of the troop ships were in the Pacific transporting troops and supplies to Vietnam.

After he arrived back in the United States, he stayed at Fort Hamilton in Brooklyn, New York for a few days getting his release paperwork processed. Then he took the subway home from the mostly Italian neighborhood in which Fort Hamilton resided. He got off the "Iron Horse" at the 116th Street Station and walked the single block to 112 West 115th Street. The PAL block was blustering with activity, the young girls were jumping double Dutch, the young men were shooting 'loadies,' and the older guys were playing street-style basketball. As he started up the stoop stairs of 112 West 115th Street, the lookout stopped him. That was when he remembered that we did not live at this address anymore.

I am quite sure Eddie had fond memories of the building and our war hero superintendent, Lonzo, but nothing like this. Now we were using the apartment as one of our Number Holes and Banks, taking in thousands of dollars per day.

Our new place at 92 St. Nicholas Avenue was on the next corner of 115th street. He continued the short walk waving and hugging many of the people that he had left three short years earlier. It seemed they were all in a time warp. Nothing much had changed, except for the added wrinkles on their faces. I still had not told him I was writing numbers.

He walked onto the tiled hallway at 92 St. Nicholas Avenue amazed at the mirrors hanging on the walls, the columned arched ceilings, and the lavishly painted walls, and started up the stairs.

He heard a voice stating, "Are you going up, sir?"

He replied, "Up? Oh, yes. Up."

The voice motioned him over to the elevator located in the middle of the lobby. Mr. Sanders, the elevator operator, closed the gate of the lift behind him and pushed the lever almost to the floor and the cab began its flight up to the fourth floor.

Mr. Sanders said, "Your mother told me to expect you. You are Eddie, right?

"Yes, sir."

"4E is to your right."

"Yes, sir."

"To the right," he repeated as he headed in the wrong direction, almost dazed by the newness of it all.

"Thank you."

As soon as he reached the front door of apartment 4E, a potpourri of assorted aromas came wafting through the cracks of the apartment's door. He knocked, then noticed a doorbell and pushed it. He heard our dog, Spot, barking, and going crazy after he took a sniff under the door. Then he heard the pitter patter of feet running to the door as it opened. Spot jumped into his arms, and his brother, Bernard, and sister Miss Vee greeted him with huge hugs. Then my newest daughter, barely one-year-old Pandora, simply stood there looking at this strange individual that she had never seen before.

He politely shook her hand, saying, "Hi, baby sister."

As he stepped over the door's threshold, he noticed white powder sprinkled lightly there. Then he returned the hugs and smiles. The scents in the air grew more intense as he walked down the hallway.

"Mommy, what's up with the powder and scents?"

"That is how I attract money into the house. It is my money entry powder and wash. The powder acts as a magnet or glue for money and the scents attract the money into the house. I have the powder and oil wash blessed by Maria at the Botanica every week. I add a few drops to the mop bucket and mop down the hallway's plastic runner every morning. It works. Believe me, it works. It has helped turn our fortunes around—from "Welfare to Wealth.""

He began to walk down the long hallway of our large four-bedroom apartment looking into rooms to his left.

Then I said, "You just passed yours."

It was the second room down, painted powder blue. It was small but very comfortable. He turned around taking a second look and saying, "Ummm."

Then we walked down to the end of the hall past an open bookcase snuggled into the corner. It contained a multitude of candles, oils, washes, and religious objects that he did not recognize. He turned to me in confusion.

I explained, "This is my good luck shrine. The green candle is for wealth, and the white candle is for purity of purpose and good luck. You write personal prayers on the candle, have it blessed by Maria before you light it, and you must never let the flame blow or burn out."

"It has burned down. What prayer was inscribed on it?" he asked.

"I prayed that you would return home safely."

"Mommy, I don't remember you ever being so religious…"

"I am not. I learned in Plains from Twin Spirits that there are powers in this universe that are far greater than we humans fully understand. This is my acknowledgement and respect of these powers."

He reached down to the bottom shelf and picked up a small sealed container, opened it, and looked in.

I immediately took it from him and replaced the lid saying, "Be careful. That is a 'Black Baby' candle. That candle is burned only to bring about the imminent destruction of your enemies, and only if you are about to be harmed by them."

"Mommy, how can you afford all of this?"

"I am writing numbers for Steve now."

"Mommy, I can see by your shrine that you realize the danger as well as the legal problems in writing numbers."

"Yes, and ha, you should not have suggested this line of work to me. Always remember, Eddie, and this goes for your brother and sisters: do as I say do, not as I do. I am throwing bricks at the jailhouse, so you won't have to. You guys must never get involved in the number business. I know it is against the law, but drinking alcohol was against the law. Running away from your slave master was against the law, and women exercising their right to vote was against the law. What is legal is not always what's lawful. Check this out," I motioned to him.

I opened the two French doors that lead into the living room, and he almost fainted. He said the room looked like one of the throne rooms of Europe that he had visited. The walls were adorned with large palace-like motifs, which were encircled by painted finger moldings that encompassed the entire room. His eyes feasted on an immaculate French Provincial cherry wood sectional sofa. It was covered in a pastel green tufted tapestry, embedded with petite beige embroidered fleur-de-lis, which stretched halfway around the room. A large mirror with a French Provincial, gold-gilded frame gracefully hung on the wall behind the sofa.

Covering the windows were large, green, and gold satin curtains that dropped from the ceiling to the floor with gold, etched curtain rods that stretched the entire length of the windowed wall. A thick, beige wall-to-wall carpet ran corner-to-corner with a marble top French Provincial cherry wood coffee table in its center. In the opposite corner was a French Provincial upholstered armchair next to a tall, crystal reading lamp.

His mouth, now wide open, said, "It is drop dead gorgeous, Mommy."

I said to him, "Today's number was 458. You are home safe, and that is now your lucky number."

He accepted the job at the U.S. Post Office on 14th Street in Manhattan and started going to Bronx Community College at night to prepare himself for attending college full time. He applied to several colleges while still in the Army, including Rochester Institute of Technology, which everyone called RIT, and they all rejected his applications. But he refused to let it get him down.

Finally, he received an acceptance letter from the State University of New York at Farmingdale, Long Island. We both hit the ceiling. I was so proud of him. However, he needed a car to get him back and forth from college on Long Island. His GI educational benefits supplied enough money to pay the car's monthly payments, but he did not have enough money for the down payment.

So, I had a plan. I told him I was taking him downtown for a movie and dinner this coming Friday. Instead, I walked him into the Pontiac dealership on Columbus Circle and 59th Street, and there it was sitting on the showroom floor. A 1966 Pontiac GTO, burgundy, with a 389 cubic-inch V8 engine, 350 horsepower, a four-barrel Rochester QuadraJet carburetor paired with a Turbo Hydramatic transmission and a Positraction-limited-slip rear end. This dog could hunt! And it was exactly what he asked for. I gave him $1,800 cash for the down payment and GM gave him a loan for the $1,200 balance. With that resolved, he was on the road in three days headed for school.

151 616 739 841

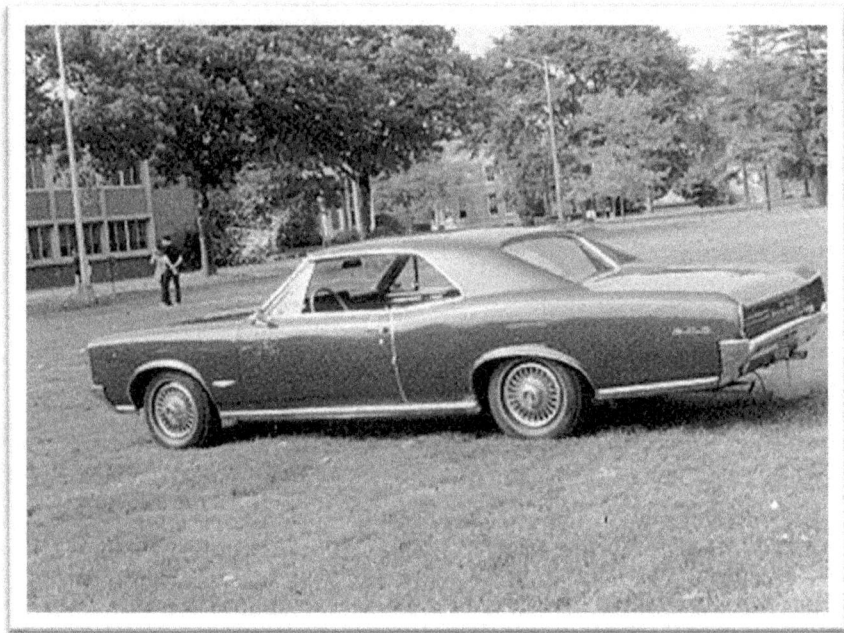

Eddie's 1966 GTO at SUNY

Champagne is done and the Hustler's Ball is over, 1966

Sugar, Red, and Nate, 1966

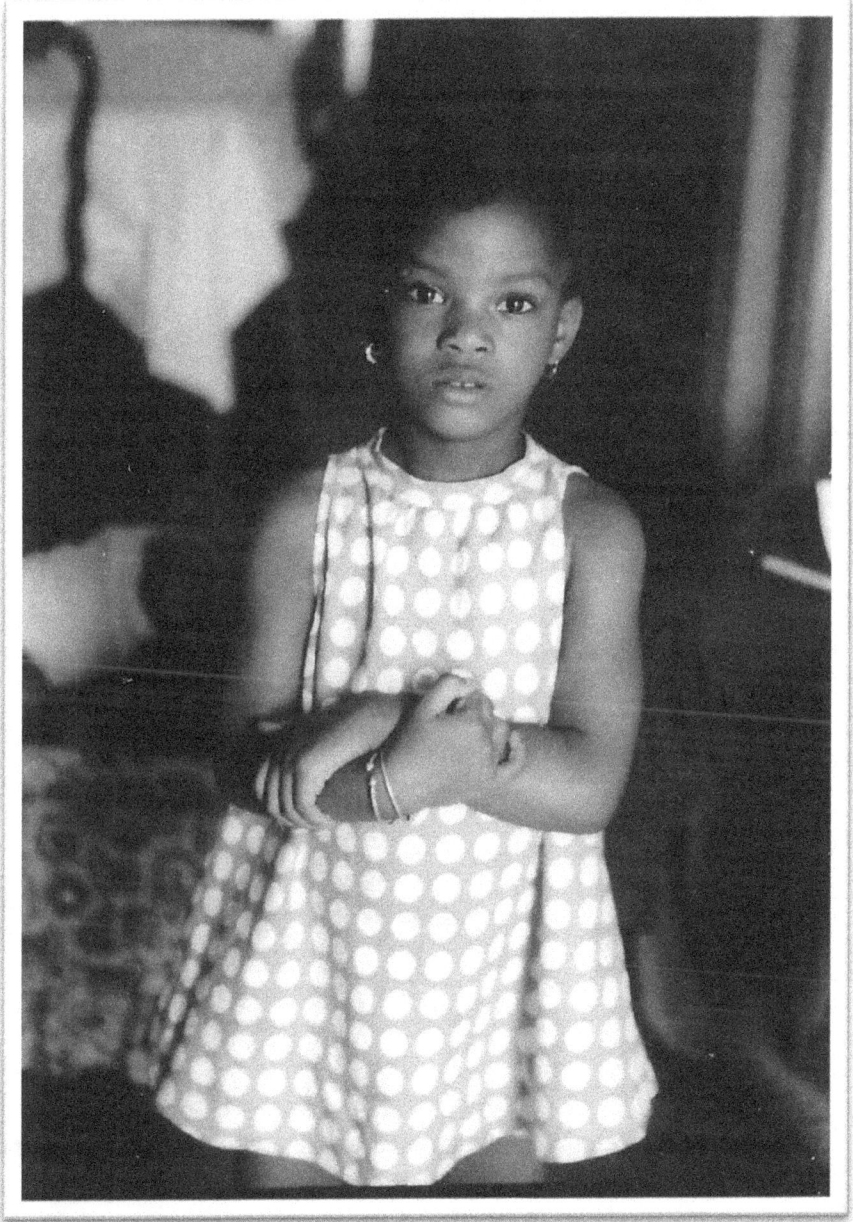

Pandora Laverne (The Little Princess) Hill-Bennett, 1966

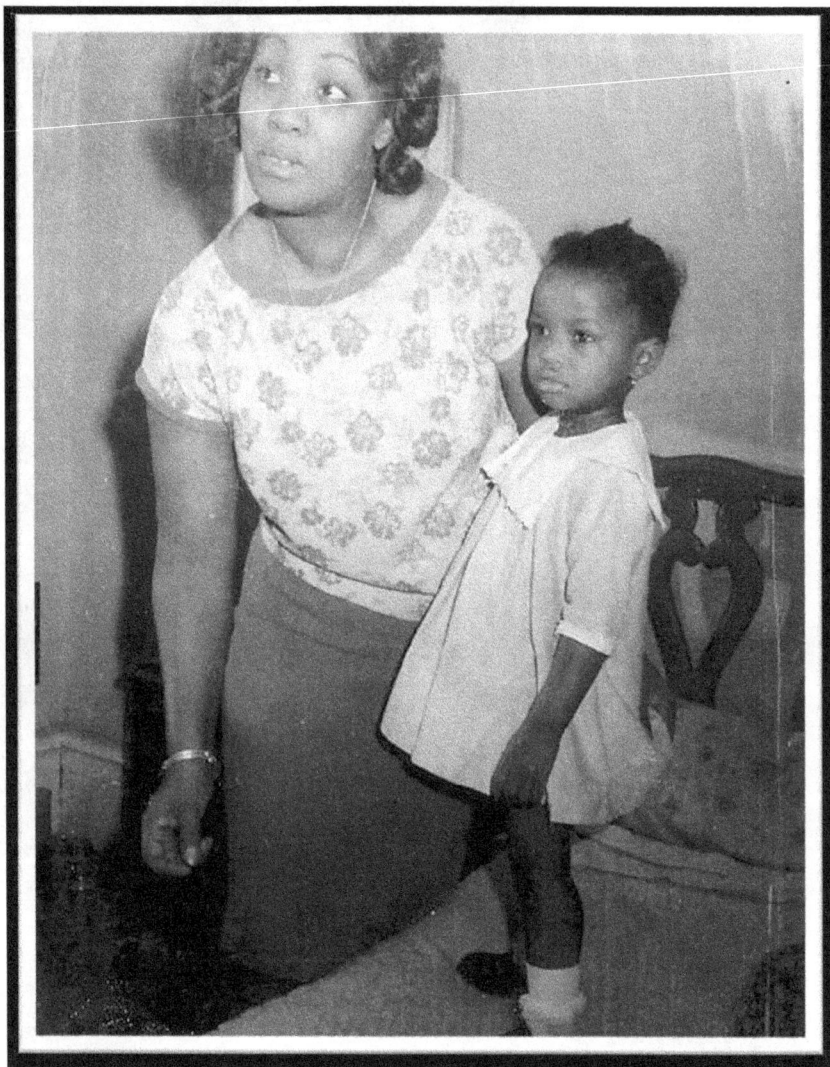

Erma with Pandora Laverne Hill, 1966

Pandora Laverne Hill-Bennett, 1966

Chapter XIII

Drugs and Numbers Don't Mix

The drug peddling on 115th Street had gotten worse since Eddie left. Heroin addiction was out of control in Harlem, and many of Eddie's high he school friends were now addicted. His best friend Teddy James was often seen nodding on the steps of his stoop at 128 West 115th Street. Teddy and Eddie had been inseparable. But as Teddy slipped deeper into heroin, Eddie started to move away from him just before he went into the Army.

Teddy was buying his drugs from a new young dealer who appeared in the next block up on 115th Street between Seventh and Eighth Avenues. His name was Charles Lucas. He was single-handedly destroying Harlem to fill his pockets. He did so by increasing the number of shooting galleries for his growing drug enterprises. He ordered his henchmen to set fire to most of the buildings between Seventh and Eighth Avenues. The vacant, burned-out Harlem buildings looked like a war zone and became a resort for narcotics dealing, shooting galleries, and prostitution.

The drug dealing worsened after we moved into 112 because of Lucas and others. He expanded his operations by opening a shooting gallery in the basement of 114 West 115th Street, the building next door to ours. Quite a few of our runners and customers were being robbed on their routes by junkies who hung out at the shooting galleries. He was also known to hang out and shoot pool with a hitman known as "Ice Pick Slim," who robbed our people. Drug dealing and numbers are like water and oil; they do not mix on street level.

Steve felt he had to address this head on. He called a meeting with Lucas on the corner of 115th Street and Seventh Avenue. There was a cute little triangle park there where we could sit on the benches and talk. He took Sugar and me with him. Sugar was armed and he took me because I had a calming effect on him that he said prevented him from losing his temper.

Lucas was a few minutes late, and his bodyguard stood across the street with Sugar. Steve and I exchanged greetings with him. He asked Lucas very politely if he would restrict his drug dealing to the north side of Seventh Avenue. Steve informed him that he had worked the numbers on the south side of Seventh Avenue for more than five years. His expansion outside of Seventh Avenue was causing him to lose customers and attract more police attention. Lucas was very disrespectful towards Steve, to say the least, but he said he would consider looking into it.

The word on the street was that Lucas was in debt to Fat Tony of the 116th Street Crew for $300,000, because of a botched drug deal. It was also being said that he was making a new drug connection directly from Southeast Asia, through a family associate who was in the military there. His associate's name was Leslie "Ike" Atkinson, a former U.S. Army Master Sergeant. This connection would allow him to pay Tony off in one fell swoop and be independent of the Mafia.

We found no change in the drug dealing next door in 114, where Big Mabelle and Jackie Wilson were frequent customers. Spot, our dog, hated drug users. It was like he could smell the drugs in their bodies and often tried to attack them. He did so with Big Mabelle as she passed our stoop on her way to get her fix. He lunged at her, ripping her dress, while I pulled back on his leash.

We also had numerous big-time drug dealers who placed large daily bets with Steve. They always requested that Steve send me out to their cars to collect their bets, like I was a streetwalker, or something. Most often, I refused to accept drug money bets and I told Steve to send someone else, as I was busy. But Steve ordered me to take their bets. They requested me because it allowed them time to tease and flirt with me. Some said I was good luck for them. Many drug dealers refused to place their bets with any of Steve's other Number Writers. Many also refused to deal with Bill because he was Jewish. And they refused to deal with Sylvester because he was a known cheat. One afternoon, Steve came into my Number Hole and announced, "Red, a hustler parked in a Lincoln outside wants to place a $100,000 straight number bet, no combination."

I said to Steve, "That is a sucker's bet. Well, tell him he needs to come inside."

Steve looked at me with his puppy-dog-begging eyes and said, "He wants you to come out to his car and write the number there."

I said, "You have to call the *East Side* for approval."

Generally, it was close to our betting cut off time, when slicksters placed their number bets trying to scam us from the race track. Steve picked up the pay phone, called the *East Side* and told them to put Tony on the phone directly. When he came to the phone he said, "Tony, I need approval to take a bet."

"Who is placing the bet and how much?"

"$100,000 and I think it is a new drug dealer trying to make a name for himself. Barnes, I believe. I'm not sure."

"Take the bet and tell Red to write it."

I grabbed my pad with a disgusted look on my face and opened the door of the candy store that I was working out of. Steve had changed my location after the last raid. The entire avenue was full of the most fabulous cars I had ever seen in my life, and they all belonged to just about every major drug dealer in Harlem. Cadillacs and Lincolns lined Lenox Avenue for two blocks waiting for me to collect their bets outside of my Number Hole. The traffic congestion caused a major problem with the local beat cops because it attracted too much attention to their beats. They were on our payroll, but the problem was with the DA's office downtown. They were the ones that received the telephone complaints and they had their own detail of police officers and inspectors. If the DA's office inspectors received a call or happened to be in the neighborhood on a given day and saw the activity, they would act immediately by locking someone up.

I walked over to the Lincoln and leaned into the open window just long enough for him to get a small whiff on my Chanel No.5 perfume, and said, "I am New York Red. I understand you gentlemen wish to place a bet."

He replied, "Pleased to meet you, Red. I am Nicky and I wish to place $100,000 on 747-straight. That is the name of the new Pan American jetliner that is rolling out of the Boeing factory in Everett, Washington soon. It is a shame that a woman as fine as you doesn't have a husband to take care of her."

Smiling, I said, "When I find a man that can write a $100,000 number, I will marry him."

His driver released the trunk and he got out of the car with two of his young hoods. They went into the trunk and retrieved two large shopping bags full of cash.

I said to him, "I can't count the money in the street."

He handed me the two bags of cash and we all walked inside the candy store together to count the money. I placed the "Closed" sign on the candy store's door. Steve and I counted the money while Nicky watched our every move, along with two of his armed bodyguards. It was 'on the money.' It was all there, not a dollar missing. I wrote 747NC, which stood for not 'combinated,' down on my yellow pad and stamped his receipt with my personal red ink stamp "NY Red" from my 18-karat gold stamp pad.

He said, "Damn Red, we need to get to know one another better."

"We will Nicky, if you keep bringing me bets like this one. Thanks."

I handed him his receipt, thanked him again for his business, and walked him back to his car. He waved his receipt in the air and the entire avenue of hustlers erupted into wild applause. I waved back at the crowd, not knowing at the time why they were applauding, as he got into his car and left.

Steve called the *East Side* and spoke directly to Tony. He confirmed that I took the bet and asked him for instructions on how to deliver his cut to the *East Side*. Tony called Steve back, told him to take his 20% cut, and to supply two-armed security people to escort me over to the *East Side*. He requested that I go immediately after the first number came out for the day. If Nicky missed the first number, we were home-free.

Then Tony called Steve again saying, "Never mind, I will send my personal limousine to pick Red up with the cash. What kind of champagne does she drink?"

Steve replied, "Piper Heidsieck."

"There will be two chilled bottles in the limo's bar, plus Italian cold cuts and pastries that I know Red likes."

The car arrived late, but with great fanfare after the last number was out. Steve assigned Sugar and Nate to accompany me by instructing them to pickup two pistols from the bank. We got into the back seats and started to party. My bodyguards went nuts in the limo. The car was fully stocked with almost everything. There was a small refrigerator with cannoli's, champagne, fruit, cheese, hors d'oeuvres and a bar packed with most top shelf liquors. The ride to the *East Side* was too short. So, I instructed the driver to head downtown on East River Drive to 14th Street, turn around, and head back uptown.

When we arrived at 115th Street and First Avenue, two nervous, burly Italians opened the door of the limo and helped me out. They requested that my bodyguards remain in the limo. They escorted me into a building, one that I never visited before. Once you got inside the building, you immediately lost all perspective and direction. It was like a maze inside. We finally arrived inside of a fabulous, large living room decorated with fine Italian furniture. It looked like a palace, much better than mine and much bigger. One of his bodyguards blew a kiss at me as I entered the room. Tony was sitting on the couch, and he greeted me with his usual heavy Italian accent.

"Red, how you doing? You had-a busy day! Great job! He should have boxed the number. He would have made some money. The number today is 477. I wonder if he had a hookup at the track, or something."

"I am doing great, Tony. Today has been busy and very interesting."

"It is all over the city. Red, you wrote the largest number bet in Harlem's history today."

I simply smiled and said, "Thank you, Tony," as I placed the two shopping bags full of money down by his side. He reached into one bag, counted out $5,000 and handed it to me. He gave me an added $500 each for Sugar and Nate. He called in his Controller, Giorgio, and we sat down next to him as Giorgio and I counted the money. Steve had recently promoted me to Controller to do accounting for his entire Bank. I tallied and proved all the Writers and Runners after the last number came out. Our Runners serviced all the apartment buildings, local bars, restaurants, barbershops, hair-dressers, nail salons and beauty parlors in our territory that stretched from 116th street to 114th street on both avenues.

Tony asked, "You want anything to eat?"

"No, Tony," I said, "I am full from the ride and I must get back to proof today's receipts."

Steve was now doing close to $60,000 a day in numbers on good days, and I took the opportunity to mention that to Tony.

"Tony, I am doing the accounting now and you are getting your rightful share of the take. And we are still having problems getting our runners and writers out of jail downtown at 100 Centre Street."

He didn't respond as I stood up and shook his hand. He appeared surprised and startled that a woman would engage him in a conversation about the business while extending her hand first to close a business deal. As I said thanks, the same burly bodyguard began to pucker his lips and to give me the sexy eye again.

As I left the room, I patted him on his crotch and whispered to him, "Signore, un piccolo pene," which was Italian for "Sir, you have a small penis."

Tony laughed and told his limousine driver to drive us back to the West Side.

After my visit to the *East Side*, not much changed with Tony getting our people out of jail. Two weeks passed and I traveled downtown with Steve to 100 Centre Street to post bail money to get Nate out of jail. After we bailed him out of jail, the judge sent a court officer to find Steve. He requested that he come up to his courtroom. Steve gave me that look and rubbed his two fingers together indicating that the judge was going to ask him for some money. At least one of Steve's Number Runners or Writers was required to be arrested and go to jail once a month or so. That way the 28th Precinct Captain could show his superiors downtown that he was doing a good job.

I was sharp as a tack in my custom made, dark violet, ¾ length suede pants suit with its mink collar, gray lizard shoes, gray lizard clutch bag, and my Henna tinted Sassoon wig boastfully adorning my head. I sat with Steve in the back of the courtroom. When the Assistant DA entered the courtroom to present her criminal drug case and then sat down. The bailiff shouted "All rise! Judge Jacob Weinstein presiding."

The judge walked into the courtroom, paused, and looked around until he noticed Steve and me seated in the rear.

Before the bailiff recognized the DA, by calling her case, the judge said, "Fifteenminute recess. Mr. Mitchell, come into my chambers with your associate, please."

We looked at one another thinking maybe he was going to lock up both of us. As we walked into the judge's chambers, he removed his robe, took his seat, and lifted his nose in the air and said, "Chanel No. 5."

I said "Thank you, Judge. You are right."

"It is my favorite. I met Marilyn Monroe at a party given by the Rameses and I instantly fell in love with her. You remind me of her."

"Thank you, Judge. I know the Rameses well. My Aunt Nora raised their children. She was their Nanny for years."

"Really? What is your name, madam?"

"It is Red, Your Honor."

"Your real name?"

"Erma. Erma Louise Hill, Your Honor."

"Yes, Nora Hill."

He turned to Steve and said, "Can we talk openly, Mr. Mitchell? We don't have much time."

Steve replied, "Yes, Judge."

"You've had three busts dismissed this month, and that's going to cost you $1,000 each."

Steve replied "Your Honor, someone else is supposed to take care of that."

"No, Mr. Mitchell, you must take care of it. But that's not the only reason I called you into my chambers. Too many officials know of you downtown because of your activities and criminal record. They see you too many times entering my courtroom as a visitor. That perfume is sinful, Ms. Hill."

"Thank you again, Judge."

"Mr. Mitchell, I need someone that is not known to court officials coming into my chambers when they are traveling with Mr. Green (they came to deliver payoff money). It needs to be someone that does not have a criminal record." Steve started to respond and the judge cut him off.

"Ms. Hill, Erma, may I ask you a personal question? Do you have a criminal record?"

"No, Judge. But I do have young children, and that is even worse."

He laughed and stared at Steve. Then it hit Steve like a hammer as to what the judge was demanding.

Steve responded, "Your Honor, Ms. Hill will be responsible for introducing Mr. Green to you going forward."

The judge responded, "No, I can't meet Mr. Green today, Mr. Mitchell. I do not have the time. Send Ms. Hill back in the middle of next week, when I will have a slower court calendar. Ms. Hill, let the court officer know who you are by passing your finger under your nose. Then take a seat in the back of my courtroom, and my court officers will know what to do."

The judge promoted me to my new job as my responsibilities continued to grow. But I willingly allowed myself to be pulled deeper into the abyss. Now, I was responsible for traveling downtown to 100 Centre Street to pay off the judges, attorneys, and post bail for our Number Writers and Runners. Steve increased my salary to $1,200 per week.

You could see that Judge Weinstein loved intelligent, attractive, and well-dressed women in his courtroom. A week later, I walked into the Judge Jacob Weinstein courtroom, dressed to kill again. I also wore his favorite perfume and I passed my finger under my nose in front of the court officer. As the judge entered the courtroom, the court officer touched his badge with his left hand. The judge took one look at me and called an immediate recess. He did so without acknowledging the Assistant District Attorney, again standing before him, and invited me into his chambers. I knew he didn't have a lot of time. I immediately handed him $3,000 in an unmarked envelope with a note naming those with court cases pending or who were locked up that week. Bail was granted within one day and all gambling charges were eventually dismissed for various reasons. Sometimes water or coffee accidentally spilled over the evidence or the DA's evidence disappeared from the court's property room. If all else failed, the judge threw the case out himself on a technicality.

The few female Assistant DAs who practiced before him quickly learned a thing or two from me. They won more cases when they started to wear stylish clothes, fixed their hair, smiled, and wore Chanel No.5.

The agreement I made with Steve that I would never go to jail took on new importance. Not only did I have young children at home to care for but I had to take care of my street hustlers now also. You cannot lock up the Controller because there won't be anyone available to bail them out of jail. This arrangement really made both the *East Side* and the DA's office extremely angry with Steve and me. We really knew we were pissing off the DA's office. Now, we made our own contacts downtown and were going over their heads. The Assistant DAs gave me dirty looks each time I exited the judge's chambers. They hadn't won one guilty case against us in months.

One hot August day, Manhattan DA Frank Smith Hogan ordered a large series of raids on Harlem's Number Banks. Our headquarters and five other Number Banks in Harlem were hit simultaneously, including Spanish Ramon's, who was from Puerto Rico, and one of the largest independent banks in New York City. They parked three paddy wagons in front of 112 West 115th Street. We thought it could be retaliation, but didn't know initially whose office was responsible for ordering these raids.

Steve was cursing as loud as he could at the police, "I paid everyone this month! I paid everyone this month!"

It was a Friday and they had confiscated $30,000 in cash, plus our daily receipts.

One police officer told Steve, "Quiet down or we will lock up the whole goddamn block, including your customers."

A funny thing about the New York State Gambling Laws was that it was illegal to write or receive a number bet, but not illegal to place a number bet. So, we knew he was bluffing.

I said to him, "Kiss my pretty yellow ass."

They knew I was not supposed to be arrested or go to jail. I had to pick up my daughter, Pandora, from nursery school by four o'clock.

The same young officer, now pissed off, said to me, "Ma'am, you are under arrest for illegal gambling," and proceeded to place handcuffs on me.

I asked the young cop, "What in the hell are you doing?"

He replied, "I am locking your yellow ass up, bitch. What do you think?"

He pushed me out of the Number Hole's door headed towards the paddy wagons. There must have been at least 200 angry customers waiting outside. This was only a few months after the Harlem riots. The customers knew that if the police confiscated their betting receipts, they would not get paid, if they hit.

I reached up with my free hand, ripped my blouse exposing my left breast, and hollered "Rape! Rape!"

The crowd surged forward, chanting, "Off the pigs! Off the pigs!" and started throwing things at the police officers.

One of the senior detectives came running over and asked the officer "What in the hell are you doing?"

"What I am supposed to do, sir?"

The detective said, "You are trying to get all of us killed. That's what you are trying to do, officer! Un-handcuff her and let her go!"

He un-handcuffed me and pushed me into the crowd. The crowd returned the favor by throwing a bottle of beer at him, hitting him in the face with it. They became rowdier and they refused to disperse, as the police requested. The crowd blocked the entrance to the Number Hole and the police had no other way out. They unhandcuffed Steve, the Writers, and the Runners and let everyone go. I was still standing in the crowd with my breast partially exposed as the officers exited the

Number Hole. They all were smiling and carrying our $30,000 cash, plus our receipts, in black trash bags above their heads, like they had won a prize fight trophy belt.

I heard one of the police officers call out to a Detective Cian Mac Muad asking him which police car to place the money in. He was the one that ordered me released. Two officers were struggling to get the money placed in their car. I knew half of it would disappear before it reached the police station. Cian ordered it placed in his car.

I called out to him, "Cian, enjoy your vacation in Brazil!"

"Do I look like I have been tanning in Brazil? You will get there before I will. What is your name anyway?" He called back out to me.

"Red. New York Red. You will see it on the receipts in the bag."

"Ok, New York Red. I think I have seen you downtown in the courtrooms. You own the city," he said.

The newspapers reported the following day that $30,000 had been confiscated in a police raid at 112 West 115th off Lenox Avenue. He turned in all the money and he didn't take a dime. Cian was one of a new set of racket detectives recently transferred into the 28th Precinct. He was an Irish cop with a strange name, Cian (pronounced "key-an") Mac Muad.

About a week later, after the last number of the day came out, he appeared waiting for me in front of the Number Hole at 112 west 115th Street with liquor on his breath and half drunk. He had confiscated an old 1959 Cadillac convertible from a convicted drug dealer that he used for his undercover car. A drunk white guy driving a bangedup Cadillac convertible by himself in the middle of Harlem wasn't much of an undercover detective. It was more of a death trap than an undercover car. We exchanged greetings and he went on spraying his alcohol-saturated breath all over my custom-made pants suit.

"I was a narcotics investigator in the DA's office and they transferred me from the DA's office downtown to the 28th. The veteran cops in the 28th Precinct automatically didn't like me because cops from the DA's office don't take bribe money. No detectives wanted to team up with me because they said they would starve to death. So, I work by myself. The reason they transferred me uptown was I have a drinking problem."

"Really," I replied nonchalantly.

"I was so drunk driving to my last narcotics raid in Queens that I wrecked my police car."

"Really? Did you kill anybody? And how did you get that odd name?"

"No, Cian is a solid Irish name with a long history. It means ancient and enduring. Cian Mac Mael Muad was the son-in-law of Brian Boru. The battle of Clontarf happened in the year 1014. Cian led his army from Munster to victory over the invading Vikings. He and Brian were both killed in this battle. Cian is now one of the most popular names in Ireland."

It wasn't unusual for me to be seen by my customers talking to police officers. Some police officers were our best customers. He appeared to be a good cop and a nice and decent guy. He was very intelligent and knew a lot about the history of number playing in Harlem. He felt the number rackets were boring and a waste of police officers' time. He said working numbers in Harlem was a dead-end career path to nowhere. Few detectives working numbers ever got decent promotions.

I said, "Cian, what in the fuck are you doing here? You are bad for business and if you are bad for business, you can't lock anyone up because there will not be any business for you to lock anyone up for, duh?"

He was so drunk that he couldn't get his last three words out of his mouth. At first, I thought he was trying to "play" me. Then after a bit, I felt he was hanging around 115th Street after work because he really wanted bribe money, after all. Bill paid all police officers on our beat.

I told him, "Cian, you may want to talk to Bill, not me. That is if you know what I am truly saying to you and you fully understand what I mean."

"I am not interested in talking to Bill. Several of my fellow police officers have recommended that I talk to Bill."

"Red, would you take my number bets?"

"I looked him directly into the face and said, "What in the hell are you trying to do, get sent to a worse precinct in the Bronx?"

He smiled and said "No."

"Cian, what in the hell do you want? I am not a rat, I don't sell pussy, and I do not date poor white boys. What in the fuck do you want, Cian?"

"Friendship."

"Bullshit! Go home to your dog, like I go home to mine. Or, go home to your wife, if you want a friend."

"My wife and I are divorced, but I have two daughters."

"Then your dog."

"I don't have a dog."

"Cian, the only friends I have are my four children, two boys and two girls. You have seen my youngest, Pandora, who is in daycare and attends dancing school. My oldest is just out of the Army and in college, and the next two are in private school."

"Private school?"

"Yes Cian, why in the fuck do you think I am out here tossing bullets in the fire and throwing bricks at the jail house? They are all doing very well."

"Red, that is great. My two daughters go to the Catholic School in Woodhaven Queens and live with their mother."

"Cian, go home to your children."

"I can't."

"Why?"

"I must have a chaperone with me to be with them. That is the only way my wife will allow visitation or allow them out of her sight."

"Oh yes, now I understand. It is because of your drinking."

"Yes, my wife is divorcing me and keeping my two young girls. Your daughters are about the same ages as mine."

He really spoke well of my two daughters, Miss Vee and Pandora, who he had seen on the block several times.

"Will you have a drink with me?"

"Cian, I do not drink with alcoholics; been there and done that. When I drink, I only drink Piper Heidsieck Champagne. You could not afford that on a police officer's salary, unless you are on the take. And since you are not on the take, your money would be better spent on your two girls."

Since I would not drink with him, he finally asked me what he really wanted.

"Red, will you chaperone a visit with my girls."

"Am I the last person on earth, Cian?"

He looked at me saying, "Yes, you are. I have no one else to count on. You don't remember, it was me in the courtroom with the ADA at 100 Centre Street, when you burst into the courtroom like you owned it. I was about to take the witness stand to testify in a drug case. Judge Weinstein interrupted the proceedings as soon as he saw you walk in. He immediately called for a 15-minute recess, asking you to go with him into his chambers. I told my wife you were a Special Assistant to Judge Weinstein and worked for the New York City Court System."

I laughed my ass off, saying, "Now, that one was pretty good!"

"She said yes to the visits, if you consented to supervise them."

He gave us a break by not locking us up, and that meant something to me. I said yes, but I really questioned whether I would actually go through with it. She finally consented to future visits without me in attendance. He kept saying he was going to give up drinking, but he never did.

Cian was catching hell from both his fellow officers and his supervisors for not producing many numbers busts or arrests. He was just not interested in numbers. He was busy observing the narcotics tariffing going on in the neighborhood. Most dope pushers in the neighborhood didn't pay him any attention because they knew he was a numbers detective. They went on with their sales, sometimes right in front of him, sometimes while he was drunk and asleep in his undercover car.

732 810 036 447

Chapter XIV

Dropping A Dime

Steve repeatedly asked the local drug pushers not to sell narcotics on our block, in front of or near our Number Holes. It was bad for business. Number players do not like being around drug addicts or pushers. Sometimes, the junkies set up number players and Runners to be robbed because they carried a lot of cash.

I said to Cian, "You have the best narcotics undercover prop on the NYPD because the pushers know you're not a threat. Do you have any detective friends in narcotics?"

He replied, "Yes, downtown."

I gave him a long stupid look and said, "Duh!"

He responded, "Drop a dime on them?"

"Yes, they will never suspect you."

He contacted a few fellow narcotics officers in the DA's office downtown that he could trust with the drug trafficking intel he observed. Within a month, the narcotics arrests in South Harlem increased sharply. The police even shut down two drug shooting galleries on our block that we begged the pushers to move. The police made sure Cian was nowhere near when they conducted their raids. I also had several customers who constantly complained to me about the narcotics trafficking on their blocks from the South Bronx to Central Park. I simply took mental notes from them without saying a word of who, when, what, or why.

I secretly and carefully transmitted the information to Cian. I knew the NYPD would transfer him from his numbers assignment, if his number busts didn't improve.

So, I suggested to him, "In exchange for my help with narcotics trafficking information, I will help you keep your undercover numbers job by giving you one number bust each month. Your contacts in the

DA's office must figure out how to get my people out on bail and their charges dismissed before or at trial."

This was awesome and it didn't cost us a dime, maybe only one dime. I killed two birds with one stone.

My visits to Judge Weinstein's chambers at 100 Center Street started to decline and he started to complain about his loss of revenue. So, I made a deal with him to place him on a flat monthly fee, regardless of the number of cases that appeared before him. We now had everyone happy. Bribery was the moral cost of running numbers in Harlem. I did not tell Steve the details, but he loved saving a bundle on his Pad-Payroll. *I didn't realize it at the time, but I was really tossing bullets in the fire. Prophet or pariah?*

For an Irish cop, Cian said a lot of bizarre things in conversations with me. They were things few white police officers would admit to.

I asked Cian, "Why are you so passionate about locking up drug dealers?"

"The Mafia says, "We smuggle this shit into the country only to sell it to Black animals." That is bullshit. My older brother Sean was addicted to heroin. He broke his ankle during a basketball game in Woodhaven, Queens five years ago. It was a painful injury. Mom didn't have the money to continue to pay the doctors for the expensive pain medication. A member of his basketball team introduced him to heroin. He died of an overdose two years ago. That is when I started drinking heavily. I looked up to him. He always jumped into the middle of a fight to beat the block's bullies off of me. He helped me with my homework after school. He even helped me study for the police department's exam. I am lost without him."

Cian went on: "Red, this is what I learned from the FBI and other high-level police agencies about the people you are working with. This is a direct quote, much of their business is in drugs. The Italian Mafia "116th Street Crew" has been operating in East Harlem for a long time. Italian immigrants began pouring into New York in the late 1890s. They brought their traditions with them, including the Mafia. A long history of Mafia Capos, the heads of Mafia families, originate from East Harlem. Giuseppe Morello and his half-brothers, Nicholo,

Vincenzo, and Ciro Terranova, arrived in 1890 from Corleone, Sicily. They soon began taking over and running the illegal gambling operations in Little Italy and in Italian East Harlem. They graduated into some of America's most distinguished and vicious mobsters. On the street, they were known as the 116th Street Crew.

After several murders of top Capos and several mob wars, the Sicilian gangs gained control over New York City. State and federal law enforcement got tough with the Sicilians, causing the loss of several, hard to replace Capos. Vito Genovese was imprisoned in the late 1950s. Mike Coppola was imprisoned in the early 1960s. When they released Mike, he was too old and the mob put him out to pasture after he served his jail sentence. The crew split, allowing Coppola's top lieutenants to break up his huge, illegal empire that included his numbers empire.

In the early 1960s, Anthony "Fat Tony" Salerno, an associate and top lieutenant who worked himself up to Capo, took over the 116th Street Crew. He based his operations out of the Palma Boys Club located at 416 East 115th Street, an address that you are familiar with. Anthony managed to hold on to and expand his empire to the South Bronx when East Harlem went from a predominantly Italian neighborhood to a Black and Hispanic neighborhood. He was able to maintain control of his numbers, bookmaking, and floating dice games that expanded further into Central Harlem and the South Bronx.

The U.S. government rewarded "The Families" for helping America fight the Nazis in WWII and fighting the spread of communism in Italy after the war. The U.S. government ordered Naval Commander Charles Radcliff to run Project Under World, a partnership with the New York Mafia families and the U.S. military. In turn, the FBI and the New York State Attorney General's Office turned their heads and looked the other way from the Mafia's criminal activities and narcotics traffic coming into the United States. The U.S. government agreed with the Mafia families to take dead aim at Negroes with their narcotics traffic. There have been little or no major FBI drug arrests of top Mafia drug figures in America for years. The numbers business and narcotics trafficking go hand in hand in Harlem at the number banking level.

One finances the other, and vice versa."

In a very angry tone I said, "Cian, that is bullshit. You don't know what in the fuck you are talking about."

He replied angrily, "You forgot about the Charles Grutzner New York Times article, didn't you?"

Steve's 54th birthday was rapidly approaching, and he asked me to accompany him to his birthday party at the Red Rooster on Seventh Avenue in Harlem on Friday night. I reminded him that I do not do bars. I have always kept a low profile that keeps me out of sight of the law. He asked again, saying it was important because his staff were all invited and his staff should attend, out of respect. The Red Rooster was one of the hottest bars in Harlem. All the major hustlers in Harlem were giving him a birthday party, "A Hustler's Ball."

I said I would go, and Steve picked up Sylvester and me in his 1966 Thunderbird at 8:00 p.m. I couldn't stand Sylvester. I knew it was going to be a difficult night for me. But I was a good soldier. I did not know why Steve hired him. He was a backstabbing, two-faced son-of-a bitch, known to squeal like a pig to the police when they cornered him. He was not good at writing numbers, but he was a damn dice shooting genius. He ran the local craps games on 115th Street.

When we pulled up in front of the Red Rooster, there were lines of Cadillacs, Lincolns, and exotic sports cars two blocks long and triple parked on Seventh Avenue. The local police simply passed them by looking the other way knowing they were paid. This was the Hustlers Ball I heard about but had never attended. I was dressed in a dark pea green leather suit with a fox collar, old gold patent-leather pumps, and a gold pocketbook with sequin fringe. The wig that adorned my head was my signature henna tinted "Sassoon." To my surprise, it was not necessary to introduce myself. The sidewalk was packed with onlookers, and almost everyone there had heard of me.

The whispers rang in my ears, "That's New York Red, the sister that wrote the largest single number bet in Harlem's history."

As the crowd pushed closer to get a better look at me, Steve simply said, "Yes, this is Red, New York Red."

There were only a few number banks in Harlem that could bank a

$100,000 bet. One was Spanish Raymond's, who was in attendance. Unfortunately, Steve's bank was too small to handle a $100,000 bet, although Steve received 20% of the take. Bets like that had to be cleared first by the Italian mob on the *East Side* to be banked. This was exactly what the independent Black Harlem bankers were complaining about.

They said, "If we worked together, we could handle a bet like that."

What I did not know at the time that I wrote the number bet, there were two $100,000 bets on the streets of Harlem that day. The first was the $100,000 number bet that I wrote. And the second was for the drug dealer whose bet was large enough to get me out of my Number Hole to write the number for him. Nick Barnes lost the first bet, but won the second $100,000 bet and almost hit the number on the first bet as well. The young pusher had succeeded in making a name for himself.

All the major Harlem number bankers, drug dealers and pimps were in attendance. I was very uncomfortable hanging with this crowd. I did not see anything wrong with writing numbers, but drug pushing and prostitution destroyed our young men, women, and our community. Most pimps deliberately got young girls hooked on heroin, forcing them into prostitution.

Prostitution and drugs went hand in hand. A few of the young women in the bar played numbers with me and some transported their pimps' bets to me. Cheryl was one of them. She was a beautiful young woman, but she could barely stand because she was going into a heroin nod. They had to take her out of the bar and sit her in one of the cars parked outside.

Steve and his staff all sat at the birthday boy's table of honor in the middle of the bar.

Sitting around us were some of the biggest number bankers in Harlem: Spanish Raymond, North Carolina Slim, Pee Wee, and Ty, to name a few. The pushers were seated at another table.

There was Uptown Joe, Mookie Roberson, and newcomers Charles Locus and Nicky Barnes, among others. Also sitting at their table was a pusher that I did not recognize. He was a tall, unattractive, brown-skinned brother smoking a cigar with a large scar on his left cheek. He kept looking at Steve as if he knew him. After we sang happy birthday to Steve, cut the cake, and danced "Doing the Dog," he came over to our table and introduced himself as Louis Taylor. He said, "My close friends call me "Fess," and he asked me if I wanted a drink.

I said, "No thanks, I have one."

He pushed his way in between Steve and me, asking, "Steve, are you going to do it for me or not? You owe me, man."

Steve tried to look the other way and avoid the question. After listening to about 10 minutes of begging, Steve finally said to him, "I will do it Fess."

He got up, left our table, and walked back to the table where the pushers were sitting, giving one of the pushers the 'thumbs up' signal. Steve was very upset for the remainder of the evening. I never asked him about his business, but I told Steve when I went to work for him that I would not be involved in any drug trafficking. He swore, on his mother's grave, that he was not currently nor would he be involved in any drug trafficking. I had worked for Steve for more than two years now, and he had never lied to me about that.

After the party was over, Fess walked over to Steve and asked, "When?"

"I will get back to you," Steve told him.

The year 1966 had a cold and snowy winter. But no matter the weather, I was out in the street collecting my customers' number bets, rain or shine, sleet, or snow. Most of my best customers had very good jobs downtown and I had to be up early in the morning to collect their bets on their way to work. I had also started collecting the night numbers again. So, it was a long day for me. I worked from 7:00 a.m. to 11:00 p.m., five days a week. Steve and I made a deal that I would net 50% of the take on the night numbers. He did not see enough return to keep his business open in the evenings or to provide me with a Number Hole, lookouts, and bodyguards. The money was working well for me. I was netting more than $6,000 a week, plus my daily salary.

I lived on the block, so it was convenient. We used my old apartment at 112 as our Number Bank in the daytime and I used it at night for our Number Hole. I took a nap between the day and the night numbers to rest a bit and take care of my kids. The long hours were not a big problem for us. The kids and I ate out a lot. I checked their homework between shifts. The police rackets squad only functioned from 9:00 am to 5:00 pm. And the night numbers were not big enough to assign law enforcement personnel to police. The night numbers came from the trotters at Yonkers Race Track. And I had my own personal protection, Spot.

Bert McKinney was a good customer of mine. She played $30 to $40 in numbers per day. I grew very close to her and she helped me out by picking up Pandora from nursery school. She didn't have any children of her own and she asked to be Pandora's godmother. I consented and she demanded to pay for Pandora's dancing school.

Pop Warner was an old pensioner who also played very heavily each day. He was too old to come by the Number Hole. So, I allowed him to come to my apartment very early in the morning to drop off his numbers, along with Bert.

Cian was doing a fantastic job tipping off his fellow detectives to arrest drug dealers that my customers dropped a dime on. However, he was still having a serious problem remaining sober. Sometimes, he was so drunk that he could not find his car. And if he did, he would kill someone, if he drove it. He frequently fell down drunk in the hallways of the buildings on the block. On several occasions, I brought him into the Number Bank at 112 to sober up. I still had a bed in the bedroom that I took my naps in and I put him in, so he could sleep it off.

One Friday, after taking my last night number, I found him badly beaten and robbed in the hallway at 116 West 115th Street. He didn't have any shoes or socks on his feet, someone had turned his pockets inside out, and he was shivering very badly from the cold rain. I took him inside my Number Hole and as I started to strip his wet clothes from him, I noticed that his shoulder holster was empty and his detective badge was missing. I covered him with dry blankets. But no matter what I did, I could not warm him up enough to stop his body from shivering. I took off my clothes and I got into the bed with him, wrapped two blankets around us, and laid there for two hours until his body warmed.

I called my kids and told them to order in Chinese food and that I would see them in the morning.

When he woke up the next morning, he did not remember a thing. I asked him, "What happened to your gun and badge?"

He didn't remember a thing, except getting into a fight with two guys that were shooting dice two doors down."

I fixed him some breakfast and teased him saying, "I stole your virginity last night."

He laughed, but I could see he was concerned about losing his gun and badge. He could lose his job over that. I walked him to the subway and gave him enough money to get home. He left his car parked on 115th Street. This was not a problem because the local cops knew who it belonged to. I called Sugar and asked him to find out from the regulars on the block what happened last night. By Monday, he got back to me and said that Sylvester was running his Friday night crap game across the street, when Cian came stumbling down the block. A couple of young punks jumped him for no other reason, other than that he was a drunk white guy, not knowing he was a cop.

After work, I cornered Sylvester on the block and told him I wanted Cian's gun and badge returned to me. I told him if I didn't get it in 24 hours, Cian would have every vice cop in Harlem from numbers, craps, drugs and prostitution here to shut everything down. I also told him that I had a $500 reward for the return of his items. The next evening, Sylvester approached me and handed me his items in a brown paper bag. I checked the gun to see if it had been fired and it had not. I gave Sylvester $500 cash and thanked him.

You can't talk enough reason into an alcoholic to stop them from drinking. I learned that with my Aunt Nora. The individual can only correct it with personal motivation and support. I called Cian the next day and gave him a good scolding about his drinking. His behavior was going to get him killed in this neighborhood. When he came by, I also reached into my pocketbook and gave him his equipment.

He gave me a long kiss and said, "Thank you. You saved my job."

I replied, "That is fine, Cian. But who is going to save you?"

He responded, "God knows, I have been trying. I ask God for

strength every morning. But my dead brother appears before my eyes, instead of God. I am going to attend an AA meeting next week. Would you come with me?" "Sure, Cian," I said.

I had attended meetings like this before with Aunt Nora. The person starts out great, but it gets lonely at night when that 'Drinking Jones' comes down. I told him I would stay in the Number Hole with him as long as I could to keep him company. He remained sober for a whole week. He started his recovery. The only cops in the 28th Precinct that would finally work with him were three well-known Black detectives known as the King Cole Trio. They established a reputation in Harlem for not taking bribes or backing down. His narcotics undercover work started receiving recognition downtown. The police department promoted him to Deputy Inspector and transferred him to head the South Bronx Narcotics Unit.

When I made my money drops to the *East Side*, I noticed a new rudeness from Tony.

Sometimes, he refused to take the money directly from me and he told his controller or top lieutenant to handle the transaction. I asked Steve about it, but he refused to discuss it. I could see that something was going on between him and Tony. However, I left it alone.

Steve's business was growing off the charts. He hired two new Runners that I broke in and supervised while bringing them up to speed. Steve's business was doing about $70,000 per day and about $6,000 in night numbers per day. Annually, that was more than $15 million per year, gross. There were just over 100 major number banks in Harlem with various levels of independence and volume under the 116th Street Crew. Some were fully independent like Spanish Ramon's, whose territory was next to ours. It ran from Seventh Avenue and 113th Street to Second Avenue and 96th Street, give or take a few blocks. Spanish Ramon's business was more successful than Steve's. If Harlem's number bankers were half as successful as ours were, then Harlem would produce close to a half billion dollars per year, gross. I turned over the night numbers to Nate, so I could spend more time with my children and Cian.

One Thursday night, I had a difficult time sleeping and Spot was barking at something all night. The candles in my shrine all blew out and there was a strange odor in my apartment. I received a short call about 7:00 a.m. from Steve's wife, Mildred.

Crying, she stated, "Someone shot Steve to death in front of our co-op apartment at 103rd Street and Central Park West."

This news hit me like a load of bricks. I could not believe it. I walked out onto 115th Street half-dressed and the block was crawling with cops. They were stopping and interrogating anyone and everyone on the street. Being very careful, I simply turned around and walked back upstairs constantly looking at my rear. I called Steve's wife back and she said the police were at her apartment and she could not talk. They asked her who was on the phone. She said it was a friend of the family and hung up. Later that evening she called me back and told me what happened.

She said, "Sylvester was his driver for the week, and he never showed up to pick him up for work. A few people walking their dogs in Central Park noticed Steve getting out of a limousine after sitting in the car talking to the occupants. He got out of the limousine, cursing one of them. Then another car parked half a block away started up and drove up to him. The occupant on the passenger side got out and fired six shots, killing Steve instantly in the middle of Central Park West.

I asked, "Mildred, who do you think was responsible for the hit?"

She said she could not talk about this on the phone. It was not secure; she would talk to me later.

When a "coup de grâce" occurs, the block becomes very hot and crawling with the police. And no illegal activity of any kind can take place. I didn't leave my house for two days. I told Cian not to be seen talking to me. I asked Mildred, what could I do?

It was all over Harlem that *East Side* assassins killed Steve, so there was no need to notify anyone. The Amsterdam News published four articles on Steve's hit beginning on Saturday, December 17, 1966. They knew more than the police did about the killers. Steve was quoted in the article saying at the funeral of his Uncle Ernest Lawson a few months earlier, "Don't shed any tears for me when I am gone."

Some of the independent number bankers sent word to me, "I told you so. You can't trust those Wops."

That evening, all of Steve's writers and runners gathered at his co-op on Central Park West. We asked Mildred if she needed protection. A few family members flew in from North Carolina, where Steve was born. They brought what they needed with them to protect Mildred. I brought Eddie Roy with me to pay his respects. Steve loved Eddie Roy. He always tried to give him money for school, but I would not allow it. He loved to see Eddie drive up in front of the Number Hole on Friday evenings from college to pick me up. He could tell when he was waiting outside by the low rumbling growl of Eddie's GTO V8 engine making his presence known.

Within a few days, Mildred arranged with Benta's Funeral home at 630 St. Nicholas Avenue and 141st Street to handle the services. There was a huge turnout of family, friends, mourners, and most of the big-time hustlers of Harlem were present. The services were conducted in Benta's Chapel because Steve did not have an affiliation with a church. The funeral procession stretched for blocks, going up to Ferncliff Cemetery. After the burial, Mildred was able to sit down and tell me what went down.

She told me, "One of Steve's longtime friends, Louis "Fess" Taylor, got out of jail about six months ago after doing time for narcotics trafficking. A few weeks before Fess started his sentence, he gave Steve $10,000 to hold for him. It became part of the money Steve used to start his number business. Steve was unable to pay him back while he was in jail. When he got out of jail, Steve offered him his $10,000 back, with interest. Fess said no, that wasn't enough to get him started back in the drug business. He felt Steve owed him a much larger favor."

I said, "I remembered Steve being pressured by some guy at his birthday party. Could this be the same guy?"

"Yes, that was Fess. Steve asked him, "How much do you need?"

He answered, "$250,000."

Steve said, "What? I'm not going to loan you $250,000."

A few days later, he came back to Steve and asked, "Would you ask Fat Tony to advance me $250,000 in junk (heroin)."

Steve said, "No, I am not in that business anymore."

He kept pestering Steve. Finally, over a month's time Steve went from a "No," to a "Maybe, I will think about it," to a "Yes, I will."

It was at his birthday party that Steve went to "Yes, I will."

"Yes, I think I heard parts of the conversation," I said, recalling that night.

"I told Steve not to do this when I overheard him in a telephone conversation with Fess discussing it. Steve and Tony's working relationship had deteriorated. Tony had been accusing Steve of shorting him on his cut of the business for years. As you know that was not true because you closed the bank every night and carried their cut to the *East Side*."

"That is true, and I told Tony several times that Steve was not shorting him when he made veiled suggestions to me during my deliveries to him."

"Finally, Steve gave in. He called Tony asking him to arrange the advance to Fess for $250,000 in heroin secured by his number business."

Tony agreed, "Okay Steve, on your word."

"Arrangements were made for him to pick up the junk from the *East Side*. Tony's nephew, who dealt in junk, told Fess to pick the heroin up on foot and alone. They made him walk around the block several times while making sure he was alone and not followed. Then they directed him to an apartment building just off 1st Avenue and 118th Street, where he picked the junk up. Tony's nephew allowed him to inspect the junk and requested that he call Steve to confirm that he received the merchandise. He walked out of the apartment building with two large shopping bags and then up to 1st Avenue. A black car pulled up to him on the corner and two detectives got out showing him their badges."

"Get in the car," they ordered.

"He looked around and determined he could not get very far running with two large shopping bags full of heroin. So, he followed their orders and got in the back seat of their car with the two shopping bags. They drove him around the *East Side* neighborhood while they talked to him."

"We know who you are, Fess. You just got out of jail. We don't know what's in the bags that you are carrying and we would hate to guess. Now, we can do two things: we can drive you to the police station, handcuff you and order two patrol officers to inspect the bags you are carrying. On the other hand, at the next stop light you can open the back door, get out of the car and leave the two bags behind. Do you understand?"

"When the car stopped at the next light, that's what Fess did, and Steve had not seen him since."

I said "But, Steve's birthday was over six months ago."

"Yes, Steve and Tony have been going at this for six months or better. Steve told Tony that he was not going to pay him a fucking dime because he was no fool. Tony set Fess up and he was stupid to fall for it. Steve knew the two cops were on Tony's payroll and the drugs were returned to Tony.

The morning Steve was shot, Sylvester was to pick him up at his usual time, 7:00 a.m., in front of our apartment building. Sylvester never showed-up in Steve's Thunderbird.

Tony was waiting for Steve to leave the house at 7:00 a.m. the morning he was killed. You know Steve. He was not afraid of anyone.

A neighbor walking his dog said, "Someone motioned Steve over to his car and Steve got in the back seat to talk to him."

I know what Steve told Tony, "Look, for the final time, I am not going to give you $250,000 or half of my number business."

Tony replied, "Bullshit! You owe me $250,000, or half of your fucking number business, nigger."

"Go fuck yourself, guinea," he said and got out of Tony's car.

"Tony's driver then flashed his headlights on and off and drove away. Another car, parked across the street on the west side of Central Park West, pulled out while Steve was crossing in the middle of the street. It stopped in front of him, the passenger got out and shot Steve six times, five in the chest and one in the head, "The Coup de Grâce." The gunman got back into the car and it sped off.

"Red, I told Steve to leave this one alone. He would not listen. But things will be all right. God gave him to me for as long as he could. We had a good life, tough times, and good times. I am going back to North Carolina to live with my family."

Mildred continued, "Steve told me if anything happened to him, he wanted you to take over the business and this is what you need to know. Steve made a deal with Tony for the block several years back. He paid Tony $20,000 for the franchise and Tony got the top 20% of the bets. That broke down to bets placed over $50. Tony didn't want the smaller bets because the singles and fives were too bulky and difficult to manage. Steve had accounts at Bankers Trust Company on Fifth Avenue and 116th Street. The branch manager got 3% to change small bills into larger ones. As you know, you walked in with large bags of $1 and $5 bills and walked out with a small package of $50 and $100 bills."

She paused for a moment. Then she told me, "You already know, Bumpy Johnson made a deal with the devil when he made his agreement with the Mafia many years ago splitting the number business in Harlem between locals and the *East Side* mob. Like many semi-independent banks, Steve wanted to get rid of the Mafia's hand in his business, but he was in no position to fight that battle."

"Mildred, thank you, but I have a lot to think about, including why I am in this business and if I am going to continue?"

I was devastated, Steve promised me that he would not get involved with drugs again, and I cried. Heroin was killing the future of too many young Black men and women in Harlem. I fought every day to keep my children from it. Now, I realized there was nothing the *East Side* wouldn't do for a dollar. Ignorance was no excuse. *Mother Nature had made her bed and now she had to sleep in it.*

908 713 516 747

Chapter XV

Fat Tony and The 116Th Street Crew

They kept calling asking, "Red, when are you going to open up? My current number man stinks."

About a month after we buried Steve, I opened my own Bank and started accepting number bets from my best customers only. These customers played on average $30 in numbers per day. I asked that they come to my apartment at 92 St. Nicholas Avenue 4E because the block was still too hot to write numbers there. Business picked up so quickly that I asked Sugar to come work for me as my runner and bodyguard. Then I added Helen and a childhood friend of Eddie Roy's, Charles Oliver.

Sylvester also came by and asked, "Red, do you have a job for me?"

I replied, "Sylvester, why didn't you come to pick up Steve the morning he got shot dead?"

He replied, "Red, two detectives pulled their car up to Steve's T-Bird, which was parked in front of my apartment building, blocking it from moving. They refused to allow me to go back into my apartment and call him. They made me sit in the car for two hours. I had no idea what was going down."

I looked at his lying ass and shook my head in disgust. I warned Steve several times that Sylvester was a lying ass-sneak and not to be trusted. "Sylvester, I'll get back to you about a job."

I knew Sylvester would inform the *East Side* that I had taken over Steve's business on 115th Street. I was surprised at how quickly the business started to gross over $10,000 per day. Cian stopped by almost every other day to check on me and to receive an intel update on the narcotics traffic in Harlem and the South Bronx. He had been sober since he was promoted and he was doing well as a Deputy Inspector of Narcotics in the South Bronx. He had six detectives working for him now.

I tried to reestablish my contacts at 100 Centre Street, but Judge Weinstein had been promoted to Superior Court Judge and he didn't work in local vice cases anymore. No police officers from the 28th would come near me. They simply sent word that I shouldn't be working the block so close to Steve's death and without the *East Side's* approval. Trying to stay out of sight, I didn't reopen any of Steve's Number Holes. I did, however, keep my old apartment at 112 as my Number Hole and Bank. I left Spot there for security reasons. My runners and writers had to do it the old fashion way: 'Street Hustle.' Anytime I was out in the street working, I always took Spot with me for protection. He was really earning his keep now. No one in their right mind would mess with me with my dog nearby.

I started to have spiritual readings several times a month by Maria at the Botanica because they started to take a dark turn. They were not good. She saw visions through the candle flames of Twin Spirits. He was struggling with his fellow Indians, who double-crossed him and their brethren, by selling out tribal lands to the white man.

Now, Maria always looked troubled after my readings and said often, "Erma, ju must always be prepared to transition to the stars. Ju time here, Erma, is standing still and it is not moving forward nor moving backwards."

Feeling tenseness in the air, I decided to send for my 'tattle-tale' sister, Freddie Mae, in Atlanta. I had not seen her in years. Just having her around for a few weeks would relieve a lot of stress from my head. She would calm me down and I would have someone I could confide in.

Eddie Roy and the children became very concerned about me also. They saw a change in my demeanor. My conversations were less fun and more serious, and I wanted to spend more time with them. They knew I tried to give them the very best of everything, food, clothes, education, a home, and most importantly, the love and attention necessary to lay a foundation that would not crack. They were all good kids and they understood why I was casting bullets in the fire.

Bernard's studies were picking up in school. Miss Vee was always an outstanding student. Pandora was my little spoiled princess. Eddie was in his final year in junior college and on the Dean's List. He drove home twice a week in the evenings from SUNY Farmingdale, Long Island, to check on me.

The kids asked me, "Mommy, what is going on?"

They heard things about Steve's death on the street and wanted answers. I gave them none. They knew I never talked about the number business with them. Eddie, who was older, had figured things out on his own.

One evening Eddie Roy pulled me into the bedroom, closed the door and handed me a brown paper bag. I opened it. It was a black Smith and Wesson revolver.

"Mommy, it is exactly what you need."

"Where did you get this pistol from, Eddie?"

"Never you mind. This is how it works. It is a .22 caliber that shoots seven rounds of .22 ammo, and that is plenty. These rounds are small and don't penetrate through the body, so don't worry about a bystander getting hit. It has no safety to worry about. All you need to do is point, pull the trigger, and don't stop until the gun goes empty.

I asked him again. "Where did you get this gun from?"

"Mommy, Uncle Sam taught me a lot of things that you didn't know about, including how to kill."

One of the grandest days in my life arrived on May 25, 1968, when I attended Eddie's graduation from college. He had a stellar career at SUNY Farmingdale. He was elected President of the Inter-Dormitory Council, and he was graduating on the Dean's List after a rough start in college. He picked me up Thursday morning in his GTO and drove me back to SUNY Farmingdale. He found me a good seat before the procession started. Unfortunately, I got up and went to the bathroom, and when I returned a lady took my seat.

I went Harlem on her ass very quickly. "Lady, you've got to get up and find another seat because I paid too much for this one."

It was a wonderful graduation ceremony. The speaker honored the Rev. Dr. Martin Luther King, Jr., who was killed in Memphis, Tennessee on April 4, 1968, about a month earlier. I remember it well. I slept in my Number Hole all night to keep the rioters from burning down the building. Cities all over America were in flames as it became known as the Holy Week Uprising. He spoke about the challenges the graduates faced in a sometimes violent and constantly changing world. But they received the necessary tools and preparation to face and overcome them. My son graduated and he was the first person in my family to graduate from college. I knew then that my work on this planet was nearing its end. The reins were about to be passed.

I never asked much of my children, except don't do drugs, don't go to jail, and don't become a burden on your family. I was so proud of him. He had tried every nerve I had, but I never gave up on him. He exceeded my expectations by a mile. Professor Bowman, his professor, recommended him for a job with Eastman Kodak on Broadway and 4th Street in Manhattan. His starting salary was over $30,000 a year.

Eddie Roy was also getting very serious about a young lady. Dale Galiber was her name and she was a beautiful young woman from St. Thomas, U.S. Virgin Islands. You would not know it though because she didn't speak with a West Indian accent. I knew it was serious because he started to eat at her house on the weekends, instead of eating my cooking at home. I didn't like many of Eddie Roy's girlfriends, but I liked her. They were friends long before he went into the Army and have been friends since.

He said, "Mommy, Dale is expecting your first grandchild and I have a serious decision to make."

"Eddie Roy, I always taught you to respect women. Even more, to love, raise and respect your children. Whatever decision you make, I will support it."

Ma Babe and Uncle Fass drilled that into the heads of all her grandsons. Even though I spoiled the shit out of him, I drilled the same into his head, and it appeared he retained those values.

He started his first job after college and he decided to marry Dale on short notice.

I asked him, "What is the reason you are getting married so quickly?"

He said, "I am getting married because I love Dale. She is the most unselfish person I know; she has good skills, is hard working, and she will be a good mother to my children. Her pregnancy isn't the reason we are getting married. It only determined the timing."

I accepted his answer and started to prepare to have the wedding reception held in our apartment. On August 30, 1968, Father Walker, assistant pastor at All Souls Episcopal Church, performed the wedding. It was there that Eddie and all my kids were baptized. Jerry Smith, his college roommate, was his Best Man, and John Leoni, his Italian schoolmate, was the wedding photographer. It was a wonderful affair.

A few weeks after the wedding, Dale started having problems with her pregnancy. Her water started leaking early and her doctor placed her on complete bed rest in Metropolitan Hospital on 97th Street and First Avenue. Dale and the baby were okay, but she was at risk of miscarrying.

The next Saturday, as I was on my way to visit Dale in Metropolitan Hospital, Cian pulled me aside and I could see he was upset. "Some people in the DA's office are still pissed off at you for going over their heads directly to Judge Weinstein to get your runners and writers off. Red, you do not have the judge to protect you anymore."

"Cian, please tell me something I don't know," I said.

"Someone is also trying to set us up. They are trying to figure out who my sources and contacts are. I believe it is Eugene Rodriguez, a dirty politician and state Senator from the Bronx, who was recently indicted for bribery and a close associate of Louis "Fess" Taylor. My last two narcotics raids in the Bronx were duds. One resulted in a shootout and one of my detectives was wounded, but not severely. Thank God, he will recover. This means one of your informants is deliberately feeding bad intel through you on purpose. They will figure out in a few days what trail my information is taking and who my main source is. Red, it is just a matter of time before they come down on you."

"Cian, the last information I gave you came from Pop Warner. He is an old man about 80 years old and he would not deceive anybody. I will handle this, and I appreciate you watching my back and the help you are giving me."

"Red, you know I appreciate you. I don't want you to feel like I don't appreciate you. Thank you for all you have done for me. I probably would not be standing here now, if it was not for you. Thanks for being here for me, but I suggest that we shut it down. It is getting too dangerous."

"Cian, I appreciate you also. I worked without Steve's protection for almost two years without any problems because of you. Tony, the local drug dealers, the police, and the DA's office downtown all appear to have stepped aside."

"Red, the operative word here is 'appear.' Please be careful."

I worked out of my cold hallway at 112 all winter from 7:00 a.m. to 11:00 p.m., until the last night number came out. My apartment was available to warm up or take a break. Even Spot didn't like working in the cold weather. But a Hustler has to do what a Hustler has to do.

Then one cold evening, I asked Bernard to go to 112 to feed Spot and take him for a walk. He did not connect the leash as he opened the apartment's door. Spot had to go so bad that he ran out of the apartment building into the street, and a car hit him and killed him instantly. The whole family was very upset. Eddie scolded Bernard to no end about Spot's death. And I lost my best friend and personal bodyguard.

The next cold Friday afternoon, after the last day number came out, a black limousine pulled up to 112 and found a parking space a few doors up on 115th Street. Sylvester walked up to the limo and said something to the passenger in the rear seat. Then he walked into 112 and knocked on my Bank's door at apartment 1C.

I looked through the peephole and said, "What do you want, Sylvester?"

"Someone wants to talk to you outside."

"Well, tell them to come inside."

He said nothing. I unlocked the door, walked to the end of the hallway, and stood in the doorway for a few minutes checking the block out. There were no other strange cars or people on the block but a black limousine. It was Tony's car. I knew who it was. No one got out of Tony's car.

I walked out on the stoop so those in the car could see me. The limo's rear window rolled down and Tony waved me over to his car. I took my time approaching it. Then a customer startled me, asking what the number was today. I replied 372. I continued to walk towards the limo, and I kneeled down to look into its rear to make sure it was Tony, and only Tony.

"What do you want, Tony?" I asked.

"How you doing, Red? I want to talk. You look great, as usual."

He was trying to butter me up. "Please, be my guest and talk, Tony."

"Please, sit in the car with me so it can be private."

"The last time someone had a private conversation with you in your car, Tony, they didn't live very long to talk about it."

I knew I was dealing with the devil himself and I had to be very careful with him. His driver got out of the driver's side and opened the rear door. Tony said, "Please, Red, we go way back."

I cautiously sat down on the back seat of the limousine keeping both of my feet firmly planted on the sidewalk with the door cracked open.

I looked the devil directly in his eyes with a long stare without saying anything. I knew this was going to be a difficult conversation, not just for me, but also for him. Mafia men have a difficult time dealing with strong Black women. They seldom give their women any authority positions in their businesses. I have never heard of, nor seen, a woman in any position of authority in their crew. Women were not respected, especially Black women.

"Tony, I am listening."

"Red, I am a reasonable man. I try to avoid conflicts, where possible."

"Baby, that is bullshit. Please, don't bullshit me. I bent over backwards telling you that Steve was not stealing from you. You continued to make everything extremely difficult for us to do business.

"Red, this block belongs to me and you have taken over the block."

"No Tony, Steve paid you for the block and he left the block to me. But I am not going to argue with you as to who owns or controls what. That argument was resolved long ago. You know the history better than I do, but that was before me. Tony, I do not need your block to write numbers. My customers come from all over the city. You may own the block, baby, but you do not own me or my customers. In case you haven't heard, baby, slavery is over."

"Red, you have taken over my block and I would like to resolve this as a friend. I will give you the block for $32,000, and you give me only 50% of the take."

"Nigger, please! You are going to give me what is mine? You really have a pair. Tony, how much money have I brought to you on the *East Side* over the past few years? Come on, baby! Give me a figure; four million, five million, and you are asking me for $32,000. Tony, that is not business. Man, that is nothing but greed!"

At that instant, Eddie Roy returning home pulled his GTO in front of Tony's limousine. He parked, got out of his car, and briefly glanced back at the limousine because it appeared out of place on 115th Street. He started to walk in the opposite direction towards our building. Then he abruptly stopped, turned around again recognizing my lizard pumps protruding from under the limousine's cracked rear door. He started to walk back towards the limousine to take a second look. Tony's driver got out of the front seat of the limo with his hand in his pocket. Before Eddie Roy arrived, his driver turned and tried to close the limo's rear door, pushing me into the car. I did not hesitate. I put the heel of my shoe into the limo's door and pushed like hell. The limo's door handle hit Tony's driver in the nuts, and he bent over moaning in pain.

I jumped out of the limo, pointed to Eddie Roy, and told him, "Eddie, freeze! Do not come any further. Turn around and take your ass home."

He stopped in his tracks and I could see his military training kicking in. He looked all around, surveying the scene and he noticed Cian standing across the street leaning against the building with his arms folded over his pistol. He calmed down, then went and sat on a stoop a few doors up from the limo. I sat back down in the limo and I continued my conversation with Tony, who was clearly rattled by the events.

Tony suspiciously asked, "Who is the guy in the GTO? Your son?"

"Tony, that is none of your damn business. On principle, I am not going to give you $32,000 for the franchise; period, end of story. Like I said, Steve left the business to me and I don't have a problem giving you your standard cut."

"No, I can't accept that, Red. Ok, ok, ok, Red, what if I give you all the drug business from Eighth Avenue to Lenox Avenue from Central Park to 114th Street?"

"What??? I know you didn't offer me that shit. You have some fucking nerve. Tony, Steve promised before I started working for him that he would not get involved in the drug business or get me involved. He violated that promise and you took his life because of it. You set up Steve and his friend in a $250,000 drug bust scam with detectives on your payroll. You did the same thing with Charles Lucas for $300,000.

But that was between you and them and I am not going to get caught up in shit like that. Tony, I'm not selling no fucking drugs. Would you sell this shit to your children and grandchildren? But you don't hear a word I am saying to you, do you? This conversation is over, Tony."

I got out of the limousine and Eddie asked, "Mommy, are you ok?"

I looked Eddie dead in his eyes and said, "The next time I tell you to go home, you better take your ass home. Do you understand me, Eddie Roy?"

And he meekly replied, "Yes, Mommy."

Tony's driver started the limo and drove off with his window cracked open. I overheard him growl, "Boss, she reminds me of that St. Clair bitch. Do you want me to send someone for her, boss?"

"No, she will keep the block warm for us."

After I sent Eddie home, Cian walked across the street and I told him what happened.

He responded, "That S.O.B. knew that I recently locked up most of his street drug dealers in lower Harlem with the help of local Black detectives, the King Cole Trio. They were the only cops that were willing to work with me in the 28th Precinct. Tony is trying to set you up and I know you ain't falling for that shit, Red. This is not good, Red, and you know their history. So, what are you going to do, sweetheart?"

"I have been talking to the owner of the small convenience store on the corner of 115th and St. Nicholas Avenue about buying his store and leaving the number business."

Then I noticed Sylvester standing in the doorway across the street watching us talk. I knew for certain now that he was on Tony's payroll and the snitch.

About three weeks later, Sylvester approached Sugar, then Helen, and told them that the block was sold by the *East Side*. The *East Side* said they couldn't work on the block anymore. Both Sugar and Helen had families, and they informed me they were quitting. I told them I understood. I fired Charles, my last runner, a few weeks earlier, because he was hiding his heroin addiction and stealing money from my customers. I worked the business back up to $20,000 per day before I closed my Bank at 112 West 115th Street. I kept all my personal customers who played at least $30 in numbers per day, and I serviced them out of my apartment at 92 St. Nicholas Avenue.

Two weeks after that, a very tall, heavyset, light-skinned brother opened a Number Hole on Lenox Avenue between 114th and 115th Street. It was one of Steve's old holes. His name was Gordon Homes. He was about 6 feet, 8 inches tall, and the meanest looking person I had ever seen. Sylvester was the first person he hired. Then other runners and writers came mostly from Brooklyn. I did not know them. He was also a new Number Banker. No one had heard of him before. His business got off to a bad start because he constantly argued with customers over their bets and refused to pay them on time. He only had one 30-watt light bulb in the entire Number Hole to write by. And the place stunk because it was not cleaned regularly. About two months after he opened, he sent Sylvester knocking on my door asking me for a meeting. I asked Sylvester what he wanted to talk about.

Sylvester lied and said, "I don't know."

I told Cian about the meeting. He recommended that I not go and he said he was going to check this guy out in the meantime. I bought a new dog, a German Shepard mix. The kids named him Nitro, but he was a puppy. I took him with me to meet Gordon and we met outside of his Number Hole because his place stunk so badly, I refused to go inside.

He said, "The people on the *East Side* recommended you to me. They said you are one of the best Number Writers in Harlem. I paid the *East Side* for the block and it belongs to me now. And I would like to hire you to work for me."

I told him, "I don't work for cheap. I will think about it."

He said, "Please, consider it."

I repeated, "I will think about it."

The word on the street was that he paid Fat Tony too much for the business and it was dying rapidly before it even got started. He had no people skills, he did not bathe regularly, and he wasn't very bright. On top of that, Sylvester was stealing from him within the first two weeks of his operation.

A month later, Homes sent Sylvester to see me again, stating that Homes wanted to talk again about his job offer. When we met, he admitted that his business wasn't doing well.

I said to him, "It is important that you treat all customers with dignity and respect.

You must be honest with them and pay them on time. They have choices. Spanish Ramon is an independent number bank two blocks away, and he has an excellent reputation for treating his customers well. Your place looks a mess and it stinks. You have got to do a better job of keeping it clean, or your customers will not come into your Number Bank to place their bets. Finally, I am available to work half days only, from twelve to four, and I must personally pay off my customers. I do not work cheaply, I get $1,600 per week, and I do not go to jail under any circumstances. Finally, who is responsible for handling 100 Centre Street?"

He replied, "The *East Side*."

I smiled and said, "You, think on it and get back to me. Let's go, Nitro."

Nitro briefly growled at him, but he was not ready for a protection role and still needed a lot of training. A few days later Gordon called me and asked, "Can you start next Monday?"

I answered, "Yes."

I felt I took advantage of him. It was Mother Nature's charge, "There are two kinds of people in the world, the shrewd and the insensible."

Yes, there was a small amount of payback and greed involved. On good days, I was still banking $6,000 gross. There was no need for me to go to work for him. I continued to receive my regular customers in the morning before I went to work for Gordon.

Cian got back to me on Gordon Homes' criminal background.

He said, "He was a major drug dealer in Brooklyn, who recently got out of jail. And the streets say he did for-hire killings. Red, you should not be working for him."

"I will do it for a short time until the store becomes available and then I will quit."

Gordon made some trivial changes to the Number Hole, including adding more lighting and adding a few more cans of vegetables to the shelves to make the Number Hole look like a grocery store. It did not fool anyone. My writing helped his business pick up, but not to a level that would make it profitable. With Sylvester's continued stealing, it only made his losses worse. He was bringing in about $10,000 per day and I do not know how much of that Sylvester was stealing. Homes held a business meeting with all his runners and writers, stating we had to do a better job of bringing in revenue.

Sylvester made a comment at the meeting, "We would be doing better, if someone wasn't siphoning off business in the mornings."

I responded, "We would be doing better, if we had honest employees who were not stealing from the daily receipts."

Sylvester continued his slander campaign with Homes behind my back, by stating things like, "Red is the reason your business is failing."

I started to notice that Sylvester was following me home in the afternoons and I no longer had protection because I didn't have Spot. Nitro was still not trained.

One afternoon, after I arrived home, I noticed two young men standing in my lobby talking to one another. I waited for a moment to see if they were going to enter the elevator, but they didn't. When I entered the elevator, they walked in behind me. The elevator operator knew what floor I got off on, so I didn't say anything. The two young men didn't say what floor they wanted to get off on either.

When the elevator arrived at the fourth floor, I got off and I noticed the two young men following me to get off too. I waited until I got past the elevator's door. Then I turned around quickly and stuck my butcher knife to the throat of the first young man. The second man could do nothing because he was blocked in the elevator door by the first.

"If I ever see you two in this building or on the street again, you will be so full of holes that the city will use your asses for water trucks to wash the streets."

I pushed him back into the elevator and told Mr. Sanders, the lift operator, who was in shock, to take these gentlemen back down stairs because they appeared to be lost. They left 92 and signaled to a car parked across the street that they had been unsuccessful.

The two detectives sitting in the car said to one another, "We will have to send grownups the next time."

I refused to say a word to Eddie Roy about what was happening because I felt it would draw him into the number business. He had grown up in the streets of Harlem. He knew how to hustle and Uncle Sam had made a proficient killer out of him. He was on his way to a great future without this street shit.

Eddie Roy came to me on July 10th and said, "Mommy, Professor Bowman was a great mentor and instructor. As you know, he helped me acquire my first job at Eastman Kodak in their Micro Film Processing Laboratory on 2nd Street in Greenwich Village. I accepted the job with Eastman Kodak with great expectations, on his recommendation. But Rochester Institute of Technology just made me an offer I cannot refuse. Based also on his recommendation, RIT has granted me admission to their photography baccalaureate program, plus a $1,500 scholarship grant with two and one-half years college credit. I will graduate with a Bachelor of Science Degree in two years."

"Wasn't RIT the school that turned you down two years ago and one of the top technical universities in the country?"

"Yes, but I have to quit my new job to go. Mommy, I didn't plan for this. I scraped together all the money I have and I am still $1,500 short in paying the tuition for my first year."

I immediately went into my number bank and counted out $1,500 and said, "Go. But what about Dale and the baby?"

"Dale is still in Metropolitan Hospital trying to save our child. Her doctors still have her on complete bed rest. I talked to her about it and we plan to move our family to Rochester after the baby is born. She is currently working for a major bank in NYC and she can get a good banking job in Rochester, while I go to school and work part time. He asked me to look out for Dale while he was in school."

He said goodbye to his brother, sisters, and me as he left for RIT at the end of August 1968 with his GTO growling.

504 518 712 527

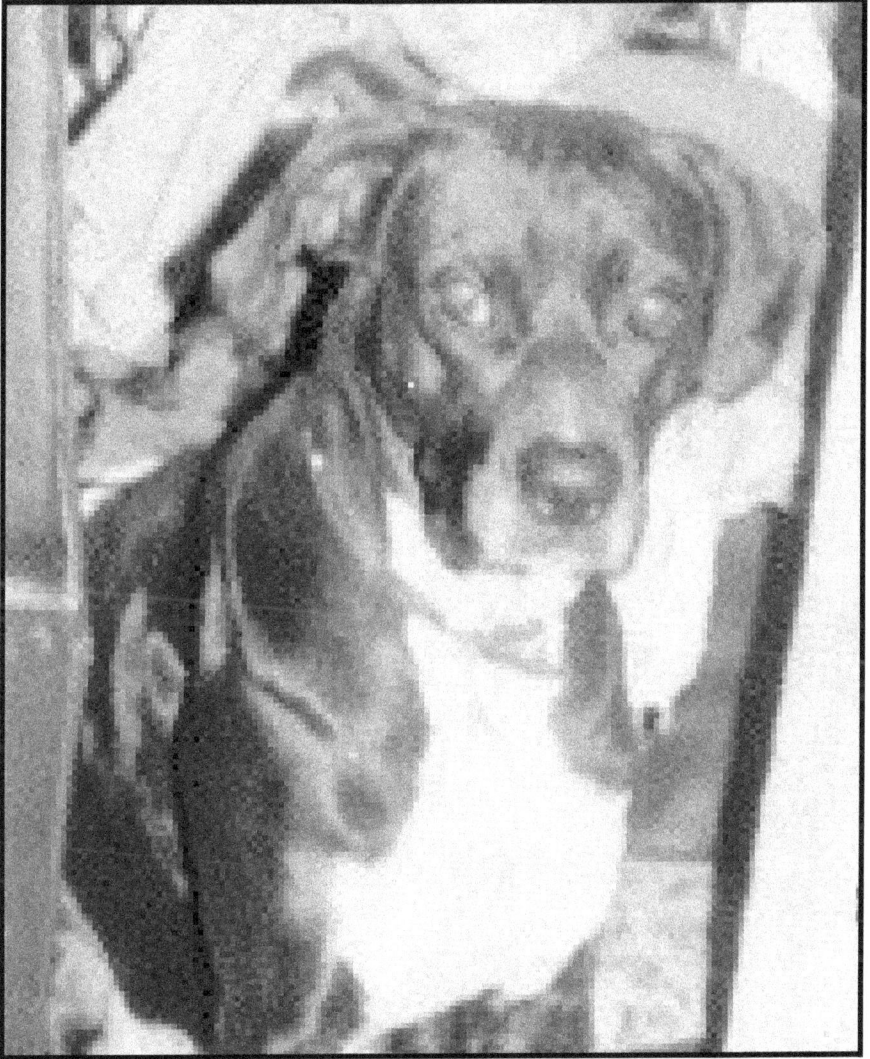

Spot

Mr. Eddie R. and Mrs. Dale P. Hill
on their wedding day in 1968

New York Red at her Number Bank,
112 West 115th Street

Chapter XVI

Traveling The Stars

On April 4, 1968, Rev. Dr. Martin Luther King, Jr. was shot by an assassin and killed in Memphis, Tennessee. On June 6, 1968, Bobby Kennedy was shot and killed by an assassin in Los Angeles using a .22 caliber pistol, the same caliber gun Eddie gave me. On July 7, 1968, Bumpy Johnson died of a heart attack in a restaurant in Harlem. King's, Bobby's, and Bumpy's deaths all occurred within four months. That troubled me, they were bad omens.

I was having very bad dreams at night about my death, but they didn't make any sense. My dream books would produce numbers that already felt as if time was standing still. This was a good time to go visit Maria at the Botanica. I hadn't received a reading in a long time. I needed to hear what she had to say.

When I arrived unannounced, she said, "Long time me no see ju. It is time for ju to see for yourself what I have seen for ju."

She asked me twice, "Are ju ready for ju travel?"

Nervously I replied, "Yes, I am."

Maria lowered her head without making eye contact and said, "I will not charge ju for this visit."

She led me into her darkened room with no windows or electric lights of any kind. She said, "Erma, you must make your own light in order to see your path. Do not be afraid of anything. I will always be here to guide ju. Please go to the bathroom first, use the toilet, and wash your hands, arms, and face. You will be traveling a while."

She closed the door and the room fell completely dark. With her hands, she directed me to a chair. Then she began to rub oils on my hands, arms, and face, preparing me for my journey. All of a sudden, my body began to get warm. I felt like I was weightless and floating in a trance.

I started to get nervous. I said, "Maria, it's dark in here. I can't see."

She took my hand and placed a long unlit match in it and calmly said, "Yes, ju can."

With her hand guiding mine, I took the long match and noticed three unlit white religious candles on the table.

I asked, "Why the three candles?"

She replied, "They are the three dimensions of your life. One for the past, one for the present, and one for the future. Which dimension do you wish to see?"

"I wish to see all three."

She told me to light all three candles. They all lit without striking the match. Above each candle suddenly appeared a bright portal of light. My voice cracked as I asked her which one should I take first. She suggested the past. I began to float back through my past struggles on welfare in New York City and the difficulties of raising three children as a single mom in an unforgiving city. Yet with determination and perseverance, I found the courage and unconventional means to move from poverty to prosperity and from welfare to wealth.

All my boyfriends appeared one by one and the various reasons I became involved with them. Sometimes the reasons were admittedly dishonest and unnecessarily selfish. Then flashing in front of me were the high times in Atlanta and Sweet Auburn Avenue, Roy Wiley, Mrs. Cunningham, The Peacock Club and my first introduction to hustling the streets. Then back to Plains, Georgia and the solid foundation laid by and the unflinching love given by Ma Babe. Uncle Fass and Mama sometimes appeared flawed but never tiring, along with Twin Spirits, Mrs. Frazier, friends, and neighbors. The rapist, Sheriff Mc Andrews' son, who received his true measure, was found lying in the rain on the sidewalk in a strange city unidentified.

Then totally to my surprise, I traveled back through my family's enslavement in Plains, Georgia and back to our arrival in North Carolina. I stopped; in the distance I saw a tall, beautiful African woman that looked familiar. She had been beaten and bruised, but she was unbroken. She was standing on an auction block naked, and white men were fondling and bidding for her. Their bids were very low. Some were saying that she was a witch and of little value because she could not be broken.

One bidder said, "She is suspected of poisoning five white men to death who were transporting her to be auctioned in a group of 50 slaves. We could not prove if or how she did it. If we could, we would put her nigger ass to death."

Another said, "She should be sent back to the Caribbean with the remainder of the unbroken niggers because she may kill her masters here, and the auction house would be sued."

I wanted to stop to see who this woman really was because she looked so familiar. But Maria said, "We must move on if we are to complete your journey."

I found myself on a slave ship that was dropping some of its slave cargo off on the Caribbean Island of Montserrat. They dropped off a group of slaves there and one man in the group she knew. Then we traveled back through time and we landed on the west coast of Africa. What African country, I do not know.

I asked Maria and she said, "Please, keep moving."

Then I saw them together, her and the man she knew were in chains being force marched to the coast by Africans who sold them to Europeans. Then we traveled back to their beautiful village, where I saw them farming, manufacturing goods, and smelting metals. Their lives were good and I saw what appeared to be their church. No, it was not a church. It was a mosque. They were Muslims—educated Muslims. There was some kind of ceremony going on. No, it was a wedding. They were being married. Now I hear gunfire; many are being killed, wounded, and captured. All before they consummated their marriage. I am listening to their language. They are screaming, crying, and throwing rocks at their armed attackers saying, "We are the Tikar peoples of what the Europeans call Cameroon! We will die before we become slaves!"

"Maria, why am I seeing this?"

She said, "Now it's time to go back."

We traveled back to North America and to North Carolina. Now, a group of six white men are taking the beaten, but unbroken woman off the slave ship with 50 other slaves. They are being force marched into the interior of North Carolina. Nightfall arrives on the road and the white men are drinking and drunk. They unchain her from the rest of the slaves and re-chain her arms around a tree. They gang rape her as she fights with every breath and strength in her body, but to no avail. Then the next day on the trail, it is raining and she is constantly falling from the beatings she took. No, no, every time she falls, she picks up some type of roadside plant and hides it under her clothing. At nightfall, the white men get drunk again and gang rape another slave woman. While they are raping the other slave, she balls up her collected herbs and casts them into their pot of soup cooking over a fire. The next morning, in horror only one of the very sick slave transporters awakens and finds five of his brethren foaming at the mouth dead.

A slave owner and planter purchases some of Twin Spirits' people's land in Southern Georgia from the U.S. government, at auction. He buys her and other slaves, so he can move his illicit enterprise there. I now have a better look at her. She looks very similar to me, almost like me. I see her giving birth to a child. She says it is a female and she is a queen. She names her Charlotte, after an English queen. Oh my God, this child is my great grandmother Charlotte Hicks Reid-Bush. I am Tikar from Cameroon, Africa.

I began to scream with joy, but Maria said we must move on and suggested we travel to the future.

I touched the future candle, then floated into the future portal. I found myself in Metropolitan Hospital on November 24, 1968; in the delivery room. Dale is giving birth to my first grandchild. She is a girl and she is beautiful. Dale is writing her name on the form for the birth certificate.

"Oh my God, where is Eddie Roy? He is not there. Where is he? I want to see him. Maria, why isn't he here? Something must have happened to him."

"Please, Erma, be calm, or you will collapse the portal. Now, please move on."

My granddaughter's name is Tamara Erma Louise. It is sweet that they named her after me. I wonder why? There is Eddie. He is at RIT taking his examinations and he could not attend his daughter's birth. I see Bernard, Miss Vee, and Pandora. They are with my mother. She must be visiting. Oh Lord, Bernard is not doing well in school, and he joins the Air Force. He liked being in the Civil Air Patrol and that is what encouraged him to join. Oh, oh, oh, Miss Vee is graduating high school and she received a scholarship to attend Fordham University in the Bronx. Pandora is with my mother; she must be visiting. No, no, I can't believe it, Eddie graduates from RIT and is working in a bank and Dale gives birth to my first grandson. Events are moving fast now. Miss Vee graduates college, marries and gives birth to a girl. She has an excellent job in computing. Pandora is living by herself and she is also working in computing.

"Erma, please move on."

Isn't that great? Tamara graduates from Spelman College in Atlanta, of all places. Now she has on a white coat. This cannot be true; she is a doctor, an eye doctor with two daughters, my great granddaughters. Tamara's name tag says ....no, I can't read. Wait a minute, I smell burning oil. I hear gunfire and explosions. I saw my grandson. His name is Tareem, and he is in some foreign country. There is a war and he is in the Marines. No, he is a Navy Corpsman in the Marines. Yes, yes, just like his father, and he survives unhurt and retires from the Navy. He has older children and a new baby. Isn't that something? I have nine great grandchildren, six biological and three by marriage.

What in the hell is going on now? Am I back in Plains, Georgia? I see nothing but red dirt. But, it's very different; there are no trees, bushes, flies or gnats. I see no hogs, houses, or roads. A woman is walking towards me. She is dressed in strange clothing with something covering her face. She is wearing a suit-no a space suit. She lifts her face visor and she is smiling at me. It appears to be my great granddaughter, Morgan. She, she, she is not in Plains, Georgia. Oh my God, she's on the planet Mars.

"Erma, our time is running short, we must go back now."

"No, no, I want to see more."

"We have no time."

I floated back to the last portal, the present. Its light started to dim and Twin Spirits reached out his hand to me.

Maria said, "No, do not reach back; you are not ready. Erma, your time with us in this dimension is dimming, but when you are ready, he will reach for you again."

I could feel a glow over my entire body. It was similar to the glow that covered Twin Spirits' body as he traveled the dirt roads of Plains, Georgia. I left Maria's feeling confident that no matter what was in store for me, I had fulfilled my purpose here on this planet. I gave Maria a $100 tip and walked back to 115th Street still on cloud nine.

Cian was waiting for me. He confirmed that the two detectives who were tailing me home in the afternoons were the same two that worked for the *East Side*. He began stopping by the Number Hole in the afternoons to walk me home when he could. He told me to call a Detective Harper of the 28th Precinct and to get it on record that I was being followed, which I did on August 27, 1968.

Sugar stopped by to see me. He found a job writing numbers for a Number Bank uptown. I mentioned to him that Sylvester and others were following me.

Sugar said, "Red, I never trusted that S.O.B. and, in a heartbeat, I would love to take him out for you. I would do him for free. I would keep my eye on him if I was you." "Thanks, Sugar."

Another strange thing began to play out about this time. I was not sure if it was related or not. A short time customer accused me of not paying him when he hit the number. His name was Marcus Gray and he was a big-time pimp that I met at Steve's birthday party. What happened was one of his girls delivered his numbers on a daily basis to my apartment in the morning. One morning, he presented a receipt showing that he hit one of his numbers. I looked at the receipt and told him that was not my stamp on the receipt. She was forging my stamp, not playing his numbers, and keeping his money to buy drugs. I told Marcus several times that was not my stamp and I wasn't going to pay him.

He started to show up at Homes' Number Hole in the afternoons to argue with me about it. This further aggravated Homes, and the atmosphere in the Number Hole became very hostile and tense. I told Cian that I was thinking about quitting, at once.

Burt, Pandora's godmother, picked up Pandora from daycare and I usually met her at the corner of St. Nicholas Avenue at 92 to take her upstairs. But her school was closed today and I brought Panzy to the Number Hole, which I normally didn't do and shouldn't have done. We had a back room where she could sit and play while I worked. I didn't allow anyone to talk to Panzy, but Sugar. I stopped leaving Panzy alone with Bernard and Miss Vee because my older children were not good babysitters. Under their supervision, they allowed Panzy access to the stove and she almost set the kitchen on fire. Luckily, it wasn't a large fire and the children put it out.

Homes' number business continued to slide and Sylvester had his ear. Homes continued to say ugly things to me concerning his failing number business.

I told him, "If you feel I am the cause of your business doing poorly, I will resign now."

He said, "No, that's not necessary," but he wasn't very reassuring about it. I suspected he talked to the *East Side* about his failing business also.

That afternoon, Cian was walking us home, Pandora in one hand and me in the other.

"Red, I believe they have figured that I am getting intel from you. I am also very concerned about you continuing to working for Homes. You should cut this guy loose now."

"Cian, I made a deal to purchase the convenience store across the street for $10,000, and I will sign the deal at the end of the month and leave."

We walked into the lobby of 92 and he asked, "You want me to ride up on the elevator with you?"

I looked around the lobby and there was no one there but us. I said, "Thanks Cian, but no."

He gave me a kiss on the cheek and his usual rolling fingers goodbye to Pandora. Pandora and I got on the elevator and Mr. Sanders took us up to the fourth floor and opened the elevator's gate.

Nitro, who was still in the apartment, heard us at once and he started to bark furiously. I looked around and there was no one on the floor, but us. I walked halfway down the hall reaching into my large handbag looking for my keys. I could not find them. I felt the gun that Eddie Roy had given me, but no keys. I walked back to the hallway window to get more light to search for my keys, but I found no keys. I told Pandora we must wait here in the hall until her brother and sister come home from school because I probably left my keys in the house. Nitro continued to bark and growl as we turned around to look out of the hallway window, which was right across from our kitchen window. I could see that I left the kitchen lights on. Then I saw a flash of light behind me reflecting in the window pane and then felt a sharp pain in my right shoulder. I screamed from the pain as my right arm went limp. Then I felt the second blow to my right lung. I turned, reaching for my pistol with my left hand, but the death blows continued in rapid secession from this towering negro with a goatee. He had swiftly attacked me with a knife from behind.

I fell to one knee trying to put myself between the attacker and my baby. The death blows continued as I continued to reach for my gun, but I failed. My right hand was of no use.

But I had made my peace with the powers of the universe. It was all in the hands of Twin Spirits now. Seeing my past and my children's future flash before me assured me that Pandora was safe. I smiled as Mother Nature delivered her final verdict and Twin Spirits reached out his hand for me to join him in the stars. I reached back and touched his hand as I fell limp, bleeding my epitaph on the tiled hallway with my unfired pistol in my left hand. The world delivered its Coup de Grâce. My term on this planet was over, but my children's term had just begun.

Prophet or Pariah
I threw bullets into fire.
Only to cement my desire
To commit my soul to aspire
By committing this feverous deed
I succumbed
To my selfish foolish needs
That would not heed.
Yet, I did not yield
To Mother Nature's speed
That one's life purpose
Must be righteous and true
For their soul to reap.

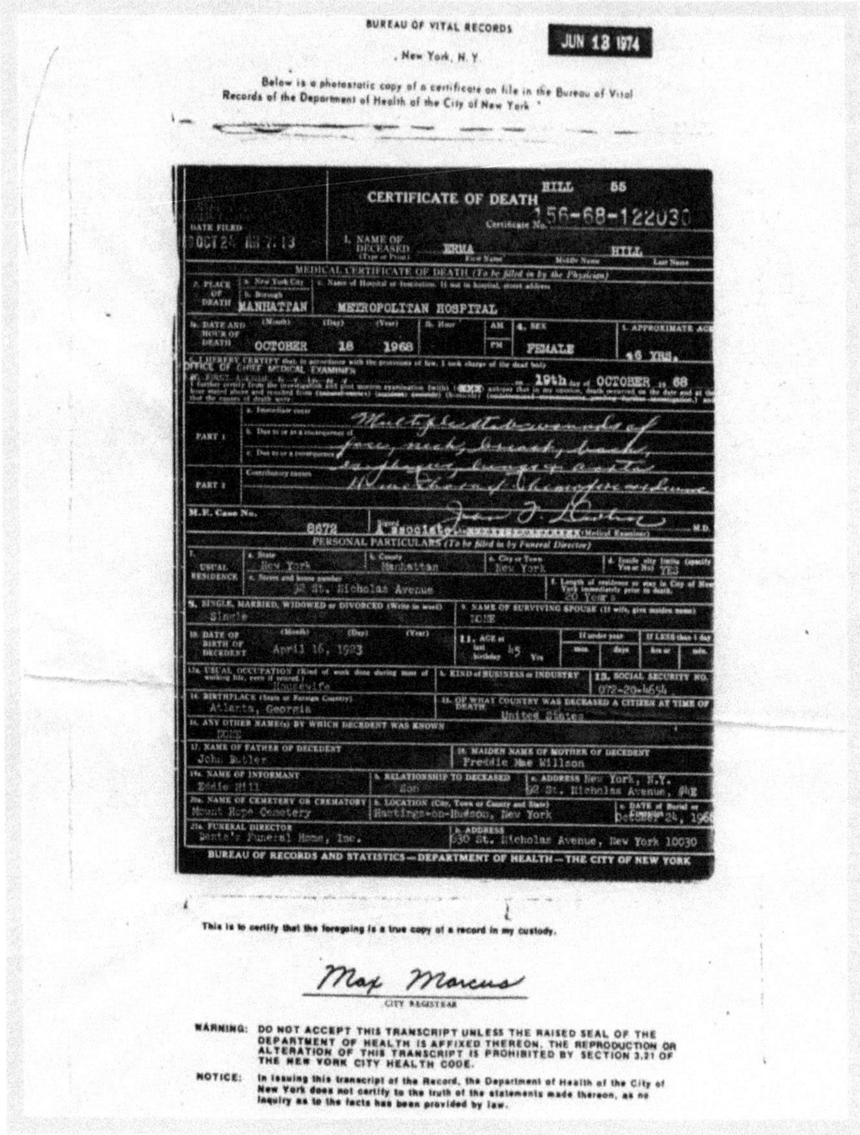

BUREAU OF VITAL RECORDS

JUN 13 1974

New York, N.Y.

Below is a photostatic copy of a certificate on file in the Bureau of Vital Records of the Department of Health of the City of New York

CERTIFICATE OF DEATH

HILL 55

Certificate No. 156-68-122030

DATE FILED OCT 24 AM 7:13

1. NAME OF DECEASED (Type or Print): ERMA (First Name) HILL (Last Name)

MEDICAL CERTIFICATE OF DEATH (To be filled in by the Physician)

2. PLACE OF DEATH: b. Borough: MANHATTAN; c. Name of Hospital or Institution: METROPOLITAN HOSPITAL

3a. DATE AND HOUR OF DEATH: OCTOBER 18 1968

4. SEX: FEMALE

5. APPROXIMATE AGE: 46 YRS.

OFFICE OF CHIEF MEDICAL EXAMINER

19th day of OCTOBER 19 68

PART I: a. Immediate cause: Multiple stab wounds of face, neck, breast, back, esophagus, lungs & aorta

M.E. Case No. 8672

Associate (Medical Examiner) M.D.

PERSONAL PARTICULARS (To be filled in by Funeral Director)

7. USUAL RESIDENCE: a. State: New York; b. County: Manhattan; c. City or Town: New York; d. Inside city limits (specify Yes or No): YES; e. Street and house number: 92 St. Nicholas Avenue; f. Length of residence or stay in City of New York immediately prior to death: 20 Years

8. SINGLE, MARRIED, WIDOWED or DIVORCED (Write in word): Single

9. NAME OF SURVIVING SPOUSE (If wife, give maiden name): NONE

10. DATE OF BIRTH OF DECEDENT: April 16, 1923

11. AGE at last birthday: 45 Yrs

12a. USUAL OCCUPATION: Housewife

13. SOCIAL SECURITY NO. 072-20-4654

14. BIRTHPLACE (State or Foreign Country): Atlanta, Georgia

15. OF WHAT COUNTRY WAS DECEASED A CITIZEN AT TIME OF DEATH: United States

16. ANY OTHER NAME(s) BY WHICH DECEDENT WAS KNOWN: NONE

17. NAME OF FATHER OF DECEDENT: John Butler

18. MAIDEN NAME OF MOTHER OF DECEDENT: Freddie Mae Willson

19a. NAME OF INFORMANT: Eddie Hill; b. RELATIONSHIP TO DECEASED: Son; c. ADDRESS: New York, N.Y. 92 St. Nicholas Avenue

20a. NAME OF CEMETERY OR CREMATORY: Mount Hope Cemetery; b. LOCATION: Hastings-on-Hudson, New York; c. DATE of Burial or Cremation: October 24, 1968

21a. FUNERAL DIRECTOR: Dante's Funeral Home, Inc.; b. ADDRESS: 530 St. Nicholas Avenue, New York 10030

BUREAU OF RECORDS AND STATISTICS — DEPARTMENT OF HEALTH — THE CITY OF NEW YORK

This is to certify that the foregoing is a true copy of a record in my custody.

Max Marcus

CITY REGISTRAR

WARNING: DO NOT ACCEPT THIS TRANSCRIPT UNLESS THE RAISED SEAL OF THE DEPARTMENT OF HEALTH IS AFFIXED THEREON. THE REPRODUCTION OR ALTERATION OF THIS TRANSCRIPT IS PROHIBITED BY SECTION 3.21 OF THE NEW YORK CITY HEALTH CODE.

NOTICE: In issuing this transcript of the Record, the Department of Health of the City of New York does not certify to the truth of the statements made thereon, as no inquiry as to the facts has been provided by law.

Erma L. Hill Death Certificate

Afterword

I was in the Rochester Art Gallery with my art class, when my Modern Art Professor at RIT pulled me aside and said, "You must call home immediately."

I called Mommy, and the home phone just rang and rang. Then I decided to call my Uncle Fred. He answered the phone crying, saying that my mother had been killed. The news caused me to waver momentarily, but my military training kicked in. In every military exercise, we practiced losing comrades. People who were your friends instantly lose their lives in the exercise. You were given no time to mourn them. You assumed command of the situation and you continued your mission's goal to overcome your enemy. I never would have thought I would be practicing this exercise in real life by replacing my mother on the battlefield. She had trained me very well and I had my marching orders. She prepared my younger brother and sisters by informing them that she would not always be with us, and that we were why she was doing what she was doing.

I remembered the look on Mommy's face as I took pictures with my friends who were graduating college with me. I had never seen such a look of pride and accomplishment on her face before. She was the first in our family to graduate from middle school, and I was the first in our family to graduate from college.

"Do as I say do, not as I do. I am throwing bricks at the jailhouse, so, you won't have to. Now, build your dreams upon my lessons learned from throwing Bullets in the Fire."

I took the next plane home from Rochester, New York, to LaGuardia. The airline gave me a priority seat in first class. When I arrived home, the remains of Mommy's blood were still in the hallway and the police chalk outline of where her body fell was marked on the ceramic tile's floor. A neighbor had taken in Pandora, Miss Vee, and Bernard, at the request of Father Walker of All Souls Church. The girls were inconsolable, and Bernard was quiet, just staring at the ceiling. Two detectives were waiting for me at the apartment's door. Detective Valone and his partner greeted me, by introducing themselves and saying they were sorry for my loss. Then they jumped directly into a lot of questions.

The first of which was: "Where were you in the past eight hours?"

I showed the receipt from my plane ticket. "I just got off a plane from Rochester, New York. My school's art professor let me know that something was wrong at home."

"Who murdered your mother?"

"I don't know who did it."

I told them as much as I knew at that time. That my mother was a Number Banker, which they already knew. I opened the apartments door and retrieved a few of her number slips from her dresser.

I said, "She never discussed her number business with me or my brother and sisters."

They stated, "Nothing was taken from her. Any Harlem robber knows number bankers carry lots of cash. We found $175 in her handbag, and it was untouched. When we lifted her body, we found an unfired .22 caliber Smith and Wesson revolver in her left hand. Do you know anything about this weapon?"

"What weapon?"

"Are you a military veteran?"

"Yes."

"We would like to talk to Pandora."

"This may not be the right time. Please, give her some time."

"Fine. Maybe you can bring her to the police station to look at some photographs."

"Maybe, in a few days."

I told them that my mother made a complaint to the police that she was being stalked. I suspected that Sylvester was setting her up. But for what I wasn't sure.

The detectives asked me to go downtown to the morgue and iden-tify my mother's body. I told them I would do it in the morning after I retrieved my brother and sisters.

The next morning before I went downtown, Pop Warner knocked on the door with his usual daily numbers bet. He had not heard of my mother's death. He handed me his number bets.

I said, "Pop, we are not in that business anymore."

He replied, "What do you mean? I don't understand."

"My mother was murdered yesterday in this very hallway."

"Oh my God, she was such a nice lady. What happened?"

"I am sorry, Pop, I must go downtown to identify her body. I will talk to you later." "I must tell Sylvester."

"Excuse me, tell Sylvester?"

"Yes, about the information."

"What information?"

"Who is selling narcotics information. I never told your mother that Sylvester was giving me information. Sylvester said she already knew he was doing it; so not to mention it and to keep quiet about it."

I asked, "Pop, how long have you been doing this?"

"A few months now."

That cemented it. Yes, Sylvester was feeding bad information to Pop Warner for my mother to pass on to Cian. I did not know who the killer was. But if Sylvester was involved, I would kill him myself.

We never found Mommy's keys. That meant someone went into her bag at work and took them. Normally, she would have walked to the door and then looked through her bag to find her keys. I went into Mommy's bedroom and started to go through her things. She kept the day's number receipts in the top drawer with the cash. There was about $4,000 there from the day's receipts. The police never entered the apartment, so nothing was disturbed or taken.

After Steve was killed, she took me over to the Bankers Trust of New York branch on 116th Street and Fifth Avenue and added my signature to her safe deposit box. It was a large box, in which she kept her Number Bank's cash reserve. The box was stuffed full of money, but I never asked her how much was inside.

She also kept a small strong box in the back of the hall closet next to her shrine, in which she kept her daily operating Number Bank cash, insurance policies, birth certificates and other important papers. She was very organized. I followed her instructions to the letter. She left no will and no letters for us. She had given her all to us before she died, and she made sure we understood what our tasks were before she left.

I questioned whether I should drop out of school to take care of my family, but that question had to wait. While looking through her papers next to her shrine, I noticed the tin can that held the "Black Baby" candle. I opened the tin can and pulled the candle out. It had Sylvester's name written on it. And she had been about to burn it.

After speaking with Pop Warner, I went downtown to the morgue. It was the first time I visited. I managed death before as a Medic in the Army. I helped clean up after the crash of an Army helicopter at Fort Rucker, Alabama that hit a high voltage line. It was a mess. The pilot and the trainer burned to death before the chopper hit the ground. We removed their remains with shovels because they were still smoking.

The morgue was expecting me, and her body was already out of the refrigerator on a gurney. She was wrapped in a black sheet and she looked as if she was taking a nap. I bent over and gave her a gentle kiss. I told the morgue attendant "Yes, that is my mother, Erma Louise Hill. He asked that I sign a few papers, and I did so and left.

I immediately drove up to Benta's Funeral Home on St. Nicholas Avenue and 147th Street and started to make her burial arrangements. Most of Harlem's elite requested that Benta's Funeral Home handle final arrangements for their loved ones. Mildred, Steve's wife, had asked Benta's to handle Steve's funeral.

The response from Mommy's customers and friends was overwhelming. The condolences poured in from all over New York City, and the wake was so wellattended that the guests had to sign on the back cover of the guest registry.

People who lived on the block donated what they could for her burial. Mommy's insurance policies handled most of the expenses.

Our family came pouring in from all over the country. The outpouring of my mother's siblings was enormous. My mother's brothers from Detroit, my grandmother and her siblings from Atlanta, Georgia. Mama Daught flew into New York City without a coat on her back at the end of October. It was very warm in Georgia, so she thought it was warm here. She almost froze getting off the plane. Uncle Freddie and her youngest sister, Lizzie Mae, took one of my mother's coats to LaGuardia Airport for her to wear. As soon as Mama Daught arrived, she stood at the apartment's door and collected guns from her sons as soon as they arrived.

She said, "This is not the time for that."

I agreed, and I told them, "I will take care of it."

We held her funeral at All Souls Episcopal Church on a Friday evening so most of her friends and acquaintances could attend. The church was packed to capacity and the overflow extended out onto St. Nicholas Avenue. I held Pandora's hand as I led the family into the church following the casket, and Bernard led the procession carrying the cross. We dressed Panzy in her favorite pink dress, the same color of the suit we buried Mommy in and the same pink silk that lined her casket.

Although Mommy was not a member of All Souls Episcopal Church, Bernard, Miss Vee, and I were baptized there. Bernard served as an Acolyte there and Father Lauder gave a rousing eulogy questioning the meaning of this act and asking who could do such a thing?

We bought a burial plot at Mount Hope Cemetery at Hastings on the Hudson. Her burial plot was in a beautiful location that overlooked the New York State Thruway.

After the funeral, I told my family members, "I'm thinking about dropping out of school to take care of my family. I must take care of my brother, sisters, and Dale, who is still in the hospital trying to save my mother's first grandchild. I have two more years to go to receive my bachelor's degree and to stay in school under these circumstances would be too difficult."

My family would have none of it. They told me their story again of *Bullets in the Fire*. They realized what a pain in the ass they were in their mother's absence while she was looking for work. They had really learned to appreciate their oldest sister for the love and care she gave them. That event also helped them realize they were all placed on this earth for a reason. They did not say any more about it until the day they were to leave for home. I noticed Mama Daught hadn't pack her bags.

She said, "Eddie Roy, I will stay and take care of your brother and sisters and help your new wife with her new baby. The family wants you to go back to school, at once."

I replied, "What about Aunt Nora in Atlanta? Who is going to take care of her?"

"Your Aunt hasn't had a drink in years and the family in Atlanta will look after her. I will be here as long as it takes for you to graduate from college."

I took care of all my mother's business within two weeks, except for taking care of her killers, but I could not believe it. What irony, and after all these years. Mama Daught was repaying her debt to her oldest daughter. She was now raising her daughter's children. What a turn of fate.

It was a hell of a thing for Pandora to see her mother being stabbed to death. I waited until after the funeral to talk to Pandora about her mother's death and take her to talk to the detectives to look at mug-shots. The detectives tried to steer her to name someone who did not commit the crime. She kept telling the detectives that the guy had a goatee, but they kept showing her pictures of guys with mustaches.

I showed the detectives a business card that Mommy received from Detective Harper of the 28th Squad on August 27 after she reported to him that she was being followed. The detectives said there was no complaint on file.

I could see that this was not going anywhere. I started writing letters to everyone and anyone who would listen, from FBI Director J. Edgar Hoover, Governor Nelson Rockefeller to Mayor John Lindsay. A strange thing happened; they all responded back. But to no avail. They never apprehended Mommy's killer.

Then I drove to upstate New York to a gun shop close to Pough-keepsie, New York, and bought a .30 caliber M1 Carbine. New York State gun laws change when you leave the city. The U.S. Marines used this weapon very effectively in close quarters combat during World War II. It was very dependable and had good stopping power at distances under 100 yards. The receiver held a 30-round banana clip and it could fire fully automatic, if you could find the illegal M2 Kit for it. On the morning that I was to return to school, I was going to take care of Sylvester. Returning to school would be my alibi, if I needed one.

I packed my clothes the night before and said goodbye to everyone, including my wife Dale, in the hospital. The next morning, I set up my sniper position on the rooftop opposite the Number Hole, between two apartment buildings with an excellent line of fire. I blackened my face and placed my Army poncho over my back to block my bodyline from being recognized by a helicopter flying over.

I saw Sylvester walking up the block about 8:05 a.m. and I waited for him to enter the Number Hole. I sighted my weapon on the stoop, as Uncle Sam trained me. He walked up the stoop right directly into my sights. Then my mother walked straight in front of him, looked directly at me, and pointed her finger directing me to go home. It was the same as she did the day she had her conversation with Fat Tony in the back of his limousine. Tears welled up in my eyes as I released the trigger. I packed up my gear in my old Army duffle bag and exited the roof. Cian was standing there on the building's stoop waiting for me. He was no aberration.

He said, "Eddie Roy, your mother was my hero. She was helping me catch the real bad guys. I am not going to stop you or arrest you. You must do what you must do. But you would have been dead in two weeks. This assassination would have your signature all over it. The *East Side* would have known they were dealing with a skilled shooter and they would come after your family first to get to you. I will do my best to find your mother's killer. What you are doing is not what your mother worked so hard for. Go back to college, Eddie, and forget about this damn street shit.

"Do as I say do, not as I do. I am throwing bricks at the jailhouse, so you won't have to. Bullets in the Fire."

OFFICE OF THE DIRECTOR

UNITED STATES DEPARTMENT OF JUSTICE

FEDERAL BUREAU OF INVESTIGATION

WASHINGTON, D.C. 20535

January 17, 1969

Mr. Eddie R. Hill
123 Shelter Street
Rochester, New York 14611

Dear Mr. Hill:

I have received your letter of January 13th
and was sorry to learn of the tragic death of your Mother.

I can certainly understand the concern which
prompted your request; however, the FBI is not empowered
to investigate this murder as we have no jurisdiction. I
regret I cannot be of help to you.

Sincerely yours,

J. E. Hoover FBI Letter 1969

THE CITY OF NEW YORK
OFFICE OF THE MAYOR
NEW YORK, N. Y. 10007

JANUARY 21, 1969

MR. EDDIE R.HILL
123 SHELTER ST.
ROCHESTER,N.Y.

DEAR MR. HILL,

THANK YOU FOR YOUR RECENT LETTER.

I AM REFERRING IT FOR ACTION TO THE
POLICE DEPARTMENT.
THEY WILL BE IN DIRECT CONTACT WITH
YOU AS SOON AS POSSIBLE.

SINCERELY,

MAYOR

Mayor John Lindsay Letter

Misc. 129

REPLY TO
CORRESPONDENCE UNIT
CA 6-3212 · CA 6-2096
TWX 212-571-1120

POLICE DEPARTMENT
CITY OF NEW YORK
NEW YORK 13, N. Y.

In Reply, Please Refer to
File No. 4341/CM
PC/373
CI/510
CD/109
28 Squad

April 14, 1969

Mr. Eddie R. Hill
123 Shelter Street
Rochester, New York

Dear Sir:

A full investigation has been made relative to your letters of January 13, 1969 addressed to the Governor of the State of New York and to the Mayor of the City of New York, concerning the death of your mother.

A search of the records of this department did not disclose any record of threats to your mother being reported. Your sister, Pandora, did identify the perpetrator of the crime, however, Assistant District Attorney Dannett stated that there was insufficient evidence on the identification of this 5 year old and that when she was questioned by the Assistant District Attorney, he believed that she could not fully tell the difference between a lie and the truth.

This matter is still under active and continuing investigation. In the event positive results are obtained notification will be made to you.

Please be assured of our full cooperation in this matter.

Very truly yours,

GEORGE P. MC MANUS
Chief Inspector

Chief Inspector George P. McManus Letter Index

Epilogue

In 1967, the New York State Legislature legalized the numbers lottery, which raised more than $34 billion for the state. It is still illegal for non-licensed individuals to take number bets in the state.

Anthony "Fat Tony" Salerno, along with the other Godfathers of the five Mafia families, the La Cosa Nostra, in New York City, were arrested by the FBI and indicted under the new RICO statutes in New York City in January of 1987. He was convicted and sentenced to 100 years in prison.

92 St. Nicholas Avenue, Apartment 4E, where New York Red last lived and the location of her last Number Bank, is now a co-op apartment building. She paid $100 per month rent for 4E. 4E is now worth $500,000.

Mama Daught remained in New York City for two years, caring for her daughter's children and helped care for her first great-grandchild. When she returned to her home in Atlanta, she took Pandora with her and raised her through high school. Mama Daught transitioned to traveling to the stars with her oldest daughter in 1985. We remain eternally grateful to her.

Pandora graduated from Frederick Douglass High School in Atlanta, Georgia, in 1981 and is now a Director of Cybersecurity for one of the largest accounting firms in America. She has no children. To this day she is still suffering with the psychological scars of her mother's death.

Miss Vee graduated from George Washington High School in upper Manhattan. She attended Fordham University in the Bronx and graduated from SUNY New Paltz with a BA in Journalism in 1977. She retired from the world's largest computer company and is now a Cloud Computing Software Consultant. She has one daughter Nikia, who is a promising entrepreneur.

Bernard left George Washington High School just before graduation and entered the U.S. Air Force. He never reconciled his mother's death and was constantly depressed.

After his enlistment and discharge, he never settled in any one location. He was shot and killed in front of a liquor store in Houston, Texas, during an argument in 1983. He left no known children.

Eddie graduated from Rochester Institute of Technology on the Dean's List in 1970 and went on to receive his Master of Business Administration degree from Fordham University-Lincoln Center in 1977. He completed executive studies at the Wharton School of the University of Pennsylvania in 1983. He retired from the world's largest telecommunications company and developed his own real estate development business. He is now an author and a "Number Hustler," not on 115th Street, but on Wall Street. His wife Dale retired at the age of 52 from one of the world's largest Wall Street banks and never worked another day. Eddie and Dale have two children, Tamara and Tareem, nine grandchildren, one great-grandchild, and one granddaughter who wants to be a surgeon and travel to Mars.

I wish to thank all of my mother's (New York Red's) customers, the residents of Harlem and the City of New York for your prayers and support over the years. Your money and resources were well spent.

To all of our family's friends, neighbors, supporters, and customers that expressed their condolences. The family of Erma Louise Hill wishes to thank each one of you.

Both Dale and Eddie took a DNA test and their ancestry is from the Tikar Peoples of Cameroon, Africa.

Tennant Contribution.

1- Mr. + Mrs. J. Williams   4H $2.00
2- Mr. + Mrs. W. Peterson   4H   1.00
3. Mr. + Mrs. F Fauntleroy   4D   3.00
   Mr. Nelson   6F   1.00
   Mr. H. Miller   1C   .75
   Mrs. E. R Harrison   1B   1.00
   M. A Joseph Jr   -   1.00
   R. Manuel   2C - 1.00
   Mrs. H. Miller   1D - 1.00
   Mrs. A. Blanchette   1.00
   Mrs. Lena Shetter   1C 2.00
   Mr.
   Mr + Mrs. J Weeks   - 1.00
   Mrs + Weeks   1.00
   Thomas + Marie Burton 1.00
   Mary Brown   2D   1.00
   Emily Hines   2B   1.00
   Barbara Zugler 2B. 1.00
   Evelyn Oliver   2B. 1.00
   Mr + Mrs. N. Shorty 1.00
   L. Adams   2G - 1.00
   Josiah Love   2F   1.00
   Joseph Baldwin   5.00
   Willie McBride 3C 1.00

92 St. Nicholas Avenue Tennant Donation

Lydia Springfield   1. 00
Bernice Porter   1. 00

Mrs. Banister   7A.   .50
C. Galern   1. 00
    Petrmand   7C.   1. 00
G. Baid   7D   1. 00
Mr. & Mrs. Oun   7H   1. 00
Mrs Nina Lessiane   7G   1.00
Lily Wright   6D   .50

Henry Brown   6E.   1. 00

M. Border   60   .50
Mrs Arnold   5C/   1. 00

K Buggess   5A   .100
Steven   5B.   100
Rosa Morgd   5K   1. 00

Emma Slater   .50

Cora Brown   135 W. 115ᵗʰ $2. 00
Mr & Mrs Franklin - 6H - $2.00
Mr Basil Smith #4H $1.00
Mr. D. W. #14   3.00

92 St. Nicholas Avenue Tennant Donation Page 2

Mrs Irma Hill pass away Friday Oct. 18, 19__

This Collection is For. Mrs Irma Hill
92 St. Nicholas Ave.

Mrs. Lilly Scott 118 W 115 St # $2.00

C. Edward Tinsley 23 St. Nic _____

Mrs. Carrie Jones 125 West 115th # 9 $1.00

Mr. James Lockard 118 W. 115th St. #__ $1.00

Mr. Leroy Simons 125 West 115th # 9 $2.00

Mr Clifford Cheatham 117 West 115th # 3 $1.00

Mr. John McCummings 301 West 114 St 2# $1.00

Mrs Abbie Taylor 109 W 115 St # 3 $1.00

Mr. James Woods 109 W 115th 2R $5.00

Mr. John Lenox Drug Store $1.00
95 Lenox Ave.

Mr. Wesley Lamont 119 W 115 L 3C $1.00

Ralph Daggs 1864 7th Av — #12 $1.00

Mrs. Helen Butler 123 W 115 St #10 $1.00

Mr. Raphel Smith 123 W. 115 St #2 .80

Mrs. Addie Brown 123 W 115th St # 7 $1.00

Mr Ralph Moore 1005 St nicholas $1.50

Mr. Harry Ray 118 W. 115th St 2E $2.00

Erma L. Hill 115th Street Donation

names

Mr. Abner Clark 124 W. 115th St. #1W $1.00
Mich James 124 W 115— $.00
Paulette Jordan 120 W. 115 #t $1.00
Mrs. Sara Richardson 125 W. 115th St. #19 $3.00
Mrs. Mattie Jones 91 Lenox Ave. #2N .50
Mr. John Fleming (Piggly Wiggly 100 St. Mkt) $1.00
Mr. Walter Cleaners, 93 St. Nicolas Ave. #2.00
Mr. Walter Mc Mullens. 89 Lenox Ave. apt 6. $1.00
Mr. Joseph Raymond 135 St. 115th St. #1D. $2.00
Mrs. Dorothy Faucette 123 W. 115th St # 1 $1.00
Mrs Lucille Briggs 123 W. 115th # 9. $1.00
Mr Raymond Smith 122 St. 115th St #3W $1.00.
Mrs Pearl Rumph 125 St 115th St apt 6 $1.00
Mr Buyford Powell, 1408 5th Ave. #10 $1.00
Miss Bonnie Day. 45 West. 110th #1E. $2.00
The James Family 124 W. 115 St #4W. $1.00

Total Amount Collected
$45.00

Erma L. Hill 115th Street Donation Page 2

REGISTER

Benta's Funeral Home, Inc.
630 ST. NICHOLAS AVENUE   NEW YORK, N. Y. 10030
AUdubon 6-4660

Register Cover

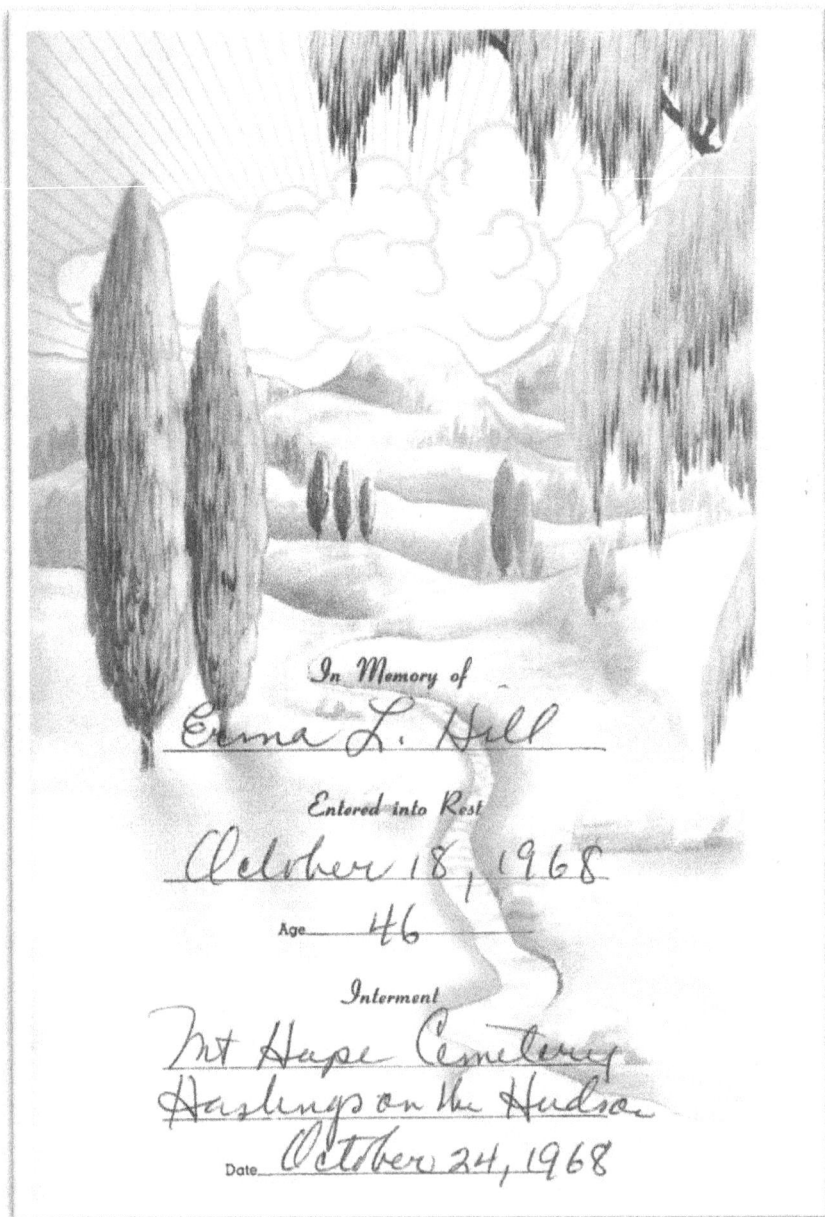

In Memory of

Erma L. Hill

Entered into Rest

October 18, 1968

Age *46*

Interment

Mt Hope Cemetery
Hastings on the Hudson

Date *October 24, 1968*

Register Page 1

Services

At *All Saul's Church*

Date *Oct 23, 1968* Time *8PM*

Officiating

Father LAudeR

Bearers

Register Page 2

Register of Friends

NAME and ADDRESS

Hayes Anna
120 W 115 St apt 4E N.Y.C.
Rev. Samuel J. Johnson
2180 8th Ave N.Y.C. 10026 apt 31
David Sim
101 W 115th St APT 6F
Eugene Graham 113 W 114 St (Slim)
Jack training au
Minnie Joe
(Mrs) Beryl Fothergill
1115 Morris Ave. Bx. 10456.
Louisa Leguna 63 Jersey Ave
Gloria Merry - 462 W. 146 St
Lucy 15 W Morris Pl
Sandra Dunaway 434 w 146 th St
Arthur Greenwood 122 W 114 St #5
Vernice Starke 147 Street
Leonard Averhart 2094 8 ave
Claudia Matthews
3 W 123 St Nyc 10027
Betty Robinson
320 East 176 St. N.Y. 10457

Register Page 3

Register of Friends

NAME and ADDRESS

Mrs. Lena Emitt 21 W 112 St
Mr Hines 117 W 115 St

A. Ford Green 409 W 159 St
Alberta Helton 711 Magenta St Bronx NY NY
J H Jones
B Bernice Johnson
Willie +

Mr & Mrs Wm Bryant 114 W 176 St 3 Far Rock NY
Miss Matilda Clarke 4 E 115 St
Mrs Katrina Ollie
1019 E 222 St Bronx NY
Flossie Prince 140 W 116 St
Mrs. W. Frierson 115 W 115 St
Mattie Emerson 70 W 115 St # 90
Lucille Wright 70 W 115 St # 8 E
Nettie Massey 1815 Amsterdam NY
J P Barlow
135 W 115 St # 2 W
Toni Bennett 120 W 114 St

Page 10

Register Page 4

267

Register Page 5

Spiritual Bouquets

NAME and ADDRESS

Mrs Josephine Leonard 8 E. 110 st N.y.c.

L. Valentine - Northeastern Academy

Bernard Rae Bennett. Northeastern Academy.

Elise Spann

Mrs Dorothy Fauette
123 W. 115 St. n y c

Mrs Lillian Colson
9 2 St Nicholas ave

Lucy Wright 104 W 145

Mrs Victoria Williams
1221 Ohio Park

Arabella Wigfall
104 Lenox ave nyc

Mrs Inez J Gains
206-54 46 Ave BaySide, N. 1. 34

Lucille Rumble 104 Lenox ave Apt 3 A

D. Hart 104 Lenox ave

Mrs Gloria Cornelius

Mrs Henry Joyner 120 w. 115 St

James Boyd 45 W 110 St 1 E

Page 12

Register Page 6

Floral Tributes

NAME and ADDRESS

Violet Allen
40 West 115 St. CA40
Mary Hays 73 W 116 St.
Lillie Sherman 156 W. 123 St.
Mrs Rose Simmons 830 E 163 St Bx59, N.Y
Mr. James Marshall 830 E 163 St Bx 59 N.Y.
Geneva Jones 830 East 163 Street
Jocelyn Mercer 830 East 163 St.
Kevin Burroughs 830 East 163 St.
Camille Bosworth 105 W 133 Apt 43
Elsie Jones 57 W 111 St —
Louise Williams 37 W 111 St
A. Wiggins 106 W 113 St
[illegible] 14 to Ave
Carl C. [illegible]
Mrs. Jean S. Smith — 141 W. 113 St.
Mr + Mrs Reginald Brown 57 W 175 St.
Mrs. Melicent Acham
Denise Acham
Mr & Mrs Taylor 101 W 115 St
#3 A NYC

Page 13

Register Page 7

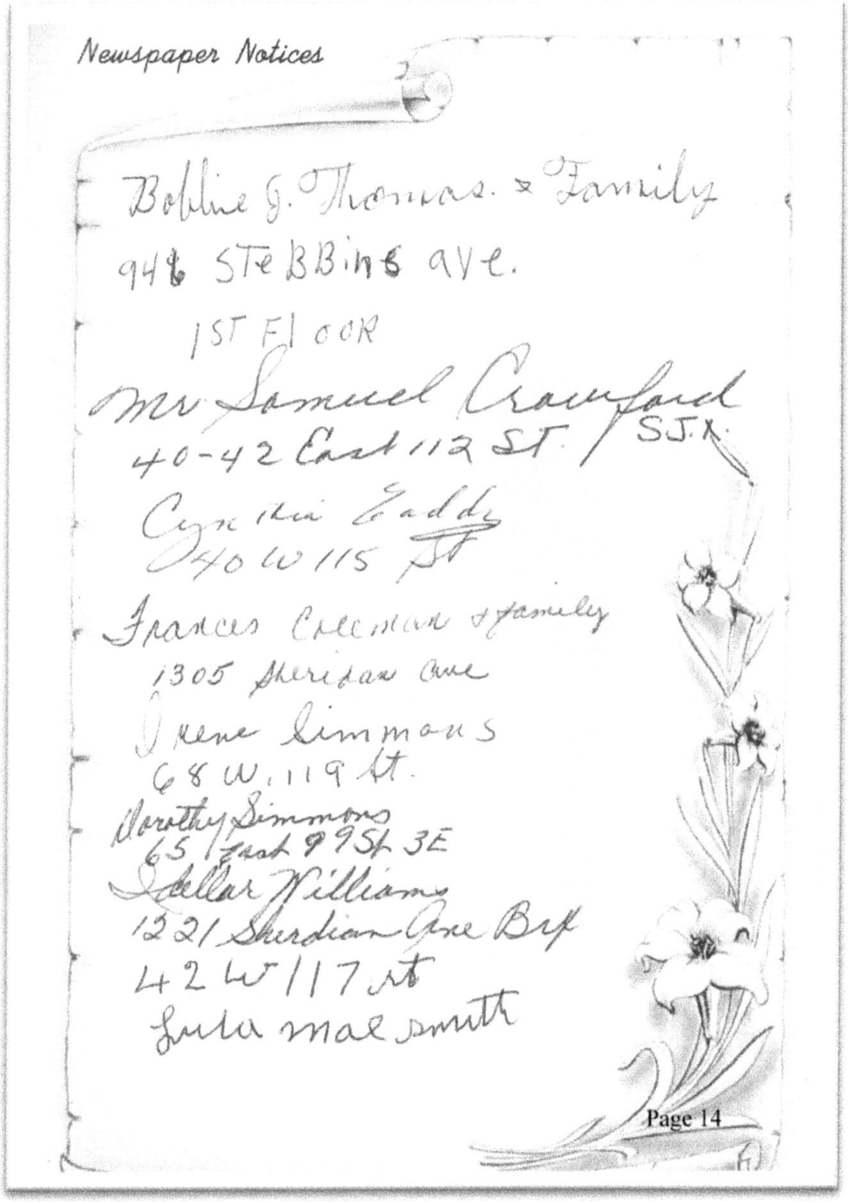

Bobline G. Thomas. & Family
948 STeBBinG ave.
1ST FlooR

Mr Samuel Crawford
40-42 East 112 ST. / SJ.A.

Cynthia Gaddy
40 W 115 St

Frances Coleman & family
1305 Sheridan ave

Irene Simmons
68 W. 119 St.

Dorothy Simmons
65 East 99 St 3E

Stellar Williams
1321 Sheridan Ave Brf

42 W 117 St
Lula mae smith

Page 14

Register Page 8

271

Esther Lenseal
130 West 115 St. N.Y. N.Y.

Paulette L. Gordon
120 West 115 St. N.Y N.Y.

V. Petinaud   92 st. Nicholas ave.
                                    N.Y.

Merretta Lister   Archie Dousdelle Jr.
Br, N.Y.   139 W. 113ᵗʰ St
Pl Lister   NY, N.Y.
Br. N.Y..

Joe Baldwin,   Sonny Hickson Jr.
92 St. nick, ave   100 W-174 st
    E. R Lofton   Bnx, N.Y.

Mrs A Faust
162 N.116 st #1 31-33 105 st
    Mrs Mckinny

Louis Marten
880 Boynton ave
    Bx

Marjorie Hill & Son
2645 Third ave

Register Page 9

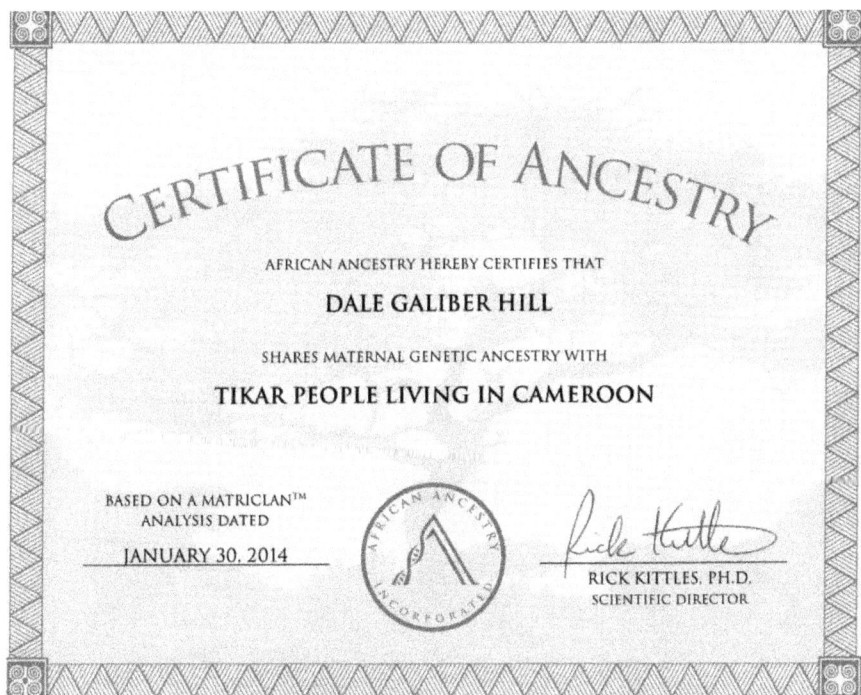

Dale's DNA Test Certificate

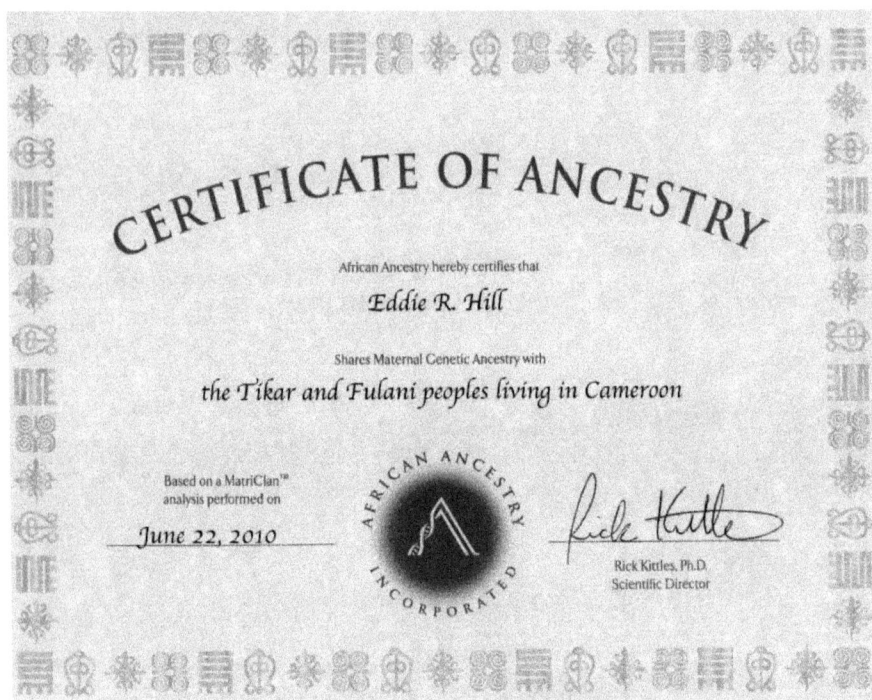

CERTIFICATE OF ANCESTRY

African Ancestry hereby certifies that

Eddie R. Hill

Shares Maternal Genetic Ancestry with

the Tikar and Fulani peoples living in Cameroon

Based on a MatriClan™
analysis performed on

June 22, 2010

Rick Kittles, Ph.D.
Scientific Director

Eddie's DNA Test Certificate

You may have noticed a series of three-digit numbers at the end of chapters 1-15.

The significance of these numbers relates to Erma L. Hill, throughout her life, and some are explained. The people who knew her best understand what they all meant.

Chapter 1	976	383	675	624
Chapter 2	761	874	058	393
Chapter 3	263	478	850	933
Chapter 4	913	483	819	532
Chapter 5	182	195	279	493
Chapter 6	032	476	635	172
Chapter 7	976	103	287	429
Chapter 8	121	597	908	084
Chapter 9	341	576	306	954
Chapter 10	437	391	615	524
Chapter 11	512	982	429	126
Chapter 12	151	616	739	841
Chapter 13	732	810	036	447
Chapter 14	908	713	516	747
Chapter 15	504	518	712	527

A Final Note
From the Author:

I want to thank you for purchasing and reading Bullets In The Fire - Biography Of New York Red by Eddie Roy. I would love to hear from you about any lessons you may have learned from reading this book.

Additionally, please leave a review of this book on Amazon.com. or on your favorite book website. If you would like more information about the author or New York Red, please contact me at bulletsinthefire.1@gmail.com or visit the bulletsinthefire.com website.

You can also follow me on social media on the following platforms:

Facebook: https://www.facebook.com/edward.roy.73

Instagram: https://www.instagram.com/bulletsinthefire.1/

Twitter https://twitter.com/BulletsFire

www.ingramcontent.com/pod-product-compliance
Lightning Source LLC
Chambersburg PA
CBHW031119020426
42333CB00012B/147